PRICES
&
CHOICES

Microeconomic Vignettes

Third Edition

David Hemenway
Harvard University

UNIVERSITY
PRESS OF
AMERICA

Lanham • New York • London

Copyright © 1993 by
University Press of America®, Inc.
4501 Forbes Boulevard, Suite 200
Lanham, Maryland 20706

3 Henrietta Street
London WC2E 8LU England

Library of Congress Cataloging-in-Publication Data
Hemenway, David.
Prices and choices : microeconomic vignettes /
David Hemenway. — 3rd ed.
p.   cm.
Includes bibliographies and indexes.
1. Microeconomics. I. Title.
HB172.H47   1993   338.5—dc20   92-34764 CIP

ISBN 0–8191–8946–4 (cloth : alk. paper)
ISBN 0–8191–8947–2 (pbk. : alk. paper)

For Nancy Lou and Brett

CONTENTS

PREFACE

Prices and Choices is a collection of twenty-six short, readable essays in microeconomics. The book is specifically designed to provide stimulating supplementary readings for introductory or intermediate theory classes. In addition, it can be used in courses on economic policy, economic analysis, or applied economics.

The book has no ideological axe to grind, but it does try to illuminate some of the limitations as well as the applications of economic theory. The primary goal, however, is to put economic concepts to work, using tools of analysis that are well within the grasp of undergraduates. Almost all of the topics covered are ones about which students have some general experience and ideas. Questions are included at the end of each chapter to supply fuel for discussion.

Prices and Choices might also be read with some benefit by both professional economists and educated lay people. All the essays are intended to provide useful insights and to require some thought and reflection by the reader. They are meant to be enjoyed, and an attempt has been made to keep them succinct, snappy, and entertaining.

Many friends, including Richard Caves, Tom Schelling, Marc Roberts, David Harrison, Ed Lazear, Suzanne Cashman, Dan Strouse, Paula Griswold, and Debbie Fallon helped me with earlier editions.

My good buddy Frederick Wales Gramlich carefully scrutinized the entire first edition and also coauthored the chapter on haggling. For this edition, I would like to thank Sara Solnick. Sara provided research support and editing for the entire manuscript and most of the definitions for the glossary.

The first edition was published in 1977, a revised edition in 1984, and the second edition in 1988. New to this edition are "Nervous Nellies," "Health Care" and "Injury Prevention." Chapters on product differentiation and skid row have been dropped.

Research for the chapters on Risk Compensation, Nervous Nellies and Injury Prevention were supported in part by the Harvard Injury Control Center, funded by the Centers for Disease Control.

Chapter 1 appeared as " 'Seek Simplicity and Distrust It': Assumptions of Microeconomics" in the *Journal of Policy Analysis and Management* 4, no. 2 (Winter 1985): 262-66, copyright John Wiley & Sons, Inc., 1985.

Chapter 14 appeared as "Quality Assessment from an Economic Perspective: A Taxonomy of Approaches with Applications to Nursing Home Care" in *Evaluation and the Health Professions* 6, no. 4 (December 1983): 379-96 and is used here by permission of Sage Publications, Inc.

Parts of Chapter 15 appeared as "Thinking about Quality: An Economic Perspective" in *Quality Review Bulletin* 9, no. 11 (November 1983): 321-27 and are used here by permission of the Joint Commission on Accreditation of Healthcare Organizations, Oakbrook Terrace, IL.

Chapter 23 appeared as "The Optimal Location of Doctors" and is used here by permission of the *New England Journal of Medicine*, vol. 306, pp. 397-401, 1982.

I BASIC ASSUMPTIONS

Economics can be distinguished from other social sciences by the belief that most (all?) behavior can be explained by assuming that agents have stable, well-defined preferences and make rational choices consistent with those preferences.[1]

INTRODUCTION

A fundamental tenet of economic theory is that the purpose of all economic activity should be to satisfy the wants of consumers. Thus, production is not valued for its own sake but solely as a means of increasing consumer utility. The economist has a tendency to identify consumption with final consumers, viewing employees, like machines, as inputs or resources; therefore, the defense of any business solely on the grounds that it "creates jobs" is given little weight by economists, who view this primarily as a using up of scarce resources.

Strong philosophic questions can be raised concerning the goal of satisfying consumer desires. Is a society that caters to every consumer whim really an ideal society? Should consumers be given everything they want? (We know, or believe, that children should not.) Are people's preferences always "good"? Aren't some desires more virtuous or of higher moral quality than others? Might not even Robinson Crusoe be somehow better off if not all his needs and desires were met? However you answer such questions, it is important to recognize the strong and controversial normative implications of this most basic of economic assumptions.

A closely related and fundamental postulate in economics is that people are rational beings. This simplifying assumption often differentiates the economic approach from that of the sociologist or psychologist. For example, when other social scientists explain criminality, they often employ such concepts as depravity, insanity, deprivation, deviance, and abnormality. These ideas are foreign to the economist. The economist depicts the individual as highly rational. A person may become a criminal but only after carefully considering the other available options. He may select a career as a bank robber but only because he perceives it as his best alternative; he may find that it pays well, the hours are good, and he is his own boss. The policy conclusions are obvious: the way to decrease the number of bank robbers is to make that occupation less attractive and others more so. Economists use the rational-action assumption to explain virtually every human choice: why people walk on the grass, pollute the environment, brush their teeth, or even go to church.

The normative conclusions of microeconomics depend on the assumptions of high rationality and excellent knowledge: the individual needs to know all the alternatives and their outcomes; he must be able to order these alternatives in terms of his preferences; and he must then choose the most preferable. It is often assumed that all this is done without cost. These are, of course, very strong assumptions.

Many consumption decisions are made not by individuals but by groups-- the family for instance. But even for an isolated individual, we may question whether behavior is normally highly rational. It is difficult to make transitive ordering of thousands of alternatives. (If you prefer A to B, and B to Z, you must prefer A to Z.) It is impossible to know all the ramifications of even the most important options, and people often find it hard not only to know what is best for themselves but also to act in the way they would like. A "weak" individual is defined as one who often is unable to do what he thinks is best. If you hear someone saying "I drink too much," or "I wish I didn't goof off so much or watch so much TV," or "Why can't I control my temper?" you may not be listening to an "economic person." Think of people you know well. Are they usually highly rational? Are you? It is interesting to consider literary figures whom all of us can know intimately. How closely do they resemble the economic person? Does a Madame Bovary seem highly rational? Or an Ahab? A Billy Budd, a Raskolnikov, a Heathcliff, or a Scrooge?

If the assumptions of full rationality and excellent information are broken, the normative conclusions of price theory may not follow, and many economic policy prescriptions become suspect. For example, if consumers do not choose rationally (or if one does not believe their wants should be satisfied), then the demand curve does not represent marginal social utility, or any such notion, and it is not clear that the restriction of supply by monopolists is necessarily bad.

A third related and vital assumption in microeconomics is that tastes are exogenous to the economic system. One might say that economists have taken John Donne's famous line and contorted it into "No! Man *is* an Island." But, of course, tastes, utility functions, and consumption decisions are interdependent among individuals; social forces do matter in our lives. The economic well-being of others can affect us directly, bringing joy or sorrow, envy or compassion. The actions of others affect our options and our happiness. Economic consumption is often most enjoyable when done jointly. Moreover, we continually compare our lives and station with others', and our perceived status can affect our contentment.

The social and economic environment certainly has some effect on an individual's tastes and preferences yet, to the extent tastes are endogenous to the system, the normative conclusions of price theory do not follow. It would surely be questionable to applaud an economic system that largely satisfies wants that it itself helped mold or create. Economist S. Alexander makes the point:

> That wants are generated by the social process, not in the trivial sense that they are affected by advertising, but in the profound sense of their dependence on the whole cultural matrix, certainly threatens the entire ethical basis of economics, striking in particular at Pareto-optimality. It challenges the principle that more is better, and opens up the question of what sort of wants we should generate, what sort of men we should make.[2]

Fundamental philosophic issues of this sort are generally excluded from consideration or discussion by the strong assumptions of the microeconomic model.

The five chapters in this section deal with issues related to the basic assumptions of micro theory. The first chapter contrasts these postulates with the quotable wisdom of some of the world's greatest philosophers. A goal of the chapter is to provide an unusual but thought-provoking perspective on the theoretical underpinnings of microeconomics.

Emotional behavior is clearly important in the real world, but it is often ignored by economists. Chapter 2 discusses temptation and tries to bring it within the purview of rational behavior. It argues that a wise individual will recognize the possibility of short-run temptation, of irrational behavior, and will attempt to structure his options and payoffs so as to minimize the expected harm. This analysis applies not only to temptation but to any emotion, such as fear, anger, infatuation, joy, or sorrow.

The economist's assumption of costless rationality means that an individual should find additional favorable possibilities or opportunities desirable. Chapter 3 describes some situations where this is not the case, where more options may prove detrimental. One purpose of this chapter on options is to discuss some of the actual problems of making decisions and living with them.

Microeconomic theory does not examine why preferences change, since it assumes them to be unchanging. Conventional theory thus does not seem highly useful in explaining fashion-- the continual and massive swings in taste that seem to occur in music, architecture, books, games, pets, and so forth. Chapter 4 focuses on changing styles in clothing. It emphasizes the importance of consumption externalities in explaining fashion change in the clothing industry. The desire of individuals to conform, and the desire to demonstrate and achieve social distinction, combine to create the constantly evolving dress styles that influence not only our expenditure for apparel but also our aesthetic perceptions.

Chapter 5 emphasizes the crucial influence social forces and pressures have over individual action. It presents two fictional tales to illustrate the potential importance of such externalities and the inefficient and undesirable consequences that may result from decentralized decisionmaking. The article also mentions how a simple postulate-- that people desire status-- can prove useful in explaining such phenomena as worker alienation and the neglect of public, relative to private, goods.

Economists clearly recognize the existence of consumption externalities but often find them "so various and so difficult empirically to uncover that we usually assume simply that they do not exist."[3] The articles on fashion and social forces argue that such an attitude is unfortunate and dangerous. It is unfortunate because it excludes from analysis much that is interesting and important; it is dangerous because the neglect of large externalities can lead to incorrect and improper normative conclusions and policy prescriptions.

In sum, the chapters in this section are designed to focus the reader's attention on some of the fundamental assumptions of microeconomic theory and to help provide a better perspective on the relationship between the model and the real world. The chapters in the remaining parts of the book apply the general economic approach to a wide variety of issues and phenomena. This first section is therefore not intended to denigrate this useful way of thinking but to highlight some of its implicit postulates and to alert the reader to the fact that some of the normative or value conclusions of economics need to be taken with a grain of salt.

NOTES TO INTRODUCTION

1. Richard H. Thaler, "Anomalies," *Journal of Economic Perspectives* (1988-1990).
2. Sidney Alexander, "Human Values and Economists' Values," in Sidney Hook, ed., *Human Values and Economic Policy* (New York: N.Y.U. Press, 1967),p.110.
3. Roger Sherman, *The Economics of Industry* (Boston: Little, Brown, 1974), p.307.

OTHER SOURCES

Frank, Robert H. *Choosing the Right Pond: Human Behavior and the Quest for Status*. New York: Oxford University Press, 1985.
Frank, Robert H. *Passions within Reason: The Strategic Role of the Emotions*. New York: W. W. Norton, 1988.

Hook, Sidney, ed. *Human Values and Economic Policy.* New York: N.Y.U. Press, 1967.

Krupp, Sherman Roy, ed. *The Structure of Economic Science.* Englewood Cliffs, N.J.: Prentice-Hall, 1966, part IV.

Scitovsky, Tibor. *The Joyless Economy: An Introduction into Human Satisfaction and Consumer Dissatisfaction.* New York: Oxford University Press, 1976.

1 APHORISMS

Seek Simplicity and Distrust It.

Alfred North Whitehead

Economics, of all the social sciences, takes the most uniform and standardized approach to human nature. Next time you hear a joke about the three economists who made four predictions, don't be misled: there is no fundamental disagreement among them about what drives behavior. All economists operate from the same basic assumptions, if not the same precise models, for any given analysis.

Good economists can apply their tools to virtually any human activity, from crime to church-going, from marriage to military strategy. Frequent use has shown that economic thinking is a powerful deductive engine of analysis. The economic framework represents an entire, self-contained world view of incentives and responses. As such, it makes a number of very strong simplifying assumptions. Many of these postulates, while undeniably useful, contrast sharply with other, enduring perspectives on behavior. This essay aims pertinent aphorisms at some economic bubbles in need of pricking.

The microeconomic individual single-mindedly maximizes utility. She bases her every action on a rational assessment of circumstances, given a consistent and relatively stable set of preference orderings. This ideal person (or firm) is reasonably well-informed, intelligent, and self-disciplined, and by definition her actions promote her well-being and thus reveal her true preferences. Good public policy is thus whatever can help this person increase her net utility; it helps her get what she wants.

Does reading philosophy, history, psychology, literature, theology, or even *Bartlett's Quotations* raise some doubts about this ideal type? You bet! One may question not only whether any individual truly has a single "maximand" or utility function but also whether she even acts as a single, consistent entity.

> The same brain may subserve many conscious selves, either alternative or coexisting.
>
> *William James*

In economics, even firms act as though they had a single intelligence, but others think even one person may not know her own preferences.

> The body has its ends which it does not know; the mind its means of which it is unaware.
>
> *Paul Valery*

Some people prefer not to know themselves.

> Know thyself? If I knew myself, I'd run away.
>
> *Johann Wolfgang von Goethe*

And most don't recognize their own self-deceptions.

> The easiest person to deceive is one's own self.
>
> *Lord Lytton*

Real people are not always consistent in their choices.

> Logic and consistency are luxuries for the gods and the lower animals.
>
> *Samuel Butler*

Nor is consistency necessarily something to be desired . . .

> A foolish consistency is the hobgoblin of little minds.
>
> *Ralph Waldo Emerson*

. . . even where it can be obtained.

> Do I contradict myself?
> Very well then, I contradict myself.
> I am large, I contain multitudes)
>
> *Walt Whitman*
> (Song of Myself)

Even if we could all behave consistently, few of us are sufficiently intelligent or self-aware to be good, rational utility maximizers.

Half of us are blind, few of us feel, and we are all deaf.

William Osler

On a more concrete level-- in the American vernacular:

Nobody ever went broke underestimating the intelligence of the American public.
H. L. Mencken

And we don't always make the best trades.

A horse, a horse, my kingdom for a horse.

William Shakespeare

Indeed, rationality itself may be overrated as a virtue.

Reason enslaves all whose minds are not strong enough to master her.
George Bernard Shaw

Moreover, most of us often lack the temperament or self-discipline to do what rationally seems best.

I can resist everything except temptation.

Oscar Wilde

Most important for policy, wants are not always virtuous. It may not be good to get what we think we want.

We desire nothing so much as what we ought not to have.

Publilius Syrus

Nor would we necessarily be happy if our desires were fulfilled.

In this world there are only two tragedies. One is not getting what one wants, and the other is getting it.

Oscar Wilde

Even apparent "utility" may not be all it's cracked up to be.

A lifetime of happiness! No man alive could bear it; it would be hell on earth.
George Bernard Shaw

Such a listing (make your own; it's fun) may seem silly. But it's also a bit disconcerting for a card-carrying economist to find so many aphorisms-- and from some acute observers-- that so fundamentally conflict with economic postulates. Of course, no list of aphorisms provides a coherent way of understanding, predicting, or prescribing all human behavior:

> Nothing is so useless as a general maxim.
>
> *Thomas B. Macaulay*

Moreover, as any student of the Bible, Shakespeare, or even Ann Landers knows, one can find a maxim to support or refute almost any given proposition about human beings.

> There is nothing so absurd but some philosopher has said it.
>
> *Marcus Tullius Cicero*

Indeed, one can even find contradictory maxims from any one source-- particularly from a source that is rich in human insight. But this is precisely my point: people are more paradoxical, more complex, and more interesting than can be captured by a simple model.

Any model abstracts from reality and hence distorts it. The simplifying microeconomic postulates are no exception: they focus on certain limited aspects of human nature. Such simplification creates a powerful analytic tool. Problems that seem hopelessly complicated prove amenable to quantitative analysis. But reliance on one tool can go too far. The current danger is that the microeconomic viewpoint is developing monopoly power. Having a single dominant perspective is a blessing for economists. Everything is grist for their mill, and no publishable problem can resist the power of rigorously applied simplemindedness. But for policy analysis, it can be a curse as well because such standardization crowds out alternative approaches and ideas. The narrowness of a single perspective is one reason why economists *qua* economists should be advisors, not policymakers.

> Nothing is more dangerous than an idea, when it's the only one we have.
>
> *Emile Chartier*

Economists might develop broader perspectives if there were alternative, full-blown deductive engines of analysis. As it is, we would do well to keep in mind the limits of the dominant model, under what conditions it is most and least reasonable. The imperialistic ambitions that economics as a discipline has demonstrated over the past few decades make this caution particularly urgent. At the very least, all of us trained in economics should show a little humility when prescribing policy:

Doubt grows with knowledge.

Johann Wolfgang von Goethe

Or at least it should.

FOR DISCUSSION

1. Do individuals need to be perfectly rational for most economic predictions to hold? How rational must they be?

2. Is the individual the most appropriate unit of analysis? Why not the gene? The extended family? The socioeconomic class? The nation? How would economic theory be affected in each case?

3. Do other social sciences (e.g., history, sociology, political science) have a unified set of basic assumptions? What are the advantages and disadvantages of this approach?

4. Forty years ago, Milton Friedman set out to repudiate "the belief that a theory can be tested by the realism of its assumptions, independently of the accuracy of its predictions." He argued that "the only relevant test of the validity of a hypothesis is comparison of its predictions to experience." (Friedman, *Essays in Positive Economics*, Chicago: University of Chicago Press, 1953, pp. 8, 9, 41) Discuss.

5. Discuss with respect to the economic approach:
   "The art of being wise is the art of knowing what to overlook." (W. James)
   "Science commits suicide when it adopts a creed." (T. H. Huxley)
   "A man in the wrong may more easily be convinced than one half right." (Emerson)
   "Analysis makes for unity, but not necessarily for goodness." (Freud)
   "Having the fewest wants, I am nearest to the Gods." (Socrates)
   "There are plenty of people for whom the crucial problems of their lives never get presented in terms that they can understand." (Chapman)

2 TEMPTATION

NO THYSELF!

My wife, Nancy, who smokes more than a pack a day, never buys cigarettes by the carton.[1] She continually runs out and is often forced to purchase from vending machines, paying some 30 percent more per pack than necessary. She argues that possessing few cigarettes helps her ration them, that if some were always lying around the house she would smoke more, which would be worse, and that her behavior makes sense.

Nancy's desire to limit the number of cigarettes in the house is an attempt to reduce temptation. A temptation situation is defined here as one in which a person must make a choice between two alternatives; one alternative is less valuable but more immediate or specific, while the other is more valuable but more remote or abstract. Nancy's behavior is designed to increase the cost of the first alternative. Embarking on a vacation deep in the wilds without cigarettes could be considered a strategic maneuver aimed at virtually eliminating the choice.

It is well known that in a two-or-more-person game, a player can be made better off by actually worsening certain of his payoffs. (The Appendix provides a simple introduction for those not familiar with payoff matrices.) Consider the single prisoner's dilemma game (Figure 2-1) with no communication or side payments. Each player has a dominant strategy, to choose option A regardless of the other's choice. Individual maximizing behavior will give the players a payoff of three each. Now if certain payoffs are *worsened*, the outcome of rational individualistic behavior can be improved. In the revised game depicted in Figure 2-2, option B has become the dominant strategy, and payoffs of five each are obtained. The argument here is that even in one-person games-- games with no externalities-- worsening payoffs or eliminating options can sometimes make the player better off. Con-

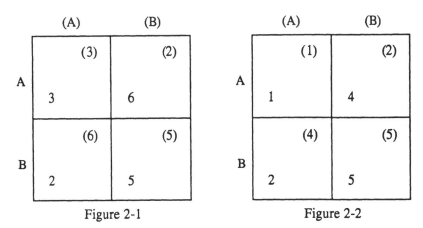

Figure 2-1   Figure 2-2

versely, adding options or improving payoffs can actually worsen the ultimate outcome.

There are a number of possible reasons why having additional choices might actually decrease one's utility. These include the costs of comprehension and calculation and the higher disutility of making the wrong decision (and crying over spilt milk) rather than having no decision to make at all. This chapter focuses on a somewhat different explanation: the problem of shorter run versus longer run benefits, of shorter run versus longer run rationality-- the problem of temptation.

For temptation to matter in the economic model, the assumption of complete rationality must be modified. More realistically, people are less rational and make worse decisions in the immediate or short run when, perhaps, they haven't had time to "sleep on it." The explanation is not that they have less information (though this is certainly possible), but that their utility calculus is less reliable. Given more time, for example, they often have longer (and more correct) time horizons. Being able to step back and examine the situation in its totality, they become less myopic.

Considering the example of Nancy and her cigarettes, we have in some respects a situation of shifting controls, actually a two-person game. It makes sense for one Nancy, who has had a chance to carefully weigh all alternatives, to change payoffs or eliminate options for another Nancy, who must make quick decisions in the face of immediate temptation.

Businesses understand and try to capitalize on the shorter run irrationality of consumers. "Impulse purchases" account for an important part of supermarket sales, and firms use packaging and display techniques as well as "magic prices" (generally with a 9 cent ending) to increase particular sales. Recognizing the more emotional and impulsive nature of snap judgments, sellers sometimes try to force instant decisions on buyers. It is in this light that such promotions as "The first twenty callers will receive free . . . " or "Offer expires midnight tonight" can be viewed. One purpose of the buyer remorse law allowing a three-day "cooling-off" period during which households may legally renege on a door-to-door sales agreement is to help consumers combat the problem of spontaneous irrational purchase.

Individual consumers have various devices for combating temptation. People on diets, for example, often buy clothes too small as an incentive to lose weight. Some have actually gone so far as to get their jaws wired shut. A number of my friends don't own television sets, largely, I suspect, because they are afraid they will watch too much. Their longer run actions prevent short-run mistakes. Sometimes I believe I might be better off if excellent diversions were not located so close to my office.

People combat the short-run temptation to spend money in a variety of ways. Some take only a limited amount to the track or the gambling casino in order to avoid losing too much money. Potential purchasers sometimes avoid attending auctions in person to prevent the excitement of the competitive bidding from driving their offers too high. Certain products and institutions are successful, I believe, largely because they help consumers delay gratification; they help them refrain from current consumption. If one were knowledgeable, and always rational, there would be little reason, for example, to prefer whole-life to term insurance. But recognizing the irrationality of some short-run decisions, one may be afraid of extra money "lying around the house" or "burning a hole in one's pocket" and correctly opt for the forced saving in the whole-life policy, even if the interest rate is low. This also accounts for low interest Christmas Club plans which were once so popular; it is a major argument for the withholding of taxes.

There are many general examples of actions designed in part to diminish the effect of short-run temptation. Collectively, Americans prohibit the three-term presidency and often prevent governors from succeeding themselves, thus eliminating a seemingly important option. Even the seat-belt buzzer can be defended as a device that helps prevent the short-run temptation "to forget it this one time" from winning out over the longer run calculation of the dangers of driving.

It may make sense for the government to help individuals combat temptation when the problem is general and there are scale economies or when it is individually difficult to make firm commitments. Partial justification can be made on such grounds for mandatory seat belt laws and perhaps for the restriction on cigarette ads. This sort of public action is, of course, fraught with danger. Rarely do we *all* want particular payoffs worsened or options eliminated. Collective deliverance from temptation, for example, is one rationale for such problem laws as prohibition and the illegality of prostitution and pornography. It is significant, however, that these laws are generally felt to be legitimate when applied to minors, who do not yet possess sufficient long-run rationality to look out for themselves.

People often attempt to help those "less rational" to resist temptation. For example, the appointment of a financial trustee to take care of the estate after death is one way to continue protecting a spouse's interests. A parent who desires to safeguard a child's virtue may refuse to provide birth control pills. The parent is afraid of condoning promiscuity and actually wants to worsen the payoffs of such behavior. There are dangers here, as in all the examples, of the individual's still finding temptation irresistible and paying more dearly. While this chapter has focused on worsening outcomes, it is obvious that the preferred strategy may sometimes be to improve payoffs in order to lower the costs of succumbing to temptation.

Temptation has been narrowly defined here. It has not been viewed as "an invitation to evil," an attempt to cheat or steal and thus to harm others. Instead, it has been described as an "invitation" to do something-- anything-- that brings immediate, often tangible, personal utility but is against one's own long-term interest. The essay ignored many tempting topics such as morality, conscience, will, guilt, and the superego. There has been no mention of the potential character-building benefits of being tempted, the potential costs of rationality, or the joys of unfettered spontaneity. The argument has been the simple one that there are different degrees of rationality and that these are sometimes related to the time of and for decision. While we are being immediately tempted, we often give long-run consequences too little weight and are enticed to do things we later regret. It thus sometimes makes sense for us to create schemes that eliminate particular options or at least make them less attractive. Certain actions and institutions are explicable as ways we help ourselves combat the dangers of temptation.

FOR DISCUSSION

1. "Consumer theory doesn't explain addictive goods too well." Comment. Is there any difference between the utility derivable from addictive goods and normal goods? What type of goods are addictive? Can people ever become addicted to comforts? To status? To making money? To consumption in general?

2. Both buyer and seller should benefit from free trade. Did Native Americans benefit from the purchase of white people's firewater? Why might they not have?

3. What is meant by the saying "He is his own worst enemy"? Is rational man ever his own worst enemy?

4. Do you ever play games with yourself or try to fool yourself for your long-term well-being? In what kinds of situations?

5. Why do people sometimes count to ten before reacting to another's objectionable behavior?

6. "Never go grocery shopping when you're hungry." Comment.

7. Why are children warned against snacks that might "spoil their appetite"? What is meant by a person being spoiled?

8. How would you go about collecting empirical evidence on temptation?

9. Even if a man pays little attention to most advertising, "their cumulative effect over time in teasing his senses and tapping repeatedly at his greeds, his vanity, his lusts and ambitions can hardly leave his character unaffected."[2] Discuss with respect to temptation. Do advertisements provide dangerous one-sided propaganda that the route to happiness is through money?

10. List a number of areas where it might make sense for government to help people resist temptation. Could laws against prostitution or bottomless dancers ever be justified on this rationale? How about fines for not locking your car, "tempting" people to steal it? What would be the benefits and costs of government's banning TV broadcasting for one hour each night?

11. Are there any cultural activities you were forced into that you have now grown quite fond of? Relate such situations to temptation situations.

NOTES TO CHAPTER 2

1. Concerned readers may wish to know that since this chapter was written, Nancy has quit smoking.
2. E.J. Mishan. *The Costs of Economic Growth* (New York: Prager, 1967): p. 130.

SOURCES

Schelling, Thomas C. *The Strategy of Conflict*. New York: Oxford University Press, 1963.
Schelling, Thomas C., "The Intimate Contest for Self-Command," in *Choice and Consequence* (Cambridge, MA: Harvard University Press, 1984), pp. 57-82.
Schelling, Thomas C., "Enforcing Rules on Oneself," *Journal of Law, Economics and Organization* 1 (Fall 1985): 357-74.
Scitovsky, Tibor. *The Joyless Economy: An Introduction into Human Satisfaction and Consumer Dissatisfaction*. New York: Oxford University Press, 1976.

3 OPTIONS

Gaining additional options is usually thought advantageous. More alternatives are generally considered to be better than fewer alternatives. One is deemed fortunate to have a large choice in deciding where to work or what to buy or whom to marry. More opportunities may be deemed valuable even if they are not taken. The loss of the possibility to eat freely may be a substantive one even for the person who chooses to fast.[1] However, an increase in options is not always an unmixed blessing. In some areas additional alternatives may have detrimental rather than beneficial effects.

SOCIAL PERSPECTIVE

Economists have long understood that increasing the discretionary power of individual decisionmakers may harm society. Competition is viewed as beneficial largely because it limits such power on the part of firms. In the model of perfect competition, sellers are forced to produce where price equals marginal cost, and their actions help lead to a Pareto optimal equilibrium-- an equilibrium where all actions that can help some people without hurting anyone else have been made. Possessing market power increases the firm's options but generally decreases the economic efficiency and well-being of the society. We don't want the firm to be able to continually charge monopoly prices and prosper. Thus, we have regulatory agencies that limit the pricing options of natural monopolies. There is a potential rationale for some sort of regulation whenever markets are imperfect. For example, insufficient consumer information is sometimes cited as creating a need for our usury, fair-packing, and pure-food laws, the purpose of which is to eliminate supposedly undesirable or unneeded alternatives.

Efficiency problems are also caused by externalities. Where there are substantial external economies, where social benefits exceed private ones, it may behoove society to bolster or subsidize the activities. On the other hand, where there are substantial external diseconomies, it may be appropriate government policy to try to curtail them. In the real world, it sometimes makes sense to outlaw rather than tax certain of these activities, so we have traffic laws, zoning codes, effluent controls, and so on. Of course, making particular alternatives unlawful merely eliminates *legal* options. The course of action may still be possible, but it is made more costly by potential moral problems, court expenses, fines, jail sentences, and the like.

We have limited the legal options concerning printing money, paying taxes, immigrating, discriminating, and selling our liquor, our votes, and our bodies. We may eventually want to eliminate the legal option of killing baby whales, carrying handguns, or having too many children. And if we discover how to choose our children's genes, we may want to limit or control that option. Or we may not.[2]

INDIVIDUAL PERSPECTIVE

Up to now we have been considering options that we as individuals might be willing to relinquish if others also gave up those alternatives. For example, we probably want automobile speed limits, provided they are applicable to most or all vehicles, not just our own. There are other options we might not want for ourselves, independent of whether or not they are made available to others.

In the model of perfect competition, where everyone is perfectly rational and perfectly informed and where it is costless to make commitments, additional independent options (options that do not affect the payoffs to other alternatives) should not prove harmful. In the real world, however, extra alternatives are sometimes troublesome or detrimental.

It is obvious that additional undesirable options can prove detrimental when they directly worsen payoffs to other alternatives. The employee may not want the option of spending a dull evening at his boss's house or having an affair with the boss's spouse. The teenager may not want the option of taking speed with his buddies. Narcotics officer Frank Serpico did not want the alternative of making easy money through graft. For the individual, the option may not be agreeable, but not taking it now has added costs: he may lose face, his job, his friends, or his life.

Additional options that don't directly worsen one's payoffs may nonetheless affect others' *expectations* concerning her actions and thus make her worse off. It is well known that in game theoretic situations, increased payoffs or additional alternatives can actually worsen results. A legal option of selling your vote may make you more susceptible to intimidation. An army's ability to retreat may make the feared enemy attack more likely. A reputation for tolerance combined with an ability to compromise may make others more strident in their demands.[3]

Even a decision unit viewed in isolation may prefer fewer options.

1. There is disutility in having had a choice and making the wrong one. Of course, we may be unhappy with the added option if we choose it and things turn out badly. But there is more than this. Having an alternative and making the wrong choice is usually worse than reaching the same outcome having had no choice at all. Psychologically, bygones are not simply bygones, and we do tend to cry over spilt milk. The utility of the present situation is decreased by the unfavorable comparison to what could have been. In addition, the wrong selection may make us unhappy by reflecting badly on our rationality, intelligence, and shrewdness. To protect ourselves we sometimes try, ex post, to change our beliefs. We try to increase the attractiveness of the chosen alternative and to decrease the attractiveness of the rejected. This opposite of "the grass is greener" syndrome is called the theory of cognitive dissonance reduction and is well known in market research literature. We try to reduce dissonance because past, unchosen alternatives *do* affect our present contentment.

2. Decisions take time, and time is a scarce resource. The thinking required for the decision may be hard. Information about alternatives is often fragmentary, and there is cost in gaining more information. There are costs in determining one's own preferences, one's own utility function. If the decision unit is a group, a family for instance, it may be difficult both to determine the intensity of each member's desires and to correctly weigh those desires. (Furthermore, family members' expectations may be changed, perhaps detrimentally, by the new option.) The decisionmaker can try to optimize which choices to consider and how much to consider them, but there can clearly be many options she can very well do without. Take a seemingly favorable opportunity the family breadwinner is offered a slightly better job, but it is in a different city. Whatever alternative is chosen and whatever the outcome, there certainly may be large psychic and emotional costs in the decisionmaking process itself. One can easily imagine that the family might have been better off without such a potentially difficult choice.

Some psychiatrists claim that too many attractive options can lead to psychic overload. As affluence increases, as customs and mores lose their stability, we may enter a state that could be termed "option shock." To quote Dr. Lipowski:

> It is specifically the overabundance of attractive alternatives, aided and abetted by an affluent and increasingly complex society, that leads to conflict, frustration, unrelieved appetitive tension, more approach tendencies, and more conflict-- a veritable vicious cycle. Such an overload and its consequences constitute a category of psychosocial stress that must have far-reaching and probably harmful effects on the mental and physical health of affected individuals.[4]

3. Individuals may just not act rationally. They may be inexperienced, intoxicated, insane, incensed, in dire straits. Society, for example, tries to prevent

the young from becoming addicted to cigarettes. Society eliminates even more options for the insane. Sometimes normal adults may simply be too weak in the face of temptation to respond rationally in the short run. A person on a diet, for instance, may strongly prefer *not* to be offered a piece of delicious chocolate cream pie-- and is probably better off without the option.

CONCLUSION

As individuals, we often like to limit others' options, especially as they affect us, and we are sometimes willing to limit our own to achieve this purpose. But independent of limitations on others, there are also many occasions when we would prefer not to have additional, even alluring, alternatives. Our added options may change others' expectations in an adverse manner. And even a Robinson Crusoe may prefer fewer options if he suspects he may choose wrongly, if a wrong choice makes him feel terrible, or if the act of choosing is itself traumatic.

FOR DISCUSSION

1. Why do many people dislike face-to-face encounters with individuals seeking charitable contributions? Will "not giving" convey a bad signal or create a bad impression? Is it ever rational to pretend you're not at home when a neighbor comes collecting?

2. Do you ever try to make it impossible to do things you don't want to do?

3. J. J. Rousseau asked: "If in order to fall heir to the property of a rich mandarin living at the farthest confines of China, whom one had never seen or heard spoken of, it were enough to push a button to make him die, which of us would not push that button?" Would you want such an option?

4. "One of the reasons for having a book of rules about when to run the risk and when not to-- when to land the disabled aircraft and when to abandon it and take to parachute-- is to relieve the man who gives the orders, the man in the control tower, of personal guilt for the instruction he gives."[5] Discuss in relation to the Rousseau quote above. Could possible guilt feelings be considered a completely separate and additional reason for not wanting options?

5. "In matters of life and death doctors are not merely operations analysts who formulate the choice for the executive; they are professional decisionmakers, who not only diagnose but decide for the consumer, because they decide with less pain,

less regret, cooler nerves, and a mind less flooded with alternating hopes and fears."[6] Comment.

6. Contrast the tendency to cry over spilt milk with the economist's advice that sunk costs are sunk, to let bygones be bygones.

7. Can the existence of an option be detrimental even if there is no possibility of a wrong choice? Explain.

8. Is there an "optimal number of options"? Is that a useful concept? Is the actual number of options generally less than the optimal number?

NOTES TO CHAPTER 3

1. Amartya Sen, "Freedom of Choice: Concept and Content," *European Economic Review* 32, no. 2/3 (March 1988): 269-294.
2. Thomas C. Schelling, *Micromotives and Macrobehavior* (New York: Norton, 1978), pp.193-210.
3. Thomas C. Schelling, *The Strategy of Conflict* (New York: Oxford University Press paper, 1963), pp. 21-76.
4. Z. I. Lipowski, "The Conflict of Buridan's Ass or Some Dilemmas of Affluence: The Theory of Attractive Stimulus Overload," *American Journal of Psychiatry* 127, no. 3 (September 1970): 273-79.
5. Thomas C. Schelling, "The Life You Save May Be Your Own," in *Choice and Consequence*, (Cambridge, MA: Harvard University Press, 1984) p. 116.
6. Ibid., p. 132.

4 FASHION

> Expenditure for display is more obviously present, and is, perhaps, more universally practiced in the matter of dress than in any other line of consumption.... The greater part of the expenditure incurred by all classes for apparel is incurred for the sake of a respectable appearance rather than for the protection of the person.... It is by no means an uncommon occurrence, in an inclement climate, for people to go ill clad in order to appear well dressed. And the ceremonial value of the goods used for clothing in any modern community is made up to a much larger extent of the fashionableness, the reputability of the goods than the mechanical service which they render in clothing the person of the wearer.[1]

There are fads and fashions in many areas: architecture, automobiles, pets, games, psychology, even diseases. Why do fashions in clothing change, and what are the effects of such change on economic well-being?

Clothing protects, but also decorates, the body. Most of the expenditure on clothes is undoubtedly for display purposes. Clothing is intimately connected with personal presentation and is thus ultimately connected with role playing and social rankings. This means, in economic jargon, that there are strong externalities in this field of consumption.

Externalities exist because what others wear dramatically affects the utility we receive from any particular item of clothing we possess. What (certain) others wear in large part determines what is fashionable, what is presentable, and even what we think fits well. While most people are not bound by fashion, all are influenced by it.

An expert on marketing and fashion writes:

> If any reader of this should doubt the power of fashion, let him try a simple experiment and note his own reactions. Let him put on clothes as worn by a past generation and then go out as casually as he can among his acquaintances or in fact

among strangers and note, first, their reactions toward him and then his feelings toward himself. There will be quizzical looks, doubtful stares and critical estimates. He will be thought queer. He will be judged as lacking in brain power and, perhaps, as an undesirable person. If he persists in his experiment, he will, if he is an employee, lose his job. He will lose his customers if he is a salesman. He will lose votes if he is a politician.... No man can belong to present-day society and at the same time be completely out of present-day fashions.[2]

THE PURSUIT OF STATUS

Most people feel the need and desire to conform to the prevailing styles. However, if conformity were the only motive behind dress, there would be little need for a theory of changing fashion; dress styles might tend to be relatively fixed. What-to-wear would be a cooperative game, reaching a stable equilibrium once acceptable custom was established.

But there are usually other social motives behind clothing. The most important of these is the attempt to gain prestige-- the desire to help ensure or improve one's ranking on some status hierarchy. The material goods most closely associated with the ego are often clothes, with fashion serving "as an outward emblem of personal distinction or of membership in some group to which distinction is ascribed."[3] This desire for distinction and prestige is a crucial cause of the volatility of fashion in a dynamic society.

Status is a relative rather than an absolute concept. In terms of status alone, the competition for prestige has characteristics similar to a zero-sum game. One individual or group gains only at the expense of another. This means that for goods consumed principally for status rather than functional utility, social and economic welfare need not be enhanced by increased production. More of the good is not necessarily better than less of it.

For the economist, "goods"-- as opposed to "bads" like pollution or garbage-- are generally assumed to bring direct functional utility. An apple can nourish us, satisfy our appetite, and taste delicious. It is an economic good with economic value because it is scarce, because everyone cannot have as much as he desires. Costlessly increasing the supply of such a good, for example, through technological advance may lower its relative price, but it should increase material well-being.

Pure prestige items, on the other hand, are valued not for their functional utility but principally *because* they are scarce or rare.[4] Increasing the supply of a status good tends not only to decrease its price but also to lower the actual prestige benefits provided by previous units. For example, much of the pleasure to be derived from ownership of an original Picasso print comes from the prestige it engenders. A virtually perfect copy, aesthetically just as pleasing, is not nearly as valuable. Limiting the number of original prints, especially by the destruction of the lithograph, may be sound business policy, but it initially seems economically wasteful. Yet, increasing production, or even discovering more originals, may not provide much social benefit. At least in terms of prestige, while new owners advance in status, they do so only as others retreat.

In *Essays in Persuasion*, John Maynard Keynes briefly mentions that class of wants "which are relative in the sense that we feel them only if their satisfaction lifts us above, makes us feel superior to, our fellows. Needs of [this] second class, those which satisfy the desire for superiority, may indeed be insatiable, for the higher the general level, the higher still they are."[5] While John Kenneth Galbraith might extend the argument, he would heartily agree that when goods satisfy only status needs, more output is not necessarily socially beneficial. "In technical terms, it can no longer be assumed that welfare is greater at an all-around higher level of production than at a lower one. It may be the same."[6]

SUMPTUOSITY

The argument thus far has been that where goods provide status and prestige, there are negative externalities in consumption. Most goods and services probably furnish both prestige and functional utility (as well as other possible benefits). With respect to clothing, prestige is generally the more important of the two. All social scientists agree that the key motivation behind most expenditures for bodily adornment is display rather than protection.

There are many reasons, most of them social, why an individual wears specific types of clothes. In terms of identification alone, clothes can help group us by age, sex, occupation, marital standing, or team membership. Clothing may also demonstrate our economic status, and it is upon this aspect of fashion that Thorstein Veblen focuses.

Veblen argues that "in order to gain and hold the esteem of men it is not sufficient merely to possess wealth or power. The wealth or power must be put in evidence."[7] The choice of clothing is often crucial for the display of purchasing power. Expenditures for dress are important for pecuniary repute since "our apparel is always in evidence and affords an indication of our pecuniary standing to all observers at first glance."[8] Fashion is an ideal arena for "conspicuous consumption"-- lavish expenditure that satisfies no real need and is merely a mark of socioeconomic status. Hence the sumptuousness of much of our clothing, especially formal attire.

Veblen emphasizes not only conspicuous consumption in bringing reputability but also the related conspicuousness of leisure. While the poor are economically forced to perform productive, often physical work, the rich are not. Thus, historically, abstention from labor was often an indication of great wealth, and the display of leisure became valued as a mark of high social standing. Therefore, says Veblen, for dress to promote status, it "should be expensive, but it should also make plain to all observers that the wearer is not engaged in any kind of productive labor," that he or she is not obliged to earn a living.[9]

Elegant apparel, Veblen argues, is contrived at every point to signal that the wearer does not habitually put forth any useful effort. "The pleasing effect of neat and spotless garments is chiefly, if not altogether, due to their carrying the suggestion of leisure-- exemption from personal contact with industrial processes of any kind."[10] Linen has been especially useful for both conspicuous consumption and leisure, for it betrays dirt at once and must be frequently renewed.[11]

Veblen explains the corset, the dress, and high heels as forms of conspicuous leisure-- demonstrations of an honorably futile existence, so far removed from menial necessities that clothes can be worn that actually impede physical labor. Similarly, refined tastes and manners are useful evidence of gentility because good breeding requires time and expense. "A knowledge of good form is prima facie evidence that that portion of a well-bred person's life which is not spent under observation of the spectator has been worthily spent in acquiring accomplishments that are of no lucrative effect."[12]

Like "good" manners, "correct" attire is determined socially rather than individually. Many consumers may correctly argue that the principles of conspicuous consumption and leisure do not directly motivate their individual purchases. Their wish is merely "to conform to established usage, to avoid unfavorable notice and comment, to live up to the accepted canons of decency in the kind, amount and grade of goods consumed, as well as in the decorous employment of their time and effort."[13] Yet, it is precisely these rules of proper and responsible behavior that Veblen argues are basically molded by the competition for status and the norm of conspicuous waste.

AESTHETIC PERCEPTION

Society not only dictates what is correct and proper but also influences what is considered aesthetic and beautiful. The prevailing fashion, for example, clearly affects our tastes. Clothes that were yesterday so attractive often seem today to have lost their aesthetic as well as social appeal. As a professor of marketing writes:

> The influence of fashion over the human mind is such as to make a style, when accepted, seem beautiful, no matter how hideous it may appear at other times when not in fashion. It is hard to believe that the hoop skirt, the bustle and the leg o'mutton sleeve were once considered very charming and highly appropriate. No doubt the present fashions will in time seem just as ridiculous and even, probably, as hideous as do those past styles seem now.[14]

Veblen argues that pecuniary criteria often underlie aesthetic judgments of what is appealing and what is fashionable. Costliness, he says, often masquerades as beauty. Fancy-bred dogs are considered aesthetic, primarily because of their expense. Conversely, beautiful flowers often are labeled common weeds because of their cheapness. Handmade items, even with marked imperfections and irregularities, are presently judged superior to machine woven ones because of their relative prices. When rayon first appeared it was both expensive and highly fashionable. Today, natural fibers are both more costly and more admired.[15]

When women were valued for their service, as in Homeric times, the ideal female was robust and large limbed. More recently, the identification of repute with conspicuous leisure has made the delicate face, the slender figure, and the constricted waist hallmarks of beauty. Today, the height of attraction is the well-conditioned body, which indicates that one can afford the expense, effort and time to work out at a fitness center. In China, the deformed feet of the female, the "golden lilies," were a mark of both conspicuous leisure and sexual appeal.

Aesthetics matter a great deal for display items such as clothing. If pecuniary values do affect aesthetic (as well as snob) appeal, this may have important implications for welfare analysis. Assume that technological improvements lead to a dramatic reduction in the cost of producing silk garments. In time, as they become more common, will they not only be less desirable for prestige and status purposes but actually feel less sensuous and look less lovely? If so, increased consumption will not make society as materially better off as might initially be supposed. However, an offsetting factor would be if those goods becoming relatively more scarce (e.g., linen clothes) began to increase in aesthetic appeal.

FASHION

Veblen's theory of conspicuous consumption and leisure appears useful in explaining much of the sumptuosity of wearing apparel. This is true not only for dynamic societies but also for those communities in which styles have remained largely static. The dress of the upper class in ancient China, for example, seems designed to display the leisure life. The long silk robe of the mandarin with its projecting sleeves served well to frustrate any attempts at manual labor. Similarly, the scholar's habit of allowing fingernails to grow to prodigious lengths advertised mental rather than physical exertion.[16]

Fashion-- the rapidly changing vogues in clothing styles-- is explained in large part by the constant *competition* for status. Such competition assumes the ability to rise in status and to use clothing as a symbol and weapon in the endeavor. The status competition may be within, or between, classes or groups, though historically interclass competition appears the more important. When there was no upward social mobility, that is, when class was unalterable, society and clothing styles also tended to be static.

In feudal society, with its traditional stratification systems, the little fashion consciousness that existed resided primarily within the upper class and seems to have been caused by intraclass status rivalry. The ceilings placed on the upward mobility of the lower classes decreased their individual distinctiveness in dress; folk costume existed rather than continual fashion change. It was when the economy became more dynamic and the social order began to disintegrate, increasing the possibility of social advance, that fashion came into its own.

As individuals from lower social groupings attempt to ascend the status hierarchy, they naturally tend to imitate the behavior and attire of those above. A psychologist writes:

> So long as a system of "fixed" custom prevails, each social grade is content to wear the costume with which it is associated. But when the barriers between one grade and another become less insuperable, when, in psychological terms, one class begins to aspire to the position above it, it is natural that the distinctive outward signs and symbols of the grades in question should become imperilled.... It is a fundamental human trait to imitate those who are admired or envied . . . and what [could be] more natural, and, at the same time, more symbolic, than to start the process of imitation by copying their clothes, the very insignia of the admired and envied qualities?[17]

In order to maintain their own distinctiveness, members of the upper class are forced to change their mode of dress. Eventually, a new upper-class style of attire emerges and this in turn is copied. This process-- fashion-- can continue endlessly, the highest class trying to differentiate itself, the lower classes in hot pursuit. As William Hazlitt wrote in 1818: "[Fashion] is a continual struggle between 'the great vulgar and the small' to get the start of, or keep up with each other in the race of appearance."[18] Since the upper class tends to desert a fashion as soon as it spreads widely, it is often said that a successful fashion sows the seeds of its own destruction.

Status rivalries are one explanation for the *continuing* change in clothing styles. Styles, of course, may change at any time for a wide variety of other reasons. The general mode of dress may be modified by the introduction of new materials, new knowledge or new ideas; it may be affected by government decree or climatic changes, by changes in people's activities or by changes in relative prices. Clothing styles can thus change with some frequency even though class structure is rigid and consumers noncompetitive.

Speed of Fashion Change

Mode of dress is but one aspect and reflection of a whole culture. The art, music, manners, morals, ideas, work, and play of a society all tend to influence what clothes its people wear. As these factors change, so might we expect clothing to change. Probably, the more dynamic the society, the more rapid will be the changes in clothing styles.

In terms of the competition for status, styles should change more rapidly the faster they spread. In Western society, followers have over time become quicker in emulating the leaders owing to the increase in living standards of the poor, the general improvements in communication and transportation, and such specific inventions as sewing machines and manufactured fibers, which have made it possible to imitate the current vogue quickly and cheaply.

As Western society advanced and became more dynamic, fashions changed more rapidly. Clothes in the nineteenth century, writes fashion author Jane Dorner, "changed more often than they had in all the previous five centuries. This constant variety was due in some measure to the fact that fashions were becoming available to a wider range of people, with the result that the upper classes were constantly seeking novelty in a bid to retain their social superiority."[19]

Another factor tending to increase the speed of style change has been growing urbanization. Urban areas have always been more fashion conscious than rural areas, in part because of the anonymity of city life, which increases the significance of symbolic display. Moreover, an urban environment multiplies the number of face-to-face encounters and thus quickens the general spread of fashion information. The growth of the cities undoubtedly contributed to the growing importance and increasing speed of style change.

Laws can be used to affect the spread of fashion and the speed of style change. The upper class does not always run away from its sartorial pursuers. It sometimes tries to stop them. During the thirteenth and fourteenth centuries, for example, the number of sumptuary laws increased dramatically as the landed gentry attempted to stop the sartorial imitations of the urban middle class.[20] England's King Edward III decreed that a man could not dress above his station:

> All esquires and every gentleman under the estate of knighthood, and not possessed of lands or tenements to the yearly amount of 200 marks, shall use in their dress such cloth as does not exceed the value of 4 marks and a half the whole cloth; they shall not wear any cloth of gold, or silk, or of silver, nor any sort of embroidered garment, nor any ring, buckle, nouche, riband nor girdle; nor any ornaments of precious stones, nor furs of any kind; their wives and children shall be subject to the same regulation.[21]

Sumptuary laws generally prove ineffective in the long run; in the short run, however, they may have some impact. In the late 1960s, for example, while dealing more with moral than status concerns, sumptuary laws regulating bathing costumes probably helped prevent the spread of the topless swimsuit phenomenon-- at least in the United States.

Some Effects of Fashion

Fads, such as Hula-Hoops, pet rocks, or Cabbage Patch Kids, can spring up independent of a predecessor and may give rise to no successor. They have no line of historical continuity.[22] Fashion change, on the other hand, is evolutionary, gradual rather than abrupt. While an individual may try to distinguish himself with his attire, he is also required to conform to the prevailing sartorial norm. Otherwise he will appear ridiculous. Styles, therefore, tend to change only at the margin. Skirt lengths, for example, may move up and down, but slowly, not radically. Similarly, hair styles may get longer or shorter, but quantum leaps are unlikely.

Fashion change is noticeable enough, of course, to make the old style look old and outmoded. Unfortunately, most fashion change does not represent an improvement; each new fashion is not aesthetically more pleasing than its predecessor once seemed; nor is it necessarily more comfortable or functional. While there is sartorial evolution, there is no clear upward progression.

Fashion may provide some utility to those people who enjoy and prefer to live in a society of flux and change. There are those who delight in the competitiveness of fashion, and those who are good at predicting new trends can clearly benefit from changing styles. But for the average person, fashion is primarily a costly annoyance.

> The average consumer is chronically distressed to discover how rapidly his accumulated property in wear depreciates by becoming outmoded. He complains bitterly and ridicules the new fashions when they (first) appear. In the end he succumbs, a victim to symbolisms of behavior which he does not fully comprehend. What he will never admit is that he is more the creator than the victim of his difficulties.[23]

Fashion is an outgrowth of the pursuit of status. While competitive consumption could theoretically result in a single, constant, but increasingly sumptuous style, in the real world it has meant ever-changing fashion. In either situation, the social costs, while not identical, are broadly similar. The average individual is continually forced into additional expenditures for items that buy little additional functional utility but only help him to remain in the same status position.

Fashion Anecdotes

There are a large number of stories and anecdotes about fashion that lend support to some of the arguments in the text, give a glimpse of the fascinating variety of historical clothing styles, and, most of all, are inherently interesting. Here are a few:

Function or Display? It was cold, and the tribesman of Tierra del Fuego wore no clothes, so Charles Darwin gave him a large piece of red cloth. Did the native wrap it around him? Not exactly. He immediately tore the cloth into strips and distributed these among his friends, who tied them round their arms and legs as adornment.

Fashion Leadership. The hiatus in English fashion that accompanied the Puritan reign of Oliver Cromwell was ended with the return of Charles II. Charles had spent much of his time in exile at the court of Louis XIV and brought back with him many of the latest French modes. But some rivalry existed between monarchs, and this was increased by Charles's attempts to break the French dictatorship over fashion. Charles's most significant innovation was half-length coat, called a "vest"-- the forerunner of the kind later worn by all eighteenth-century gentlemen. The vest was described by John Evelyn in his diary of October 18, 1666: "It being the first time his Majesty put himself into the eastern fashion of vest, changing doublet, stiff collar, bands and cloak into a comely dress after the Persian mode, with girdles or straps, and shoestrings and garters into buckles, of which some are set with precious stones."[24]

Louis, the Sun King, to show his superiority in matters of fashion decided to mock Charles's attempts at fashion leadership. How? Louis had all his footmen, and only his footmen, wear Charles's newfangled "vest." This made Samuel Pepys "mighty merry, it being an ingenious kind of affront."[25]

Style Evolution. Trousers for women made their debut in America in 1849 with the Rational Dress Campaign of Amelia Jenks Bloomer. The "Bloomer costume" was a cross between a pair of cossacks and long knickerbockers, with a short skirt modestly worn over the top as a concession to convention. Although Amelia crisscrossed the country lecturing on its advantages, the bloomer had little initial success. The idea was too far ahead of its time. However, some thirty years later, when bicycling became a feminine pastime, the bloomer gained wide acceptance. As Ada Ballin wrote in *The Science of Dress*:

> The feeling against the Bloomer costume was very strong, for although it had many good points about it, it represented too violent a change from the fashion of the time and ladies would not adopt it for fear of appearing ridiculous. Reform to be effective must be gradual, and it takes some time for the public to become accustomed to a new idea even in dress.[26]

At the same time the bloomer became acceptable, the bustle lost its appeal. The bustle was a pad worn under the skirt to swell the fullness of the rear end. The bustle made it difficult to stand upright, awkward to walk, and positively dangerous to sit down. Bicycling is credited not only with popularizing the bloomer but also with destroying the bustle.

Sports do not always hold the upper hand to fashion, however. Though roller skating, or "rinking," was quite popular among women in the late nineteenth century, as skirts grew tighter in the 1870s and 1880s, skating became impossible and had to be temporarily abandoned to await the advent of the looser Edwardian styles. Female tennis also suffered fashion difficulties. Stiff corseted clothes were common on the courts until champion Suzanne Lenglen shocked Wimbledon in 1922 by appearing in a "short" (midcalf) skirt. Ten years later, on the same courts, Alice Marble astonished the world by appearing in shorts! Many people thought this was going really too far for the sake of the game.

Fashion Extravagances. Styles often tend to the extreme. We have witnessed this in our own era, with the stiletto heel for women and the micro-mini dress. Other examples: In the 1880s the bustle had reached such an extent that it jutted out like a shelf "whereon a good-sized tea tray might be carried."[27] During the reign of Louis XVI, hair styles had risen to such a degree that Marie Antoinette (known for her taste and elegance) had a coiffure that rose thirty-six inches above her head. And in the 1550s, the bodice for a time became so deep cut as to expose the nipples.

Men, who have often been more style conscious than women, have also had their style extremes. In the 1550s, fashionable trousers became so stuffed with rich materials that a scandalized German Protestant church placed the "trouser devil" into its list of devils. A century earlier, before the advent of stocking-pants, fashionable coats became so short that when a man bent over he exposed his bare posterior. An English sumptuary law, passed in 1475, proclaimed: "Nobody below the rank of Lord, Esquire, or Gentleman may wear a coat, cape or smock so short that when he stands erect it fails to cover his private parts and buttocks, in which case he pays a fine of twenty shillings."[28] The privilege of exposing oneself in public was thereby reserved for the upper classes.

Deleterious Fashion. We are often shocked and bemused by tribal customs such as the filing down of front teeth, the flattening of foreheads, or the plate-shaping of the lips. These and other forms of self-mutilation are performed for religious reasons (teeth are filed to permit free passage of the soul), to demonstrate abstention from physical labor (the elongated head indicates that heavy burdens cannot be carried there), and for other motives such as the practical one of avoiding slavery (a female with distorted lips is less in danger of being kidnapped for concubinage).

We should not forget, however, that Westerners, primarily through fashion, have also disfigured and deformed the body. Attention has focused principally on the waist and on the feet.

Many shoe styles restrict and deform the foot. They are thus deleterious to the health. High heels are among the worst, leading to podiatric disorders, calf muscle shortening, sway back, and so forth. The constriction of the waist by corsets and girdles causes even more serious medical problems. Circulation and breathing are impeded, creating all sorts of difficulties from headaches to fainting spells. A shrinking of the rib cage also increases pressure on the internal organs; additional troubles are caused and compounded by the limited possibility for physical exercise.

Western fashion is not only often uncomfortable but also downright debilitating and dangerous. The typical business suit of the 1920s, it is said, prevented proper ventilation of the body. Moreover, the collar and tie interfered with the free movement of the head, restricting neck and shoulder muscles and giving rise to headaches and fibrositis. The nineteenth-century crinoline is an excellent example of the problems created by fashion. This stiff petticoat, which expanded the full dress skirt, was not only restrictive and cumbersome but also risky. The diaphanous material frequently caught fire, and one woman in a crinoline was actually blown into the sea, where she drowned.

Oh, the suffering in the name of good taste.

CONCLUSION

The general microeconomic model normally assumes that individual utility functions are independent, that individual consumption functions are independent, and that tastes are exogenous. Such postulates are unrealistic for the clothing market, and thus the model, and its welfare implications, may not be very useful for the consideration of fashion.

Fashion is a complicated phenomenon, influenced by many factors. This chapter has focused on one important cause of style changes in clothing: the competition for status. Status rivalry seems quite useful in explaining the *continual* changes in styles, especially in societies that permit upward social mobility.

For most people, what-to-wear is a mixed-motive game involving elements of both cooperation and competition. The typical individual desires to clothe himself in the general manner of his contemporaries; he does not want to be considered odd. Within that prevailing style, however, he may want to be thought to dress extremely well, to be sartorially superior to the others. Veblen argues that his primary motivation is the desire to be considered highly placed on a socioeconomic hierarchy. The competitive use of clothing as an emblem of personal and class distinction is an important cause of changing dress styles, or fashion.

Mixed-motive games, or games with negative externalities, can often result in inefficient outcomes. In the case of fashion, it is possible that the entire society could be better off if the conspicuous consumption aspects of clothing and bodily adornment were eliminated. It is suggestive that utopians from Plato to Sir Thomas More to Mao Tse-tung dressed all their citizens alike, generally in plain, undecorated, and durable cloth.

FOR DISCUSSION

1. Why do soldiers wear uniforms? Why do parochial school students? Girl scouts? Prisoners? Priests? What would be the costs and benefits to society if everyone were compelled to dress in virtually identical clothes?

2. Make a long list of goods and services and try to decide whether "fashion" exists in each item. Is there fashion in mothballs? Ironing boards? Steel? Brooms? Art? Soap? Books? Stocks? Why is there fashion in some areas and not in others?

3. Which of the items on your list are primarily status goods? Does there seem to be any connection between status goods and fashion? Do you think that status items loom large or small in the U.S. economy? In the Native American economy? In the People's Republic of China?

4. "The consumption of alcohol and tobacco, and some indulgence in fashionable dress . . . by workers are commonly classed as productive consumption, but strictly speaking it ought not to be."[29] Comment. How can one differentiate "productive" from "nonproductive" consumption?

5. Trinkets were among the principal items offered by Old World traders to the Native Americans. Assuming free, uncoerced trade, where both parties to the transaction should benefit, did the exchange of corn, tobacco, or land for these tokens of bodily adornment help the Native American society even in the short run?

6. Do sellers cause or influence clothing fashion? How? Which ones? Were fabric manufacturers particularly happy about the miniskirt?

7. Can rapidly changing fashion be considered "worse" in the clothing than in the automobile industry because of the lack of well-organized *used* clothing markets?

8. If Veblen is correct about the importance of conspicuous leisure in dress styles, why haven't clothes been even more cumbersome and confining? Surely human ingenuity could devise something even more constricting than the corset. Similarly, why aren't clothes even more sumptuous than they are? Does the theory of conspicuous leisure have something to say concerning this question?

9. What kind of *empirical* studies might be done to help verify or refute some of the assertions and arguments in this chapter?

10. What is the effect of fashion on the clothing industry? How would the market structure, conduct, and performance be different if (a) there were no competitive consumption or (b) the competition took the form of increasing sumptuousness rather than changing styles?

11. Why are designer labels currently placed on the *outside* of so many garments?

NOTES TO CHAPTER 4

1. Thorstein Veblen, *The Theory of the Leisure Class* (New York: Mentor, 1953), p. 119.
2. Paul Nystrom, *The Economics of Fashion* (New York: Ronald Press, 1928), p. 9.

3. Edward Sapir, "Fashion," *Encyclopedia of Social Sciences*, vol. 6 (New York: Macmillan, 1931), p. 140.

4. Dwight Robinson, "Economics of Fashion Demand," *Quarterly Journal of Economics* 75 (August 1961): 378-95.

5. John Maynard Keynes, "Economic Possibilities for Our Grandchildren," *Essays in Persuasion* (New York: Harcourt, Brace, 1932), p. 365.

6. John Kenneth Galbraith, *The Affluent Society* (Boston: Houghton Mifflin, 1969), pp. 138-54.

7. Veblen, *Theory of Leisure Class*, p. 42.

8. Ibid., p. 119.

9. Ibid., p. 120.

10. Ibid.

11. Quentin Bell, *Of Human Finery* (London: Hogarth Press, 1948), p. 24.

12. Veblen, *Theory of Leisure Class*, p. 49.

13. Ibid., p. 87.

14. Nystrom, *Economics of Fashion*, p. 9.

15. Alison Lurie, *The Language of Clothes* (New York: Random House, 1980), pp. 126-28.

16. Bell, *Of Human Finery*, p. 38-41.

17. J.C. Flugel, *The Psychology of Clothes* (London: Hogarth Press, 1930), p.138.

18. William Hazlitt, quoted in Robinson, "Economics of Fashion Demand," p. 379.

19. Jane Dorner, *Fashion* (London: Octopus Books, 1974), p. 9.

20. Rene Konig, *The Restless Image: A Sociology of Fashion* (London: George Allen & Unwin, 1973), p. 140; Joanne Finkelstein, *The Fashioned Self* (Philadelphia: Temple University Press, 1991).

21. Dorner, *Fashion*, p. 13.

22. Herbert Blumer, "Fashion," *International Encyclopedia of Social Sciences*, vol. 5 (New York: Macmillan, 1968), p. 344.

23. Sapir, "Fashion," p. 143.

24. Dorner, *Fashion*, p. 24.

25. Ibid.

26. Ibid., p. 72.

27. R. Broby-Johansen, *Body and Clothes: An Illustrated History of Costume* (London: Faber & Faber, 1966), p. 143.

28. Ibid., pp. 124-25.

29. Alfred Marshall, *Principles of Economics* (1920).

5 SOCIAL FORCES

STORY I

Once there was a duchy called Irvana that lay in the fertile valleys of the Vagi Mountain. The people there were happy, friendly, and hard working. They had great freedoms and a very reasonable living standard. They were a proud people, proud of their villages, their homes, and their work.

One fateful summer, a native son named Nicholai returned to the town. Nicholai had been the brightest young man of Irvana. He had left the duchy to gain further education and had become a successful businessman in the outside world. Nicholai came back to Irvana because he loved it. He remembered the beautiful white villages and green fields; most of all he remembered the people-- proud, free, and happy. Yet, upon his return, his heart filled with sadness. It was not that the duchy had changed much. It was, he felt, that it had not changed enough. The people were still strong and content, but they had not moved with the times. There had been a few improvements, certainly, but only a few. Irvana had not taken advantage of many new technological advances. Nicholai did not want his country to be backward or to be considered out of date.

Nicholai felt he could help Irvana. He saw how he could increase its output, using machines and modern techniques to replace hand labor. He would build his own modern factories as an example and a prod for Irvana to change its inefficient ways.

Not only was Nicholai a clever man, but he had also gained some measure of wisdom. He had seen problems of advancement, problems of pollution and congestion. Never would he endanger his beloved green fields and pretty villages. He would not dirty the air or water, nor would he let his factories impose undue costs upon his neighbors. He would use his financial resources and his prestige and power to help Irvana grow materially, while eliminating the major costs of change.

But economic growth can affect society in countless ways. It can change people's attitudes, their outlook, their morality, and their contentment. All sorts of scenarios are possible, some good, some bad. Here, beginning with a happy people, we have cause to fear. Let us pick one possibility out of many and spare Irvana much worse fates.

Nicholai built some factories. The problem with his jobs was that they did not satisfy the workers. Compared to other work in Irvana, this was dull, monotonous, and routine. It did not demand workers's minds or command their hearts.

Nicholai at first had trouble finding workers. Most craftspeople clung stubbornly to their outmoded ways. But he found some, enticed into boring jobs by higher wages. Those workers found themselves with higher income, higher wealth, higher consumption. Nicholai paid well and shared profits. His reputation for fairness and efficiency had not been overblown.

Now a touch of envy lurks in every heart. People care about prestige and their neighbors' attitudes and power. How smart a person is, or how strong or how good, is relative to other people. There are few absolutes. In economic terms, worth is often based on what the market pays. And this creeps into the evaluation of the person's own self.

Those who originally joined with Nicholai left their nice jobs for ugly ones. For them, the higher wages more than compensated. These new jobs brought increased wealth and living standards-- both absolutely and relative to their neighbors. They could buy things their neighbors could not, do things their neighbors could not. Their money, sad to say, could also buy political power and favors. Relative wealth was paramount here. But most important, the houses, clothes, and furniture of the factory workers were superior to others'. Their status rose, not only with consumption but also with their wealth itself.

Part of the reason these workers shifted jobs was to increase their status. Let us assume that without that change in relative position they could not have been persuaded to do the boring work of Nicholai's factories. The gain from the absolute increase in consumption would not have been enough.

To the extent these workers rose in status, others fell. Craftspeople could not purchase what factory workers could (though some tried). They could not enjoy the costly activities with their friends. Their children wondered why other children had more. Could not they too?

So more workers switched to the boring but higher paying jobs. And then some more. As more and more families opted for high income and consumption, it became harder still for those left behind. Each worker felt increasing pressure to work in the factories. Soon almost everyone worked there. Those left outside the factories were, indeed, outsiders.

The valleys of Irvana are still fertile and the fields green. And the townsfolk, because of Nicholai, are richer in material goods. But workers dislike their jobs, and there is less laughter and less happiness in the villages. All people cannot increase in status. Each person remembers the old days before Nicholai's factories, and each longs for the past. All wish they could return. All together. Individually, they cannot.

FOR DISCUSSION

1. Do you feel any pressure to be "successful"? What if you aren't?

2. Is it generally true that the more of one's friends who do something, the harder it is not to? If more and more friends "goof off," is it harder to study? If more and more acquaintances try pot, is it harder to abstain? As more and more families watch TV, is it harder not to? ("Did you see the Superbowl?") Is it easier to do calisthenics alone or in a group?

3. How does Story I relate to a prisoner's dilemma game? Are there any similarities to what happened to Irvana and "neighborhood tipping," the marked transformation of neighborhoods from the predominance of one ethnic group to that of another?

4. Why does the poverty line shift over time?

5. Is the competition for prestige at all comparable to the competition for military power? If Irvana didn't advance, wouldn't it just become bait for more prosperous and militaristic neighbors?

6. "If we begin with an ideal world, almost any change is likely to prove unfortunate." Discuss in relation to Story I. Relate to the economist's use of the model of perfect competition.

7. Is tennis more fun to watch now that players are better? Is pro football, basketball, baseball more enjoyable for spectators than college equivalents? If participants spend more and more time and expense getting better vis-a-vis opponents, is this a move toward greater social welfare?

8. Isn't "progress" usually beneficial? When is it not? Are these just minor exceptions? What do you mean by beneficial?

9. Does the status of a job (other than its pay) matter in work selection? Do people choose optimal jobs? Is high mobility a good thing?

10. Why do you think so many teenagers drink and smoke? Is it purely for functional utility, or is it also for prestige, standing, and the need to conform? Is the amount of smoking optimal from an economic standpoint?

STORY II

"Five meters is not too tall," said Fred Johnson, and his nostrils flared in anger and determination. *"My son is not going to be a runt."*

Fred stood up, but his back remained bent. He began rubbing his spine. Martha, his companion, kept quiet to allow his anger to pass.

They were alone in the waiting room.

Fred was over three meters tall. He was large for any age-- except his own. He stood head and shoulders above his own father, who always stated his height in the ancient system of measurement. Fred's father was *"six feet small."* Both father and son wished they were taller.

"You don't know what it's like to be a man-- and be too short," continued Fred. He paused for effect but kept rubbing his back. He wished that he were home, under the massage machine. He would like to ask Martha to help him rub, but that would never do. He was mad, and he wanted to remain so. Anyway, Martha was busy fiddling with her knee supports.

"I'm too short," said Fred; *"Now hush, Martha, you know that it's true."* Martha had not batted an eye. She was steeling herself for the speech she knew was forthcoming. Her knees hurt, but she must maintain her composure. This was an important argument to win. Her son's future life was at stake.

"If I had only been taller I could have been somebody," continued Fred. He stopped his incessant self-massage for emphasis and eyed his companion. *"You know I could have.*

"Tall people have all the advantages," complained Fred. This was his lifelong gripe. *"Tall people are the best athletes. Christ, why shouldn't they be? Height's an advantage in everything. People look up to tall people."* Martha started to smile, but checked herself. *"They're respected. They get the best of everything. They get the best jobs, they get the pick of the girls--"*

"Fred!" Martha interrupted sharply. Fred blanched.

Martha stood up. She had sat still too long, and her back was throbbing. Fred immediately straightened up, as he always did when he and Martha were standing. It was fortunate that the waiting room ceiling was high. Though Fred was not a tall man, he frequently bumped his head in old buildings.

Martha bent over, in part to ease the strain on her aching back, but more in order to remain at a lower altitude than her companion. Then she lowered her voice and spoke strongly but quietly. She knew that Fred blamed all his failings on his stature. He had never forgiven his parents for making him below average. But she had to convince him.

"Why did we go to a height advisor," she asked, *"if we weren't going to take her advice?"* The height advising business, begun immediately after the genetic breakthrough that had allowed height selection, had mushroomed in the past

decades-- a mushrooming closely paralleling the rapid increase in average height, an increase termed the height inflation. Martha had always felt that there was an insidious connection between the advisors and the inflation. It was Fred who had insisted that they see an advisor. But the advisor, instead of advocating increased size, had warned about the drawbacks of excess absolute size, while minimizing the importance of being relatively tall.

"We should never have gotten a woman advisor," snarled Fred. "What do women know about height?" Martha hunched over a bit further. She always wished that, for Fred's sake, she were smaller than he.

"She came highly recommended," reminded Martha. "The Asworths used her, and the Walkers." She paused. "We could have always gotten a second opinion. We might still get one. Perhaps they will let us postpone this appointment. We could come back tomorrow, or--"

"Nonsense!" cut in Fred. "We are here, and the time has almost come. We know something about the statistics and the trends, and I, at least, know what it's like to be too short. My son is not going to go through what I went through, what I go through. He is not! He is not! He will be five meters, and he will be tall!"

Fred was practically yelling. Martha closed her eyes, tightly. She was trying to calm her tremors. Her knees ached, her back throbbed. Worse still, she felt dizzy and lightheaded. She wasn't sure she was thinking clearly. She hoped it was just her blood pressure medication. Damn that medication. That was another problem about being too tall.

She sat down; Fred sat beside her. He seemed contrite. She knew that he was sorry he had raised his voice. She put her hand on his knee and started rubbing. Fred closed his eyes.

"I just want our son to have every advantage," he murmured.

"So do I," she said softly. "So do I." Martha thought of her son-to-be. This was to be the only child they could have. They had been a little unlucky in the drawings. But she was by no means bitter. While some families might have as many as six children, others were not even permitted a single offspring. This was to allow some diversity in family size, while checking the overflowing world population. She had been thankful when her time had come, and she had not emerged empty handed. And a boy! It was what they would have chosen. Now she secretly wished it had been a girl. Fred would not have been so inflexible about a girl's height. He still believed- - as did many-- that the woman should be shorter than the man. There weren't any good reasons for this belief, except that was the way it always had been. And since many people wanted it this way, it was the way things had generally remained.

"Fred," she said. "Really. Think of the physical problems. Knees, back, ankles, heart. We weren't built to be so tall."

"We weren't built to walk upright either," snapped Fred, "yet it hasn't hurt us much." Fred was sitting down. He paused. "Look, I know there are problems, now."

Fred emphasized the "now." "But science will solve these problems. It just takes a little time. There's a lot of money going into height research. Soon we'll just have one little operation at birth that will correct everything." Fred had stood up, bent over, and was rubbing his back. "Even the really tall won't need those awful spinal operations every year. One little operation will correct everything."

"You don't know that," cried Martha. "You may be dooming our son to a life of agony, just to be tall." She continued. "And think of the social problems caused by the height inflation. The old buildings have to be converted or torn down. The old furniture is no good. Nothing old is much good now," she said. "And the height inflation has all the problems of the old population explosion, and you're the one who always said that we should--"

She was interrupted by the opening of the waiting room door. A man entered. A large man. Another patient. Fred immediately straightened up, stood tall, and looked the man in the neck.

The man seemed friendly, introduced himself as Jim, and then asked, "You here for a spinal operation too?"

Fred shook his head.

"No, of course not," said Jim, looking down at Fred. Fred was too short to require that operation. "Of course not." And Jim sneered.

The sneer did it. Shortly thereafter, when the doctor came in, Martha signed for five meters.

The next day Fred met Jim at the prearranged location. Fred was smiling. "Thanks," he said, as he handed Jim a packet of money. "You were great. It worked perfectly. My kid's gonna be tall!

"But I was worried," he continued, "you were almost too late."

"Sorry," replied Jim. "I think I must have passed out for a bit on the way over. You know. The blood pressure medication."

FOR DISCUSSION

1. Relate Story II to Story I. Relate it to options.

2. How tall would you like to be? Does it depend on how tall everyone else is? Would you like to be below average in height? Above average? Can more than a majority of people be above the median height? What do you think would happen to average size if people could choose their children's height? What will be the effects when couples can choose the sex of their children?

3. What would correct government policy be in Story II? What should it be currently, given that individuals can choose how many children they have?

SOCIAL FORCES

Man is a social animal. He lives in a society of others and naturally is influenced by them. His attitudes are influenced by the attitudes of that society; his perceptions are affected by the perceptions of others. Similarly, his economic choices and decisions are largely molded by social values and pressures.

All people have a few basic physical needs, such as oxygen, water, food, and warmth. That these needs can be very cheaply provided is demonstrated by the fact that incredibly poor people, beginning with the cave dwellers, have been able to survive. Over and above these necessities, man typically has a choice about what desires to attempt to satisfy; he must also decide the manner in which to satisfy them. Society exerts a major influence over all such decisions.

When dining with others, for example, Westerners must normally eat meals with specific utensils-- knives, forks, spoons-- on a plate or in a bowl; liquids are to be drunk from a cup or glass. And there are myriad other customs to be observed. Wearing apparel is similarly specified. The Western male must usually wear shoes, socks, pants, even underwear; particular shirts, trousers, coats, and ties are required for formal occasions. It is generally not necessary for government to enforce such prescriptions. Each individual's desire to conform, to be included rather than excluded, is normally sufficient.

This clustering of action (and attitude) is called *custom*. For any individual, the existence of custom brings both benefit and cost. Custom decreases the range of socially acceptable choice while making the actions of individuals in society more predictable and coordinated. Two points deserve special emphasis here. First, custom clearly influences human social behavior, including economic behavior. Second, there is no automatic mechanism, no "invisible hand," to ensure the correct amount of custom or to ensure that the location of the clusters will be optimal from some social criteria.

Economists do not usually discuss customs or focus on social influences. The person in the economic model is a rational type who follows her own self-interest and has a single measure called utility that she attempts to maximize. Moreover, it is generally assumed that her preference function is not directly affected by the consumption path, work pattern, or general lifestyle of others. Preferences are data, exogenous variables, uninfluenced by economic outcomes.

This heroic assumption can lead to fruitful insights, but it seems to assume away much that is interesting in the real world and can result in misleading and incorrect conclusions. This chapter argues that preferences are largely interdependent and mentions some normative implications of introducing some consumption externalities into the general microeconomic model.

If a person's preferences depend, in part, on the economic actions of others, what is the exact nature of that relationship? There are many plausible assumptions that might yield worthwhile hypotheses. Here we argue that a person cares about her relative position in society. For example, if an individual finds her relative income or wealth declining, ceteris paribus, her utility decreases. This kind of interrelationship has been examined by such economists as Veblen, Duesenberry, Galbraith and Frank. For one thing, people are concerned about their status in society, and this is a relative rather than an absolute concept. A person's economic status or prestige depends heavily on her relative income and relative consumption levels. Even a person's sense of individual worth is affected by the relative values the economic system places on her contribution.

In order to uphold her position in society, a person must meet certain forms; she is expected to behave in certain prescribed ways. To the extent that her social standing depends upon her economic position, she will be expected to consume at a certain level. The kind of house she lives in, the car she drives, and the parties she gives should reflect her position. A business executive cannot skimp on the liquor she serves her guests, or the car in which she chauffeurs her clients or peers, or even the clothes she wears in their presence. In order to maintain her status, her position, her job, she is often forced into a certain lifestyle. And her required consumption expenditures will increase as society grows richer.

Relative consumption also matters for reasons of direct functional utility. The value of certain goods and services (vacations, plays, dinners, etc.) may be enhanced by consuming them with friends and neighbors. If a person's relative income falls, she may find it increasingly difficult to accompany higher income friends desirous of consuming higher quality and more expensive items. As contemporaries increase housing expenditures, the individual may find it impossible even to live in the same neighborhood.

A person's economic status affects whom she meets, whom she marries, where she lives. It affects her opportunities. A person, even one not particularly gratified by economic power or satisfied by material possessions or enthralled by conspicuous consumption, may rightly care about her place in the economic hierarchy.

If one's ranking matters, one's relative as well as one's absolute position, then there are externalities, and decentralized decisionmaking may well lead to suboptimal results. If, for example, it is relative consumption that gives prestige, then ceteris paribus, total consumption expenditures will be too large. If it is private rather than public goods that buy status, our mix of purchases, as Galbraith has argued, may overemphasize personal possessions. If our income, rather than our leisure or the kind of work we do, promotes respect, then we may tend to work too hard and at the wrong kinds of jobs.

CONCLUSION

Man is a social animal and is dramatically affected by his social environment. His preferences are influenced by the economic actions of others. Advertising is but a minor source of such influence.

There are many ways that another's actions may affect an individual's preferences. One interesting and plausible way is that, for a variety of reasons, people care about their *relative* wealth, income, and consumption.

Some important normative implications derive from this assumption. The most crucial is that, even assuming perfect competition, economic "progress" may lead to inferior equilibriums. Story I illustrates how social forces may cause worker alienation. In Story II, man cares about his *relative* height. This story emphasizes how growth (in a literal sense!) may prove inimical to society. The point of both stories is that social forces create externalities, and where important externalities exist, decentralized and competitive actions may lead to undesirable results.

FOR DISCUSSION

1. "Conventional welfare analysis stands and falls with the theory of the immutable isolated consumer. If wants can be influenced, what do we mean by the satisfaction of wants?"[1] Comment. Who should decide what wants to satisfy? Since man is a social animal, with preferences molded by the environment, does this really mean that all of conventional economic welfare analysis is uninteresting or misleading?

2. "The more truth there is in this relative income hypothesis-- and one can hardly deny the increasing emphasis on status and income-position in the affluent society-- the more futile as a means of increasing social welfare is the official policy of economic growth."[2] Comment. Aren't we better off, happier, than our great-grandparents? Don't we have better food, housing, sanitation, medication, and so forth? Do you think that the importance of status and income position increases as the society grows richer?

3. "It is thus not so much the utility of cash earnings which provides the initial incentive to men to make them start clearing large areas of bush and plant cash crops, but rather a desire on the part of a few enterprising men to prove themselves as entrepreneurs and ultimately to accumulate more assets and thereby either confirm or establish their position as 'big men.'"[3] Comment. What are the implications of this for government policy designed to promote progress? What are the implications for human welfare?

4. Does what brings status (wealth, power, strength, intelligence) differ among different societies? If so, what accounts for this difference? Does the economic system influence what kinds of things bring prestige and respect?

5. Think of another way social forces affect preferences other than through prestige and status desires. What are some economic implications of this effect?

6. Given that social pressures do affect preferences, what are the implications, if any, for public policy?

7. Are there customs and clusters that you find less than ideal? Are the current calendar, the English language, the customary system of measurement, the typewriter keyboard, and the location of cities optimal? How do you feel about wearing neckties or high heels, going to cocktail parties, and tipping cab drivers? Can or should anything be done about such customs?

NOTES TO CHAPTER 5

1. Stanislaw Wellisz, "Discussion on the Doctrine of Consumer Sovereignty," *American Economic Review* 52 (May 1962): p.287.
2. E. J. Mishan, *The Costs of Economic Growth* (London: Staples, 1967), p.120.
3. Scarlett Epstein, "Innovation of Cash Crops in New Guinea Subsistence Economies," reprinted in H. W. Arndt, "Prestige Economics," *The Economic Record* 48 (December 1972): p.585.

SOURCES

"The Doctrine of Consumers' Sovereignty." *American Economic Review* 62 (May 1962). Papers and comments by T. Scitovsky, J. Rothenberg, A. Berson, S. Wellisz, W. Baumol.

Duesenberry, James. *Income, Savings and the Theory of Consumer Behavior*. Cambridge, MA: Harvard University Press, 1949.

Frank, Robert H. *Choosing the Right Pond: Human Behavior and the Quest for Status*. New York: Oxford University Press, 1985.

Fromm, Erich. *The Sane Society*. New York: Holt, Rinehart & Winston, 1955, chapter 5.

Galbraith, John Kenneth. *The Affluent Society*. Boston: Houghton Mifflin, 1969, chapter 11.

_____. "Economics as a System of Belief." In *Economics, Peace, and Laughter*. Boston: Houghton Mifflin, 1971.

Hook, Sidney, ed. *Human Values and Economic Policy*. New York: N.Y.U. Press, 1967.

Schelling, Thomas C. "On the Ecology of Micromotives." *Public Interest* 25 (Fall 1971): 59-98.

Schumacher, E. F. *Small is Beautiful*. New York: Harper & Row, 1973.

Veblen, Thorstein. *The Theory of the Leisure Class*. New York: Mentor, 1953.

Weisskopf, Walter. *Alienation and Economics*. New York: Dell, 1971.

II EXCHANGE AND PRICING

INTRODUCTION

At the heart of microeconomics lies price theory. Economists emphasize the importance of prices in a market economy: the crucial information they relay to prospective buyers and sellers and the role they play in rationing society's scarce resources. Many types of pricing and exchange relationships exist in the real world. This section examines a few.

Chapter 6 discusses gift giving, where price equals zero, and describes the role of gift exchange in primitive and modern society. The next four chapters deal more directly with pricing and pricing methods: haggling, scalping, tipping, and the cover charge. The general procedure is to explain where such phenomena are likely to occur and to describe some of their principal economic effects.

6 GIFTS

Gift giving and receiving form an important component of our social life. We receive gifts from birth, when we are showered with presents, until death, when well-wishers provide the bereaved with flowers or other tokens of concern and affection. Virtually all the important social events of our lives are marked by the receipt of cards or gifts: weddings, birthdays, anniversaries, graduations, bat mitzvahs. Even a house purchase may bring housewarming presents. The giving and receiving of cards and gifts accompanies many of our general holidays, such as Mother's Day, Valentine's Day, and Easter. Much of the magic of Christmas is intimately connected with the making, buying, wrapping, giving, and opening of presents. Gifts may also be given for no apparent reason, occasion, or event but simply as surprise tokens of love.

Many goods given gratis might be considered as gifts, such as treating for drinks or having friends for dinner. Many services are also provided free of charge and could conceivably be categorized as gifts. Much of our social exchange-- of favors, respect, ideas, even recipes-- have elements of gift giving. The focus here is upon the material present, often identifiable by its special wrappings. The emphasis is not upon the normal social exchange of favors or the various forms of charity, from the giving of alms to the poor to the donation of blood to the Red Cross.

Gift giving can be contrasted with exchange by barter. Barter requires the relinquishing of one good in order to secure another. In gift exchange, on the other hand, the giving up has a voluntary component. While there are often strong social pressures to return gifts, there are no legal sanctions against noncompliance, for no binding contract has been entered into. In barter both parties determine what will be exchanged, and haggling is permissible. In gift exchange it is the giver who unilaterally selects the exact good that changes hands, though there may be hints, customary rules, or other pressures that affect her choice.

Although the gift giver has more discretionary power over what good, if any, to relinquish, she has less real freedom to withdraw from a continuous process of exchange. While the pressures to engage in specific market or barter exchanges are generally small, there is usually a strong social obligation to accept an offered gift. The acceptance of a gift helps create or affirm a cordial relationship. To refuse a gift usually engenders ill will. The acceptance of a gift produces further pressure to reciprocate in some manner. It is therefore entirely possible for an individual to become trapped in a system she had no desire to enter into. Even refusal to return something as innocuous as a Christmas card greeting can have undesirable social ramifications.

It is the social aspects of gift giving that most differentiate it from market transactions. Among other things, gifts can serve to express affection, promote fellowship and solidarity, and reaffirm social worth. Such social effects are largely absent in market transactions, in which parties to the exchange are playing economic rather than social roles.

While gift giving is primarily a social event, it does have important economic consequences. It influences the kind of goods demanded as well as the timing of purchase and possibly even the household's consumption/saving choice. One dramatic illustration of the impact of gift giving on business is the effect of Christmas on retail sales. In December sales of apparel stores in the United States jump some 65 percent over normal months; sales in general merchandise stores virtually double. Overall December retail sales are consistently more than 20 percent above the normal monthly average.[1]

This chapter is divided into three parts. In the first, a major implication of microeconomic theory regarding gifts is examined. Unfortunately, because of the social nature of gift giving, classical economic theory is not terribly useful for understanding the role of gifts in society. The second part describes the importance of gift exchange in a number of tribal societies. Viewing gift giving from different cultural perspectives can help illuminate some important aspects of gift exchange in modern society. The final portion discusses the qualities of those specific types of goods that are often purchased as gifts.

GIFTS AND MICROECONOMIC THEORY

Economists have largely ignored the phenomenon of gift giving. The general economic approach, however, is that a person is a rational being and will therefore try to give that amount and those particular presents that will maximize her own utility. Perhaps the principal implication from micro theory regarding gifts is that, except for strictly monetary presents, the custom is economically inefficient. The argument parallels the well-known analysis of the inefficiency of government housing subsidies. Such programs are inefficient because direct income subsidies that cost the government no more than the specific product subsidies can provide greater utility to the recipients. If they wish, the recipients can spend the whole of their extra income on housing. If they spend only a part on housing, economists presume they prefer the expenditure pattern they selected for themselves. Similarly with gifts. A gift of $20 should provide at least as much material benefit as the gift of a $20 necktie.

The conclusion that monetary gifts are always more efficient than material ones requires some very strong assumptions. One assumption is that the recipient's consumption pattern does not affect the giver's utility. A related and more crucial postulate is that the act of caring and giving, of bestowing the proper present, doesn't directly affect the recipient's utility; she would be at least equally content had she just enough additional income to have purchased the good for herself. This postulate is generally incorrect in that it ignores the essential social nature of gift giving. In the real world, since individuals do not have complete knowledge, they often desire the signals and symbols of affection and esteem that gifts can provide.[2]

There are other assumptions implicit in the conclusion that gift giving is inefficient. One postulate is that an individual's preferences are always best known to herself and that she can act rationally with respect to them. This may not be the case if there are problems of personal temptation or if there is an unwillingness to buy oneself desired commodities because they seem "frivolous." A further assumption is that the transaction costs of market exchange are negligible. Again there are exceptions in the real world. On a trip I might see something unusual and inexpensive that a good friend might like. Buying it as a gift could prove more efficient than any available market arrangement. I know she would have trouble purchasing it for herself. Contacting her immediately has costs. There may be problems with my buying it on the hopeful assumption that she will repurchase it from me. Formal or informal contractual agreements making me her purchasing agent can run into difficulties. While market transactions are usually more economical than gift exchange, if explicit contracts are costly to make or enforce, then reciprocal gift giving may prove more efficient than market exchange. This may be a usual circumstance for many primitive societies.

GIFT GIVING IN PRIMITIVE SOCIETY

Nineteenth-century German economist Bruno Hildebrand's three-stage theory of economic development emphasizes the importance of the medium of exchange. The first stage is represented by a natural or barter economy, which is gradually supplanted by money exchange and finally by credit. Studies of tribal society belie this simple schema. Gift giving is often an older and vastly more important form of exchange than is barter in primitive economies, and it thus should be placed at an earlier stage. Moreover, a fundamental ingredient in many gift-giving arrangements is the supposedly advanced notion of credit. As Marcel Mauss perceived, gifts generally require countergifts, and often, time must elapse before presents can be returned.[3] A posthaste gift return is often considered improper, for it implies a refusal to stay indebted. In the words of a French maxim, "Excessive eagerness to discharge an obligation is a form of ingratitude." Similarly, an exact-return payment may be considered an affront, suggesting a desire to transform a social relationship into a businesslike one.[4] Gift exchange thus frequently entails an implicit, albeit unusual, form of credit, where the original recipient remains under some obligation until the gift is repaid. While there are no formal contractual arrangements, some countergift is often dictated if honor and reputation are to be preserved.

The *Kula*

Gifts accompany virtually every ceremony in Melanesia and are also provided for a wide variety of privileges and services. Gifts are given to the garden magician, to village mourners at funerals, to unmarried girls for sexual favors, and so forth. The Melanesian vocabulary contains an enormous number of words specifying particular categories of presents.

The *kula*[5] stands at the apex of this Melanesian gift-exchange system. It is public and ceremonial, rooted in myth, backed by traditional law, and surrounded by magic. Yet, in its essence, the *kula* is simply a passing from hand to hand, between designated partners, of prestigious but generally useless objects. The exchange of *kula* items takes place in a circular fashion around the islands. Necklaces are passed clockwise from island to island; armshells are passed counterclockwise. These *kula* objects have little practical value other than for decoration, and even here they are often too valuable or cumbersome to be worn. But first-class necklaces and armshells are more than mere valuables. Each has a name, a personality, a past, and perhaps even a legend attached to it. To possess one is considered exhilarating yet comforting. Their owners may handle and gaze at them for hours. Moreover, while they are never kept for any length of time, temporary possession provides the owner with prestige and perhaps renown. The *kula* valuables form a favorite subject of tribal conversation, gossip, and gloating.

Kula exchange is usually reserved for village chiefs, who have a number of lifelong *kula* partners in other tribes. Their ceremonial exchange of necklaces and armshells often requires large overseas expeditions; herein lies the great economic significance of the *kula*. The expeditions facilitate large amounts of exchange among the islands in the form of gift giving and barter. The *kula* thus promotes both economic trade and political friendship, creating a vast network of relationships among potentially rival tribes.

A relationship similar to the *kula* often exists between common tribesmen in neighboring maritime and agricultural villages. Vegetables and fish are exchanged by specific partners in ceremonial and reciprocal gift giving. This exchange, known as *wasi*, promotes economically beneficial division of labor among the islanders.

The natives also engage in barter but sharply distinguish this from *kula*, *wasi*, and all other forms of gift giving. Barter, or *gimwali*, is generally held in low esteem by the Melanesians. *Gimwali* lacks the social aspects of gift exchange. There is no ceremony, magic, or special partnership. When asked about certain transactions, whether they belong to one class or another, a native is apt to say in a deprecating tone, "That was only *gimwali*." It is significant that villagers will barter, but not exchange gifts, with members of tribes that are usually treated with contempt.

Gimwali can be done with strangers and in a free manner. Gift giving, on the other hand, requires social intercourse and often an elaborate form and manner of presentation unnecessary in barter exchange. When criticizing indecorous or hasty procedure during *kula*, a native may say, "He conducts his *kula* as if it were *gimwali*."

While sharp bargaining occurs in *gimwali*, direct haggling is never permitted in gift exchange, for it would demean the entire process. In gift giving, however, there is sometimes implicit negotiation to help ensure that both parties are happy with a reciprocal exchange. Even in *kula*, since village chiefs have a number of partners in other tribes, "bait" may be used to show an interest in or to bid for a partner's newly acquired armband or necklace. Second-grade treasures, such as pigs or axe blades, are often given to solicit specific *kula* valuables.

In *kula*, *wasi*, and many other types of gift giving, return presents are socially obligatory. It is sometimes impossible to return equivalent gifts immediately, and often it is bad form to attempt to do so. The requirement of delayed reciprocity helps create an obligation and trust relationship that unites villagers and tribes. Trust is more important in reciprocal gift giving than in barter or legal credit since there is no direct means of redress should return gifts appear niggardly. While there is sometimes dissatisfaction with particular gift exchanges, most natives try to return a good equivalent. Social pressures are powerful among the islanders, especially in gift giving, since generosity is a principal virtue and meanness the most despised vice. Moreover, a reputation for fairness and generosity is useful in attracting a more munificent stream of presents.

The *Potlatch*

Gift exchange also plays a pivotal role in the life of Indians inhabiting America's northwest coast. Social ranking seems almost an obsession for these natives, and position is constantly challenged or reaffirmed at complex ceremonies known as *potlatches*.[6] The great *potlatches* are winter festivals that last for weeks. They are marked by the lavish distribution of gifts by the host and sometimes by the actual destruction of valuables in a competitive show of wealth.

Potlatches are often given at critical life events: birth, adoption, puberty, marriage, death. There are also face-saving, totem-pole, and vengeance *potlatches*. For some tribes, the house-building *potlatch* is the largest and most important type. Visitors from other villages remain for a considerable part of the winter and help construct a dwelling. There is much ceremony and festivity, culminating in the presentation of valuables to the numerous guests.

At a major *potlatch*, the host is aided by his *numaym*, which is principally a paternal descendant group. Past gifts of blankets and other valuables by the host to his *numaym* obligate them to repay on demand, at phenomenal rates of interest. These repayments provide the host with enough property to distribute among outside guests to bring honor to his name and to his *numaym*.

The goods distributed at the *potlatch* consist almost entirely of treasure items of little practical value. They are not intended to satisfy the comfort wants of the guests but first and foremost the status demands of the host. The social ranking of the host, or of his progeny, largely depends on the relative size of his *potlatch*. Social standing resides not in the accumulation of wealth but in its public disposition. *Potlatch* gifts are thus different from payments for work done. Instead, they may be considered as prestige investments, goods bestowed on guests in their capacity as *potlatch* witnesses.

The *potlatch* is the principal method among the Indians by which relative rankings are not only established but also validated. While the host is judged by the size of his *potlatch*, guests are ranked by the relative value of the gifts they receive. The inequality of the gifts reflects the host's judgment of relative social worth.

While general gift exchange is common among the natives and usually associated with fellowship and good spirit, the *potlatch* is sometimes used for economic warfare. A perceived slight or insult by one close in status but from a different *numaym* may be met by a *potlatch* challenge-- to see who can give away or, more often, destroy the most valuables. Failure to match one's rival is tantamount to defeat. This is the motivation for the spectacular vengeance *potlatches* used to ruin an opponent. The spectators are the ultimate judges in these ostentatious displays of conspicuous destruction.

The vengeance *potlatch*-- vast destruction of property to destroy a rival-- is the monster child of gift exchange. The usual *potlatch*, however, is a time of ceremony and festivity, often accompanying a major social event. It is sometimes the occasion for joint constructive work, as the building of houses or totem poles, and in aboriginal times it may have served as an important method of income distribution. Before contact with white traders, the natives were more numerous and less prosperous. It is believed that gifts given during *potlatch* contained more utilitarian items that helped alleviate short run misfortunes. The aboriginal *potlatch*, as well as serving prestige functions, may also have been a form of disaster insurance, distributing essential food and wealth and preventing violent attack by neighboring *numayms*.[7]

Gift exchange is vastly more important in these primitive societies than in the modern economy. Yet, gift giving in developed countries remains a significant phenomenon, with somewhat similar motives and effects. For example, gifts can build friendships and goodwill; they often help solidify kinship relationships. At weddings they are one aspect of the creation of linkages between the uniting families.[8] Ostentatious gift giving can be used to preserve rank and increase prestige. A debutante's coming-out party, for instance, can be perceived as primarily an investment in status.[9] And our exchange of gifts at Christmas has been likened to a gigantic, friendly *potlatch* involving millions of families and with many budgets ending in fundamental imbalance.[10]

GIFT GOODS

It has been estimated that purchased gifts account for more than 4% of the typical household budget.[11] Goods received as gifts are somewhat different from commodities that would be purchased for oneself, and it is not possible (nor perhaps desirable) for individuals to compensate completely for this fact. In other words, gifts influence the type and kinds of goods purchased and produced in our economy.

The social aspects of gift exchange are of utmost importance. The content of a present is generally subordinate to its significance as a token of the social relationship. Moreover, the manner of giving is often as important as the gift given. Virtually anything can be given and welcomed as a present if it is given in the right spirit. Nevertheless, certain types of goods are more presentable and acceptable as gifts than others.

Flowers are an appropriate gift for almost all occasions, as, to a somewhat lesser extent, are candies. Flowers are beautiful and fragrant; there is the implication that these are beautiful things to brighten the lives of beautiful people. As Emerson wrote in his curious essay on gifts: "We love flattery even though we are not deceived by it, because it shows that we are of importance enough to be courted. Something like that pleasure, the flowers give us what am I to whom these sweet hints are addressed?"[12] The rationale for candies follows the similar logic of sweets for the sweet.

Gift giving is a sign of social relationship, and what we give may be considered a signal of how we view the recipient. Thus the appropriateness of flowers, candies, and so forth. Conversely, it is often fitting to give something representative of oneself. Emerson argues that a poet should bring his poem, the miner a gem, and the shepherd his lamb.[13] An extreme instance of self-presentation through gifts is the display of masculinity on the part of a new father in the giving of cigars.[14]

While it is the thought that counts, the relative value of the gift also matters. It matters since the gift is a presentation of oneself, an indication of one's generosity, and a signal of one's affection. The value of the good may be reckoned by the time spent by the giver in making the present or in selecting the most appropriate item, or it may be determined by the price. There are, of course, limits of good taste on the maximum price since there is often a social obligation to repay gifts and because it is considered vulgar to try to buy friendship or affection. These are items the value of which is destroyed if bought or sold in the marketplace.

Because affection becomes tainted by marketplace values, it is customary to tear off price tags before giving store-bought presents. Similarly, it is the mean person who precisely computes the price of goods received. Nonetheless, the conspicuousness of gifts, and the signal attached, requires that they usually be generous. A Chinese proverb says: "In ordinary life you must be economical; when you invite guests you must be lavish in hospitality."[15] A dinner guest not only receives ample portions but is given better than the usual fare.

Gift goods are generally near the top of the line. They are often brand-name items with well-known trademarks for superior quality. One gives an expensive Parker pen as a graduation present, not a collection of Bic pens. Manufacturers cater to the need for known prestige goods for gift purposes. Lancer ads show hosts quickly recognizing and appreciating their guests' gifts of this particular wine. Hallmark creates the card "for those who care enough to send the very best." Gift giving generally rewards the high-quality product differentiation advantages of the well-known, established firm.

Presents are usually luxuries. Gift shops are packed with frills and knickknacks. It is often in bad taste to give something too useful to a poor friend or relative, for it smacks of charity. It may tend to rob the gift of its sentimental value and humiliate the recipient with the implication that he is being treated as a needy person rather than as an intimate.[16] As Emerson writes: "We wish to be self-sustained. We do not quite forgive a giver. The hand that feeds us is in some danger of being bitten. We can receive anything from love, for that is a way of receiving it from ourselves; but not from any one who assumes to bestow."[17]

The suitability of any particular gift depends on the occasion and the relationship of the parties concerned. The closer the relationship, the wider the latitude of choice of gifts (and usually the more appropriate the present). Many items are too personal or too expensive to be given by mere friends or acquaintances. Some presents require intimate knowledge of one's tastes, decor, sense of humor, and so forth. The more distant the relationship, the more important the implicit rules of gift giving, the more likely are gifts to be luxury items of well-known high quality.

CONCLUSION

Social exchange, the exchange of courtesies, pleasantries, ideas, and favors, is pervasive. Gift giving is an aspect of social exchange involving material goods. In primitive society, gift giving is also often the dominant method of economic exchange. Even in our advanced society, the exchange of gifts has important effects on our economic and social lives.

It is the social ramifications of gift giving that sharply differentiate it from market exchange.[18] In primitive societies, gifts play a total social role, encompassing aspects of the religious, magical, economic, judicial, and moral.[19] Among the Melanesians, gift giving is "one of the main instruments of social organization, of the power of the chief, of the bonds of kinship, and of the relationship in law."[20] In all societies, gift exchange is a powerful force helping to bind social groups together.[21]

Gifts also bring various recipients and donors into comparison. This is demonstrated in a most dramatic fashion by the *potlatch* ceremonies, whose principal function is to create and preserve social status rankings. But comparisons created by gift giving are present in all societies. Modern parents, for example, try to give equivalent presents to their children to emphasize equal love for them all. Conversely, to avoid the invidious comparison of whether mother or father cares more, it is a common practice for parents to give gifts jointly.

The role gifts play in status comparisons is enhanced by the high visibility of much gift exchange. Large ceremonial gatherings are integral components of the *potlatch* and *kula* exchanges. In modern society, gift exchange is also somewhat conspicuous. Presents usually are opened before some kind of audience, often including the donor. Indeed, one reason gifts are wrapped is to provide an element of mystery and surprise and to allow the giver to witness the recipient's initial reaction. General conversation, especially around Christmas, is often directed to the exact nature of presents given and received. This conspicuousness of gift giving influences the type of goods exchanged. In both primitive and modern society we find that gift goods are generally luxury items of well-known high quality.

FOR DISCUSSION

1. "Never borrow money or do business with a friend." What is the basis for this adage?

2. Does the marketplace decrease the value of certain services? Which ones? Why is there a tendency to look down on paid companions, gigolos, and prostitutes?

3. What are the pros and cons of a society in which gift giving is the principal method of exchange?

4. "In spite of the success of a business society in increasing productivity and in providing for human wants, it has a tendency to undermine itself because of its inability to generate affection. It is a positive-sum game in which everybody benefits, but in which the game itself is apparently so lacking in emotional effect that it does not produce loyalty, love, and self-sacrifice. Very few people have ever died for a Federal Reserve Bank."[21] Do you agree? Aren't many businesspeople quite protective toward their corporations? Aren't there any social ramifications of pure economic exchange?

5. Relate gift exchange to the business practice of reciprocity.

6. What is the relationship between gift exchange and geographic mobility?

7. Do you think the McDonald's gift certificate is highly profitable? Why or why not? How about one for Dunkin' Donuts? For Saks Fifth Avenue? For Tiffany's? Why give a gift certificate instead of money?

8. Why is there a Mother's Day? Which groups had an incentive to create one?

9. What are the principal economic effects of Christmas?

NOTES TO CHAPTER 6

1. U.S. Department of Commerce, *Survey of Current Business: Business Statistics* 72, no. 5 (May 1992): S-8.
2. Paul Webley and Richenda Wilson, "Social Relationships and the Unacceptability of Money as a Gift," *Journal of Social Psychology* 129 (1989): 85-91; Colin Camerer, "Gifts as Economic Signals and Social Signals," *American Journal of Sociology* 94, Supplement (1988): S180-S214.
3. Marcel Mauss, *The Gift* (New York: Norton, 1967), pp. 1-45.
4. Barry Schwartz, "The Social Psychology of the Gift," *American Journal of Sociology* 73 (July 1967): 6.
5. Most of the material in this section on *kula* exchange comes from Bronislaw Malinowski, *Argonauts of the Western Pacific* (New York: Dutton, 1950). Secondary sources include: Paul Bohannan, *Social Anthropology* (New York: Holt, Rinehart & Winston, 1963), pp. 229-39; Cyril Belshaw, *Traditional Exchange and Modern Markets* (Englewood Cliffs, NJ: Prentice-Hall, 1965), pp. 12-52; C. A. Gregory, "Gifts," in John Eatwell, Murray Milgate and Peter Newman, eds., *The New Palgrave Social Economics* (New York: W. W. Norton, 1989), pp. 109-18; and Mauss, *The Gift*, pp. 18-31.
6. A great deal has been written about *potlatch*, some of it contradictory. Material in this section comes from a variety of sources, principally: F. H. Boas, *Kwakiutl Ethnography* (Chicago: University of Chicago Press, 1966); Helen Codere, *Fighting with Property* (Gluckstadt, Germany: J. J. Augustine, 1950); George Peter Murdock, *Rank and Property among the Haida*, Yale Publications in Anthropology #13 (New Haven: Yale University Press, 1936); H. G. Barnett, "The Nature of Potlatch," *American Anthropologist* 40 (July 1938): 349-57; Ronald P. Rohner and Evelyn Rohner, *The Kwakiutl* (New York: Holt, Rinehart & Winston, 1970), pp. 95-105; Stuart Piddocke, "The Potlatch System of the Southern Kwakiutl: A New Perspective," *Southwestern Journal of Anthropology* 21 (Autumn 1965): 244-64; Douglas Cole, "Underground Potlatch," *Natural History* (October 1991): 50-53; Bohannan, *Social Anthropology*, pp. 253-65; Belshaw, *Traditional Exchange*, pp. 20-29; and Mauss, *The Gift*, pp. 31-37.
7. D. Bruce Johnson, "The Formation and Protection of Property Rights among the Southern Kwakiutl Indians," *Journal of Legal Studies* 15 (January 1986): 41-67.
8. Belshaw, *Traditional Exchange*, p. 50.
9. Bohannan, *Social Anthropology*, p. 259.
10. Claude Levi-Strauss, *The Elementary Structure of Kinship* (Boston: Beacon Press, 1969), p. 57.

11. J. Davis, "Gifts in the U.K. Economy," *MAN* 7 (Fall 1972): 408-29; Thesia Gardner and Janet Wagner, "Economic Dimensions of Household Gift-Giving," BLS Working Paper 221, Department of Labor, October 1991.

12. Ralph Waldo Emerson, *Essays*, Second Series (Boston: Houghton Mifflin, 1865), p. 154.

13. Ibid., p. 155.

14. Schwartz, "Social Psychology of the Gift," pp. 1-11.

15. Alpha C. Chiang, "Religion, Proverbs and Economic Mentality," *American Journal of Economics and Sociology* 20 (April 1961): 258.

16. Peter M. Blau, *Exchange and Power in Social Life* (New York: Wiley, 1967), p.111.

17. Emerson, *Essays*, p. 156.

18. David Cheal, *The Gift Economy* (New York: Routledge, 1988).

19. Mauss, *The Gift*, p. 1.

20. Malinowski, *Argonauts*, p. 167.

21. Levi-Strauss, *Elementary Structure of Kinship*, p. 59.

22. Kenneth Boulding, *Beyond Economics* (Ann Arbor Paperback, 1970), p. 235.

7 HAGGLING

A remarkable feature of contemporary economic life is that market exchange can transpire very naturally without verbal exchange. A final consumer may simply take an item from the shelf, some money from his pocket, change and receipt from the clerk, and then leave the store. If words accompany the purchase, they may refer to the weather or to whom a check should be made out. Sometimes the qualities of the product are discussed. Talk may include mention of price, but this is normally only by way of idle chatter over its level, inflation, or a missing tag. Haggling is the exception rather than the rule in most consumer goods markets.

Most final goods in the United States are sold at standard terms and standard prices. This is also the case for many intermediate goods. The terms are offered on a "take-it-or-leave it" basis, with "give-and-take" effectively precluded. Economists, except when discussing labor markets, often assume the existence of this standard form of contract "negotiation."

There is no haggling, nor any reason for it, in the world of perfect competition, where decisionmakers face horizontal demand-andsupply curves. Nor will haggling occur if only one of the participants has market power and already knows the reservation price of the other. But haggling is possible where the reservation price is not known or where both parties possess some degree of market power (and there is something to bargain about). Looking at real world markets, this seems to suggest that haggling is possible virtually everywhere.

In a simple scenario of price determination, either buyer or seller announces a price. In this chapter we assume it is the seller, which appears to be the more usual situation; the analysis is symmetrical in either case. If the buyer dislikes the seller's initial figure, he may make a counteroffer. If this bid induces the seller to modify his announced price, haggling has occurred. In other words, it takes two to haggle. The communication required for haggling need not be oral, though it generally is, and

This chapter is coauthored by Fred Gramlich.

it can involve the quality of the item or the terms of the contract as well as, or instead of, the price.

FACTORS AFFECTING HAGGLING

Personal Preferences

Some people enjoy haggling; they relish the opportunity to outwit an opponent. They love the reputation for shrewdness they may gain from haggling. On the other hand, many people are poor bargainers. Others may regard it as an intrusion of self-interest upon goodwill. One does not usually haggle with family or friends because this asserts the narrow individual interest over the social relationship. Those who wish to make a conspicuous display of wealth may also wish to refrain from a bargaining process that may indicate something of a penny-pinching mentality. Finally, the rich and powerful may dislike haggling with the poor because of the unattractive distributional implications.

Emotion and Dependence

The dynamics of haggling can generate emotion and sometimes unpleasantness or bad feeling. A buyer desperately wishing not to antagonize the seller may avoid the risk by not quibbling. Most consumers will not bargain over the price of a new alternator for their car at a gas station in unfamiliar territory late at night. Nor is it usually wise to haggle with a doctor over the price of an urgent operation for acute appendicitis. The patient is too dependent upon the outcome of the operation, and haggling may affect that outcome.

The Value of Time

Bargaining takes time, and time is an important economic resource. Rich buyers, particularly those with a high earned income, are likely to value their time highly and not waste it bickering over the price of exchange. Those with lower time costs-- the unemployed, the retired-- are more likely to bargain. The wealthy, on the other hand, are more likely to purchase the time of others to represent them in potential price negotiations. The value of time varies over time. A buyer may not haggle if time is short: he has a plane to catch; he is late for an appointment; he is eager to get into a performance but needs a scalped ticket; and so forth.

The value of time also varies for institutional sellers. Stores with busy periods will have a policy not to bargain. Not only does it waste the employee's time, it wastes the time of everyone in the queue at the counter, and this affects the attractiveness of the store. Since it takes at least one person to man a shop, small stores with occasional business are more likely to be receptive to bargaining.

The Value of Goods in Exchange

If the purchase is of small value, there is little potential gain from haggling. Thus, there is little haggling over low-price retail items-- a newspaper, chewing gum, a cup of coffee-- since the potential gain to either buyer or seller is incommensurate with the added time cost.

Conversely, a buyer of large quantities may find it pays to haggle about terms, quality, and price. This may also lead to better deals in subsequent purchases. The seller finds the threat to change suppliers unless concessions are forthcoming more menacing if made by a large buyer. Since purchases are generally larger for producer than consumer goods, these are often the markets where haggling occurs.

Institutional Control

There are strong reasons to expect haggling to be less prevalent in retail markets where stores are large. Haggling creates problems for the coordination and control of the large organization. Revenue projections are more difficult, tax calculations more arduous, employee theft more likely. A customer thus finds he cannot haggle with the salesperson, for the clerk is not allowed to bargain. He must follow orders.

In order to haggle, decisionmakers must be involved. Those doing the bargaining must have some power or incentive to set the ultimate price. The owner-salesperson in a small store has this power and may have the incentive. The clerk in a large chain does not. Indeed, one way a seller can attempt to discourage haggling is by making communication with decisionmakers difficult.

Subsequent Dealings

Haggling can affect the buyer's or seller's reputation, influencing other transactions. A retail seller's reputation for allowing haggling may attract an unappealing mix of customers. Bargain hunters with time to burn may flock to the seller, while the rich avoid him.

A low-price outcome in one transaction may strengthen the next purchaser's bargaining position. Sellers are thus more receptive to haggling when transactions are secret or the exchange is part of a close-out sale. In general, sellers are more prone to haggle about unique rather than standardized goods. With unique items, such as secondhand goods, haggling is less likely to lead to disgruntled customers because postpurchase comparisons are more difficult; the seller's future negotiation position is also less jeopardized. One reason large buyers can gain price concessions is that they are in some sense unique. The seller can agree to grant such concessions to others-if they purchase as much.

Price Discrimination and Oligopolistic Coordination

Sellers may promote haggling as a useful method of price discrimination. For Italians selling leather goods in the open markets of Florence, haggling allows them to distinguish between the ill-informed tourist and the sharp-eyed connoisseur. Similarly, used car and furniture dealers in the United States can increase their profit if they are able to employ haggling to help determine demand elasticities.

Haggling makes price coordination more difficult, however. Oligopolists may therefore attempt to ban haggling and other forms of price concessions. If they desire to promote price discrimination, it will be through other, less destabilizing methods.

MARKETS FOR HAGGLING

Housing and Labor

Two important areas in which haggling often occurs in the United States are housing and labor markets. A house is generally the major consumer durable purchased by a family. A used house is unique and usually sold by another family, whose business is not selling houses. The large number of sellers and the expensive and unique nature of the product, combined with the immediate availability of decisionmakers, imply that haggling might be a common feature of this market, which is indeed the case. A principal exception is the builder of many similar, geographically clustered homes, who might wisely refuse to haggle with any single prospective buyer.

For rentals, there is generally less haggling when the renter is an individual family interested in an apartment in a large complex of similar units. On the other hand, where rental space is unique (a room in someone's home) or the renter is special (a drawing card at a shopping center) or the renting organization is willing to occupy a significant percentage of the space available, negotiation is more likely.

When a laborer works full time for a corporation, it is generally, though not always, the corporation that sets a price around which haggling may or may not occur. An individual laborer without unique skills may be unable to bargain successfully about the offered conditions of employment. On the other hand, one with rare talents -- a twenty-game winner, an outstanding executive-- may have the power to haggle or actually to set his own price. When labor is organized, workers have the power to bargain about wages set by management. Indeed, U.S. law requires "good faith bargaining"-- haggling-- in such situations.

IS HAGGLING GOOD OR BAD?

In a sense, haggling is wasteful; it takes time, can generate adverse emotions, and may disrupt planning. Exchange at some arbitrarily determined level between the reservation prices of the participants might be more efficient. But such a solution is generally neither practicable nor desirable for both parties. Each has an incentive to understate his true willingness to deal, and either or both may believe a better personal outcome can be achieved through haggling.

Haggling often causes price discrimination, which can have both beneficial and detrimental efficiency effects. Price discrimination of intermediate goods can allow inefficient firms in the consuming industry to survive while efficient ones are failing. On the other hand, discrimination in final goods markets often has the effect of increasing the output of monopolized industries, thereby increasing allocative efficiency.

Since information is often gained and exchanged during haggling-- especially concerning particular buyer needs regarding deliveries, payment terms, and so forth-- such negotiation can improve economic efficiency. Consider a situation in which each seller has his own standard contract form. If market information of buyers is incomplete, or if there are costs of changing suppliers, even a relatively competitive market may diverge from efficiency. Without haggling, sellers may not have sufficient incentive to offer those special terms that particular buyers would find most advantageous. This situation is not unlike the case in which prices exceed the competitive level solely because information limitations remove the advantages to price reductions. When haggling increases information, it may also increase social welfare.

The distributional effects of haggling are not clear cut. Rich buyers with large time costs may have less tolerance for haggling and thus be willing to pay higher prices. Conversely, the rich may have achieved their financial position in part by being good bargainers. The rich are also more likely to purchase expert negotiators to bargain for them. In addition, the rich buyer or large firm is more likely to buy in large quantities and is thus more able to extract pecuniary price concessions through haggling.

The welfare effects on third parties are also mixed. The presence of haggling makes collusive arrangements among oligopolists harder to maintain. But it may also make it more difficult for potential entrants to obtain accurate price information; thus, entry becomes riskier and less likely. For consumers, the absence of precise price information makes comparison shopping and rational buying more difficult.

Whether or not others haggle affects the expectations and actions of buyers and sellers. For example, because most people haggle over new cars, list prices tend to be set well above average price. This forces all potential buyers either to haggle or to be discriminated against. Conversely, if no one bargains about typewriter prices, it is difficult for any individual purchaser to make much headway. The stability of either haggling or standard pricing arrangements may prove harmful or beneficial to any particular individual, depending on his situation and proclivities.

POLICY

The government requires haggling in labor markets when management confronts a union. The good-faith bargaining rule is used as a way of ensuring that management deals with the elected collective representative of the employees rather than with the workers individually. It is not haggling per se that is valued but enforced managerial recognition of the union's legitimacy.

Government also sets prices in certain markets, thereby precluding haggling over rates. But in general, the U.S. government has taken a largely laissez-faire attitude toward bargaining. When haggling occurs, usually no one has forced the two to tangle. But because haggling requires at least some market power, one of the participants might prefer standard terms and prices to haggling.

Haggling can affect efficiency and equity. Its third-party influences are varied. Ideal government policy toward haggling is probably noninterventionist. The potential benefit from government action is not likely to be large, while the monitoring and enforcement costs are probably prohibitive.

CONCLUSION

Haggling is a pervasive economic phenomenon, though somewhat less prevalent in developed countries where time costs are high. The large established sellers found in advanced nations sometimes try to eschew haggling because it makes planning and control (and collusion) more difficult.

Market structure characteristics affect the likelihood of haggling. Haggling may be most common when bargaining power is somewhat equally distributed, as in the case of bilateral monopoly. In retail markets, haggling occurs most often when sellers, like buyers, are small. Haggling arises normally in many intermediate goods markets because purchasers, like sellers, are often large. When power is disparate, the stronger party has the power to impose, and may prefer, take-it-or-leave-it conditions. There are, of course, exceptions to this rule, as when a large seller finds it advantageous to price discriminate via haggling.

Theoretically, the economic effects of haggling are many and varied. However, the dearth of economic evidence regarding haggling makes it difficult to assess its real-world importance. But given the likely costs and problems of any attempted government regulation, we can surmise that the current laissez-faire policy is probably a wise one.

FOR DISCUSSION

1. Do you expect to find haggling over airplane tickets? Doctor fees? Christmas trees? Used books? Banquet speaker salaries? Explain. Might it matter who the buyer is (e.g., an individual or a large corporation)?

2. "The market for television advertising time is elaborately organized. While networks have posted rate cards, negotiated agreements are the rule on *major* sales. An advertiser can get a better deal if he risks waiting to buy until a week or two before show time" (Richard E. Caves and Marc J. Roberts, *Regulating the Product* [Cambridge, Mass.: Ballinger Publishing Company, 1975], p. 104). Comment. Might you have predicted this situation?

3. What factors determine whether buyer or seller normally sets the price? Does it matter who does?

4. Should the federal government be willing to haggle about its employees' wages? Should it negotiate or haggle over its purchases of paper clips? Of roads? Of spaceships?

5. Is haggling more a cultural or an economic phenomenon? Knowing just economic information but little about the social aspects of the nation, could you predict the amount of haggling and where it is likely to occur?

6. "Never look a gift horse in the mouth." Relate to gifts. Relate to haggling.

7. If other consumers haggle in a particular market, does this affect whether or not you will? Why?

8. How would you go about gathering data and doing empirical research on haggling?

8 THE COVER CHARGE

There is a wide variety of pricing strategies and arrangements in the real world, including sales, specials, loss leaders, discounts, haggling, bundling, tying, and minimums. The pricing arrangement discussed in this chapter is what nightclubs call the "cover charge" and economists classify as the "two-part tariff." Here, the term "cover charge" is used to describe the fixed price that allows access to certain goods or services, usually for a particular period, following which the consumption of the commodity is generally variable among users. Thus, the ticket price for a basketball game is not considered a cover charge, but the fee for entering an amusement park is.

THE BUYER'S PERSPECTIVE

Consider the simplest case. There is a cover charge, but there is no additional cost to the customer. The potential purchaser is attempting to compare this scheme with one in which there is no cover, but there is a variable charge depending directly on consumption. This choice is nicely illustrated by the American tourist's decision of whether or not to buy a Eurail Pass.

The Eurail Pass provides unlimited train travel in Europe for a limited amount of time. The question to be considered is whether or not it is a worthwhile purchase. We will assume there is only one other alternative: traveling by train at the normal fare.

Before the fact (ex ante), if the traveler knows that she is definitely going to spend more than the cost of the pass on rail travel, she should purchase the pass. However, even if she is planning to spend less on rail travel at regular prices, she may want to buy the pass, given some elasticity in her demand. Neglecting various complications, owning a Eurail Pass makes additional out-of-pocket expenses for train travel equal to zero. This can lead to additional travel and greater utility.

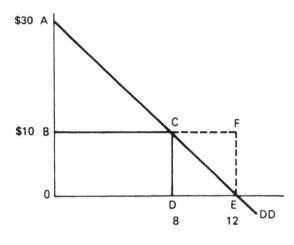

Figure 8-1

Figure 8-1 gives an individual's demand curve DD for rail travel. Let us ignore income effects, or assume the income elasticity is zero, so that DD is a constant utility demand curve. With normal fare OB the customer will purchase OD amount of train service and gain consumer's surplus given by triangle ABC. It is clear that if the Eurail Pass costs less than rectangle OBCD, it should be purchased. But once the individual owns a pass, the additional price for extra travel in the period equals zero, and OE of train travel will be consumed, providing the additional benefit of triangle CDE. Thus, the pass should be purchased as long as its cost does not exceed quadrangle OBCE. In other words, an individual initially planning to spend only $80 on rail travel at normal prices may nonetheless find a Eurail Pass costing $90 to be a wise purchase (Figure 8-1).

On the other hand, the after the fact (ex post) knowledge that the amount traveled OE would have cost more at normal prices (rectangle OBFE) than did the purchase of the Eurail Pass does not confirm that buying the pass was a good decision. The price of the pass can be less than rectangle OBFE and still greater than quadrangle OBCE. In other words, receiving $120 worth of rail service for a Eurail Pass that cost "only" $110 does not show that the purchase was a wise one.

Other real-world examples of a cover charge with no variable out-of-pocket expenses might include "all-you-can-eat" dinners, entry-fee free-ride amusement parks, WATS telephone service, or membership in American Express, health clubs, or the Automobile Association of America. Prepaid health plans may also be included in this category.

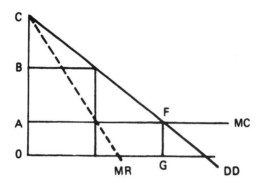

Figure 8-2

THE SELLER'S PERSPECTIVE

Consider a monopolist selling a single product, with no fear of entry. For simplicity, assume a constant marginal cost, OA in Figure 8-2. Theory tells us that if the firm cannot price discriminate, it maximizes profits by selling that amount where marginal revenue equals marginal cost, charging price OB.

Now let the firm impose a cover charge. This option can increase the company's profits. Let us examine the simplest case, in which all customers are identical, with demand curves DD. Again we assume that income effects are negligible. In this case, by pricing at marginal cost, and with a cover charge equal to triangle ACF, the firm can truly maximize its profits. Total revenues for the firm are the summation of rectangles AOFG (unit sales) plus the sum of all triangles ACF (cover charge). The firm produces that amount where (unit) price equals marginal cost.

The cover charge may be considered a form of price discrimination, a special brand of volume discount. Each customer is sold the first item at OA plus the cover, while each successive purchase costs only OA. Were there a fixed cost, equal to the cover, associated with selling to each customer, this pricing arrangement would be "cost justified."

If customers do not have identical demand curves, the seller maximizes profits by setting unit price equal to marginal cost but charging a different cover for each buyer, just sufficient to exhaust her consumer's surplus. This has the same net effect as perfect price discrimination and, like all discrimination, requires some ability to prevent resale of the commodity. It is also similar to perfect price discrimination, or any pricing scheme that appropriates the entire consumer's surplus, in that the solution can be a bit precarious. Increasing the cover charge to any buyer by as much as a penny eliminates all sales to that customer.

THE SOCIAL PERSPECTIVE

Classical microeconomic theory holds that, with no externalities, the optimal amount of production for each industry occurs where demand equals marginal cost. Should price be set above marginal cost in only one industry (e.g., mass transit), individuals will use too little of that service. A consumer deciding whether to use her own car or public transport for an additional trip will be comparing the marginal cost of additional car miles to the price (greater than marginal cost) of additional transit miles and, from the social perspective, will too often use her own vehicle.

For a company with decreasing costs, a single price per unit set equal to marginal cost will leave revenue less than total cost. Subsidies are then necessary for the firm to survive. But most government subsidies conflict with the efficiency or equity goals of society. The two-part tariff has been discussed by economists as a solution to this problem. Like straightforward price discrimination, it has been suggested as a way for the regulated natural monopolist to provide the optimal amount of output while avoiding the problems of subsidization. In the real world, regulated telephone services and electricity and water supplies are often priced to include a flat fee, with additional charges related to the amount of consumption.

The allocation of resources will be efficient with a two-part tariff if unit price is set at marginal cost and the cover charge does not cause any potential customer to eliminate all her purchases. If the cover charge does cause some buyers to leave the market, the two-part tariff will not result in the best allocation of resources. For the case of a uniform cover, the second-best solution may require a lower cover charge to keep more buyers in the market and a unit price that diverges from marginal cost.

Providing the consumer with the option of either a fixed fee or a unit charge (the Eurail Pass) also affects economic efficiency. This alternative will usually increase consumption but not necessarily by the right people. The Eurail Pass owners buy too much from the viewpoint of society, consuming as long as their demand is positive, even though their marginal benefits are less than the marginal cost of production. And those not opting for the flat rate will purchase the correct amount only if unit price is set equal to marginal cost.

CONCLUSION

The cover charge is an interesting pricing arrangement that can often increase profits. It is employed in a variety of circumstances. One is the situation in which sellers find exclusion of nonpayers feasible and desirable. Tennis clubs and amusement parks provide examples. Fixed charges can be used to cover common costs, such as the large fixed costs of telephone companies, electrical utilities, and other natural monopolies. And flat fees are sometimes supplied to reduce consumer uncertainty and to spur efficiency in production. This is part of the logic behind prepaid health plans and the efficiency in production. This is part of the logic behind prepaid health plans and the single charge for complete orthodontic work. These are just some of the areas where the cover charge is found in the real world.

The term "cover charge" is not very precise. An admission to the circus or the movies is probably not a cover charge. On the other hand, the initial fee for stepping into a taxi or a fixed price for local telephone service probably is. But how about rentals of cars, bikes, buffers, or parking spaces, where the price varies with time rather than actual use? And how about the plumber who demands some fixed amount for any time worked between zero and one hour?

Whether such practices are or are not considered cover charges is not crucial. What is important is that such real-world pricing schemes be analyzed and understood.

FOR DISCUSSION

1. If you were president of Tiffany's, would you charge people simply for walking into the store? What would be the effect if you did?

2. Is a ski lift pass a cover charge? What is the effect of this pricing arrangement? Why aren't ski lifts priced per ride rather than per day? Is a subway fare system that allows complete travel between all points for a single price a cover charge? Why aren't passengers charged per length of the ride (as they are in the Bay Area Rapid Transit)?

3. "Some nightclubs have too much business on weekends, so they add a cover charge applicable only to these crowded periods. Such action encourages customers to come in during less busy periods of the nightclub's operation" (Douglas North and Roger Leroy Miller, *Abortion, Baseball & Weed* [New York: Harper & Row, 1973], p. 133). Comment. Why not raise liquor prices and have a minimum? During busy periods why do many restaurants have a minimum but usually not a cover? Why don't they set a limit on how long clients can remain at a table?

4. Contrast overtime wages and cover charges.

5. To get access to Dun & Bradstreet company financial information, there is a fixed fee as well as a unit price. Why do you think D & B set prices in this manner? Might they have any problems preventing the resale or distribution of their information?

6. Can a perfect competitor impose a two-part tariff? Why or why not?

7. What should be public policy toward the cover charge? Should a patent-based monopoly be permitted to impose a two-part tariff?

SOURCES

Musgrave, Richard and Peggy, *Public Finance in Theory and Practice* (New York: McGraw-Hill, 1989).

Ng, Yew-Kwang, and Mendel Weisser. "Optimal Pricing with a Budget Constraint-The Case of the Two-Part Tariff." *Review of Economic Studies* 41 (July 1974):337-45.

Oi, Walter. "A Disneyland Dilemma: Two-Part Tariffs for a Mickey Mouse Monopoly." *Quarterly Journal of Economics* 85 (February 1971): 77-96.

9 TIPPING

A tip may be described as a gift, usually a small amount of money, given voluntarily for a service rendered. It should be noted that the gift is small, not entirely compulsory, and is given after the service has been performed.

WHO IS TIPPED?

Tipping is partly determined by custom and thus varies from country to country. Japan, New Zealand and Iceland are still relatively tip-free, while in Egypt and Brazil, almost everyone seems to require a tip.[1] On the other hand, in Belgium, cabdrivers are not tipped, and in Finland barbers are never tipped. Indeed, in Finland, it might be considered an insult if a tip were offered, for the tip can imply a distinctive class or hierarchical position between the parties. The Finn may reasonably believe the offer demeans both himself and his job, for, even when the practice is widespread, a tip may denote a lack of status. Miss Manners[2], Emily Post[3] and Letitia Baldridge[4] advise that room waiters are tipped but not hotel managers, skycaps but not reservation clerks, stewards but never a ship's officer. It is perhaps significant that "boys" and "girls" jobs are often tipped: delivery boys, shoeshine boys, hatcheck girls, and so forth.

Tips are thus given for some services in the United States but clearly not for all. The service generally has to be menial and physical (porter, bellhop) rather than more skilled or of higher status (doctor, lawyer, accountant). The service is usually personal (barber, caddy, waiter, masseuse). Thus, cab drivers are tipped but bus drivers aren't. Ball park attendants may be tipped if they perform a special service such as cleaning your seat. The same is true for strolling restaurant musicians if they play your request. On the other hand, personal services not personally paid for or performed by fellow workers, are definitely not tipped (trainers, makeup artists, secretaries).

Finally, face-to-face contact is generally important. Home-delivery newspaper boys are tipped regularly if they collect personally, not if the bill is sent by mail. Garbage collecters and answering services may provide more or less personal service, but they are not tipped. Sometimes, however, a Christmas "bonus" is given. For nurses, houseparents, and even secretaries who provide face-to-face continuous intermediate-status service, a "gift" is often appropriate. There is something less demeaning in these lump sum bonuses or gifts. Thus, high-fashion hair stylists in big cities expect Christmas bonuses from regular customers rather than weekly tips.

Jobs requiring tipping are often those a servant might perform personal, menial, low-status services requiring face-to-face contact. While this describes most instances when tipping is in order, there seem to be a number of occupations, especially borderline ones, where custom makes the determination. For example, ship stewards are tipped, but airline stewards are not. It is not entirely clear whether movers should be tipped. Repairpeople, however, generally aren't, nor are sales personnel.

CUSTOMARY NATURE OF TIPPING

Perhaps the most outstanding feature of current tipping is its customary nature. Social conventions largely tell us not only whom to tip but how much. Tipping is often virtually obligatory, and indeed, the tip has been incorporated as a compulsory service charge in many European restaurants. The worker is no longer clearly inferior to the consumer. Convention creates an implicit, though vague, contract among near equals.

For the worker, the custom of tipping might be viewed as the service equivalent to piece-rate pay. Rather than the contracted objective criteria of the employer, however, the service worker has to depend on the whims and generosity of the consumer, a special problem with nonrepeat customers. The conventionalization of tips thus benefits the worker, stabilizing the expected return for service, making income slightly more predictable, and enabling a wiser choice of occupations. At the same time, of course, extra service could be rewarded with an extra large tip.

With respect to tips, the customer usually simply wants to do "what is right," what is expected. That is why he reads Miss Manners. He tries to tip whom it is customary to tip, the customary amount, in the customary manner. If service is adequate, he generally wants no unfulfilled expectations, no hurt feelings. He may not want to be overly generous or appear vulgar, but he also does not want to cheat anyone or appear cheap. And if he is "risk averse," he may especially not want to grossly undertip anyone and have that person create a scene. Given a variety of national customs, this could be a partial reason tourists generally tip heavily. There are, of course, other reasons for large tips: to be known as a big tipper, to reward excellent service, and so forth.

One of the real drawbacks of tipping is the problem it creates for fair-minded people. They are required to learn the correct amount and procedures for tipping-- and sometimes they err. Tipping also creates minor problems for rational buying decisions since two prices (one quoted, one conventional) must be discovered in order to learn the full cost of purchase.

WHY TIPPING?

Popular belief holds that *tip* derives from eighteenth century English usage and stands for the words "to insure promptness,"[5] but tipping was known as far back as the Roman era and is probably much older. The word *tip* itself may come from stipend, a bastardized version of the Latin *stips*, meaning gift.

The tip begins as an incentive and reward for good service. It allows the buyer to withhold partial payment until the quality of the service is observed. This is more helpful the less sure he is of the reliability of the worker. The demeaning nature of the tip partly derives from this point there is an implication that the worker is perhaps untrustworthy or lacks good work habits or high ethical standards. In part, too, the tip may be demeaning in that it is the buyer who unilaterally determines the amount of the tip, the worth of the act. (There may also be an aura of charity for the poor, but working, person.) A contract specifying the various graduations of service quality and their price would clearly be less demeaning. Given the small nature of the service, however, and the small amount of the tip, the "transaction costs" are generally too far out of line to make this a feasible alternative.

For the employer of the worker (for those workers not self-employed), the tip performs a similar function. The quality of the employer's product is somewhat tied to the quality of the worker's services, as dinners are to waiter services, room accommodations to bellhop services, ship travel to steward services, and so forth. The employer wants reasonable service to be provided but may be unable to supervise the worker directly. The customer is best able to judge the adequacy of a simple personal service, and the custom of tipping provides an immediate positive monetary incentive to the worker; complaints provide a negative incentive. Total remuneration is thus, hopefully, more closely allied with service quality than if a flat rate were paid. Again, though, there may be an implicit distrust of the worker, especially compared to the trust given to the customer.

It is not surprising that tipping has often been attacked for its "undemocratic" and demeaning nature. The institution, however, remains strong. Miss Manners "abhors the custom of tipping"[6] and Emily Post believes that "tipping is undoubtedly an undesirable and undignified system, but it happens to be in force."[7] Their advice is, of course, to tip. Tipping seems to be a custom that individual action cannot readily eliminate. Collective action, however, has sometimes been effective. In the airline industry, tipping of stewardesses was never permitted; which of course is easier than stopping an established custom. Communist countries met with some early success in eradicating tipping,[8] but even China has now decided to permit it unofficially.[9]

It is not at all clear, though, that the elimination of tipping is socially desirable. Tipping can perform a useful function, and the main social drawback, its demeaning nature, can easily be overstated. The question is largely one of attitude. It is doubtful, for example, that the current tipping of barbers, waiters and waitresses, and cab drivers dramatically decreases either their dignity or their social prestige. These people are now tipped principally because it is expected, because it is the custom.

More Effects of Tipping

Tipping can be an important component of workers' pay. For example, it is estimated that more than 60 percent of the total earnings of the more than 250,000 waiters and waitresses employed in large establishments come from tips. On the other hand, only 2 percent of chambermaids' earnings derive from this source.[10] When compared to a straight wage, pay that includes tips will be more variable. To the extent that there is risk aversion, workers should demand a slightly higher average wage than they would otherwise. This is also the case if the job is indeed demeaning. A countervailing factor is the greater ease of income tax evasion with tips, thus increasing effective take-home pay. (According to a 1986 IRS report, the only type of revenue with a lower compliance rate was illegal income.)

Where there is tipping, the base wage (employee) or the basic service cost (self-employed) should be less than in its absence. In the case of a waiter, since a large part of his income comes directly from the consumer, the restaurant can give him less. One effect of tipping, then, where the worker is an employee, is that when business declines, he is less of a burden or fixed cost. His income, however, fluctuates greatly. Where there is tipping one might therefore predict fewer "firings" and more "quittings" than where there is not.

Looking at it another way, the income of the worker depends on the base wage, the generosity of the customers, and the success of the enterprise. The more standardized the tip, the more important becomes enterprise success. We have here a crude form of profit (actually sales) sharing. This is carried the farthest in European restaurants, where the service charge is automatically added to the bill.

It is illuminating to contrast the tip with the sales commission. In the latter, income depends on making immediate sales, the understanding being that walk-in customers generally must be "sold," or non-walk-in customers found. Tipping usually occurs when it is fairly certain that walk-ins will buy or have already bought (restaurants, hotels, ships, taxis). The function of the tip is to help ensure adequate service. The emphasis may be more on future sales. Both the tip and the commission are forms of sales sharing and thus both decrease "overhead costs."

From the employer's perspective, tipping may be beneficial; it reduces supervision costs and direct-wage expenses. The desirability of tipping is also affected by state and federal laws. It was only in the mid-1980s that Congress began requiring employers to pay federal unemployment and Social Security tax on tipped income. And it can matter whether tipped income is included when states determine whether minimum wage requirements have been met.

An interesting economic effect of tipping is that it causes price discrimination against the soft hearted and the big tipper. If bigger tips are directly related to inelasticity of demand, tipping could prove one minor method by which firms could increase their profits.

It is important to distinguish areas where services are likely to be repeated (barber) and those where they are not (taxi). In the former, past performance and the expectation of future contact helps generate a fairly stable system of acceptable pay for acceptable service, though there may be some continuing "jockeying for position." While each separate "unwritten contract" between barber and customer may well be different, a constant small tipper, ceteris paribus, can generally expect less service than a big tipper.

With nonrepeat games the situation is less stable. A worker may well vary service depending on how he sizes up the customer-- on what he believes is the customer's tip-service schedule-- and on the cost of different levels of performance. In nonrepeat games, the worker has much less information and is more likely to categorize incorrectly. The same is true with the first encounter of a repeat game, though the worker, with similar information, may well select a different level if he expects repeat purchases. For a customer for whom misclassification is likely and may create problems, some sort of signal is in order.

In nonrepeat games, the customer is mostly on the honor system to tip adequately. (The worker, though, still has the threat of expressing disapproval or creating a scene.) The conventional nature of the tip, and its small size, protects not only the worker but also the transient customer, making him less likely to be distrusted and more likely to receive adequate service. The conventional rules themselves, necessarily simple and easily understood, may create minor problems. For example, if a restaurant tip is expected to be 15 percent of the bill, a small purchaser may have to distinguish himself if he is to receive service equal to those ordering an expensive meal.

Overall, the custom of tipping probably has had only the most minor effect on the total price of most purchases. If business is steady and the tip standardized, the tip becomes similar to a small surcharge. If tipping conventions are less rigid, and workers are risk averse, the total price of purchase may be marginally higher with tipping. More important, the less rigid the conventions, the more the potential for price discrimination.

CONCLUSION

Those occupations for which tipping is prevalent are usually low paying, or else the small amount of money involved would have no allure. The service performed is often personal and simple: the tipper alone benefits, is best able to judge the worth of the service, and can do so immediately. The task is often menial, and there may be an implicit superior-inferior status relationship in the act. Face-to-face meeting helps to facilitate payment.

The custom of tipping tends to make pay more proportional to service actually rendered. Since a straight wage for variable work is not unusual, however, with tipping there is the possible implication that the worker may be a bit untrustworthy, or at least needs an immediate tangible reward to work effectively. For many tipped jobs today, any such conclusion is probably unwarranted.

Some occupations receive tips largely because it is the custom. Other occupations that might well be tipped are not. It is doubtful, for example, whether any startling changes would result if tips were eliminated for waiters, barbers, and cab drivers or begun for ushers, flight attendants, and gas station attendants. Perhaps even more interesting is speculation on whether we might like to withhold partial payment until service is complete and then somewhat unilaterally determine the worth of services performed by plumbers, garage mechanics, TV repairers, doctors, mail carriers, actors, salespeople, and so forth. At least one of the many problems is that as tips increase, the incentive for the customer to "cheat" increases, as does the price discrimination against those who don't. This is undoubtedly one reason that, from the point of view of the customer, tips are never a large part of total cost.

Overall, the effects of tipping are varied but probably fairly minor. The principal function of the tip is as an incentive and reward for good service. And though much tipping is largely obligatory and conventionalized, an extra-large tip can be given for extra or exceptional service, a small tip for poor service. The obligatory nature of tipping permits this "punishment" for bad performance. Perhaps the greatest drawbacks of tipping are its potentially demeaning nature, the search problem it causes well-intentioned travelers, the occasional nuisance of tipping (e.g., needing the right change), and the difficulties that can arise if implicit rules of tipping are not clear or are not followed.

FOR DISCUSSION

1. A British survey concerning tipping concluded that "it tends to decrease management control, increase recruitment problems, and irritate and embarrass many customers."[11] If most people dislike tipping, why does it continue to exist? Why won't individual action simply put an end to it?

2. If others tip, does this affect the likelihood that you will tip? Why? How do you determine how much and whom to tip?

3. Why would Communist countries try to abolish tipping? Is this easy to do? Is tipping likely to spring up again? Why or why not?

4. What would be the principal effects if tipping were abolished for barbers in the United States? For waiters?

5. Do you expect there to be more tipping in a developed or a less developed country? Why? Do you expect tipping rates to be higher in New York City or in Muncie, Indiana? Explain.

6. Why is tipping based on a percentage of the sales price as opposed to the quantity of service rendered? For example, waiters may do as much work for breakfast as for dinner, yet they receive far less in tips. Is this fair? Is it efficient?

7. Diners sometimes give money to the maitre d' in hopes of getting a good table. Contrast this payment with a tip. Who has the upper hand? Contrast the bribe to the tip.

NOTES TO CHAPTER 9

1. "The Golden Rules of Tipping," *Conde Nast Traveler*, September 1989, pp. 118-125.
2. Judith Martin, *Miss Manners' Guide for the Turn-of-the-Millenium* (New York: Pharos Books, 1989).
3. Elizabeth L. Post, *Emily Post's Etiquette* (New York: Harper and Row, 1984).
4. Letitia Baldridge, *Letitia Baldridge's Complete Guide to the New Manners for the 90's* (New York: Rawson Associates, 1990).
5. *Encyclopedia Americana*, 1973 ed., s.v. "Tip."
6. Martin, p. 374.
7. Post, p. 394.
8. Good Housekeeping, *Today's Etiquette* (New York: Harper & Row, 1965), p. 332.
9. "Tipping Takes a Trip," *Time*, August 3, 1989, p. 32.
10. Bureau of Labor Statistics, "Wages and Tips in Restaurants and Hotels," U.S. Department of Labor Bulletin 1712 (Washington, D.C.: Government Printing Office, 1970); Bureau of Labor Statistics, "Industry Wage Survey: Hotels and Motels," U.S. Department of Labor Bulletin 2055 (Washington, D.C.: Government Printing Office, 1980).
11. *Why Tipping?* Economic Development Committee, National Economic Development Office, Millbank Tower, London, 1972, p. 8.

10 SCALPING

This essay analyzes scalping, the buying of tickets in order to peddle them at higher than official prices. First we examine why tickets are so often underpriced at the box office, which attracts the scalper. Then we discuss the efficiency and equity impacts of making scalping illegal. In 1990, Pennsylvania began penalizing convicted scalpers with a $5,000 fine or two years in jail.

UNDERPRICING AT THE BOX OFFICE

Consider a monopoly that is selling tickets for a professional football game or a rock concert. Assume, for simplicity, that the number of tickets is fixed, and all seats are homogeneous. In Figure 10-1, capacity cannot be expanded and is given by Q_c. The demand for the particular event is DD. The profit-maximizing monopolist, unable to price discriminate and unconcerned with future sales or entry, sells that amount Q_o where marginal revenue equals marginal cost, changing price P_o. If price is set much lower, below P_c, demand for tickets exceeds supply. With no transactions costs, there is an incentive for scalping once official rates fall below this level.

In Figure 10-2, with high demand relative to capacity, $P_o = P_c$, a price the least bit below the profit-maximizing level creates excess demand, increasing the likelihood of scalping.

We can imagine scalping occurring in the real world even though there is no excess demand for tickets, even though the event does not sell out. For example, purchasers may be misinformed about the price or availability of tickets, or scalpers could conceivably offer their tickets at more convenient locations. Low box office prices, however, seem to be the principal cause of scalping.

A seller may price tickets below P_c for a variety of reasons, including incompetence, internal institutional problems, non-profit maximizing goals, or government decree. We assume that the official seller is a flexible, rational,

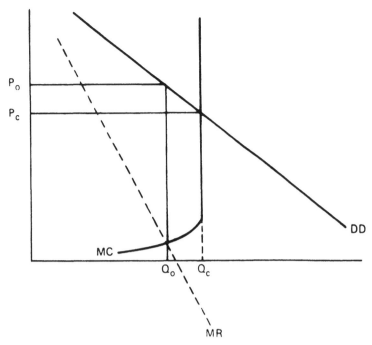

Figure 10-1

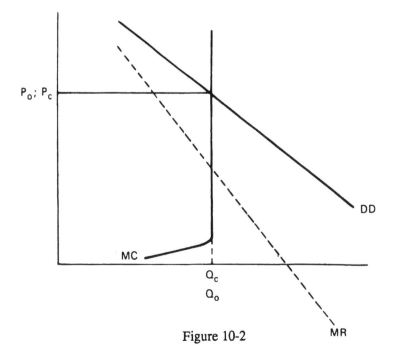

Figure 10-2

unconstrained profit maximizer. We also assume, however, that there is some uncertainty with respect to the nature of demand.

If there is demand uncertainty, it is easy to understand why tickets are sometimes overpriced, sometimes underpriced. When demand is high relative to capacity, as in Figure 10-2, we should often expect tickets to be priced so low (below P_c) as to create excess demand and promote scalping. Real-world considerations generally cause the producer of an event to prefer to underprice rather than overprice tickets.

The producer of an event is typically selling more than one item. A rock group expects its concerts to enhance record sales. The concerts (hopefully) shift audience preferences favorably, increasing the demand for the group's recordings. (The causation also runs in the opposite direction, with record sales changing preferences and increasing the demand for concert tickets. The effects are mutually reinforcing.) Since profits from the albums are positively related to tour attendance, the maximization of total profits may mean the pricing of tickets below P_o in Figure 10-1. Yet, there is still no reason to charge prices below P_c, which sells out the arena, and in Figure 10-2, the profit-maximizing price remains unchanged. However, when facing demand uncertainty, the rational seller should tend to underprice rather than overprice tickets. Given high demand for the concert (Figure 10-2), overpricing decreases profits not only from ticket sales but also from the sale of records. In the spring of 1975, for example, the Rolling Stones released a number of new albums to "capitalize on the tour hysteria."[1] The hysteria might have been less if concert sales had been overpriced at $50 rather than underpriced at $10.

A concert takes time, during which there is a captive audience to whom other goods and services can be sold, such as programs, souvenirs, and particularly refreshments. Focusing on the sale of food and beverages, assume, for simplicity, that the desire for such general refreshment is unaffected by concert attendance. Attendance does, of course, increase demand for the particular food and drink provided at the concert. The ticket seller monopolizes such sales only during the period of the concert and only for the captive concert audience.

A rational buyer should determine the total cost of both concert and potentially desired concessions before purchasing the ticket of admission. The profit-maximizing prices to be charged by the monopolist then depend on the interdependence and elasticities of demand. For example, the ticket seller could conceivably charge a high price of admission while subsidizing the concessions. In the real world, the normal strategy seems the reverse. Concessions are generally priced quite high, while there may be an underpricing of admissions to attract customers to the arena. One reason for this strategy is that real-world customers are not perfectly rational; they tend to be a bit myopic, neglecting to include all related costs when making their ticket-pricing decisions. (Consumer myopia is apparent in other areas. For example, the prices of make-specific automobile replacement parts are large relative to cost. On the other hand, the new car itself may be priced a bit below the simple monopoly level to entice and lock in the potential buyer of replacement parts.)

Not only do entertainment producers sell a variety of complementary items, but they often create many similar events. A particular rock group's concert, for example, is generally performed in a number of cities, and sometimes a number of times in the same city. The quality reputation of a rock group becomes crucial in attracting fans to subsequent events. One indication of quality, among many, is past attendance. Continued sellouts indicate to potential ticket purchasers that a particular rock group is in fashion and may even be very good. Since buyers are more influenced by attendance than by total ticket revenue information, there is an incentive to set prices for a particular event below the short-run profit-maximizing level, P_o. (There may also be a temptation to inflate attendance figures.) And while there is no reason to price below P_c, if P_c is not perfectly known, the possibility of underpricing may be preferable to that of overpricing, especially if being "sold out" becomes an important informational variable for potential purchasers.

Let us draw together the argument thus far for the tendency to underprice. Even as we near capacity, extra revenue from selling one more ticket may be high compared to marginal cost (Figure 10-2). We expect low marginal cost since there is little expense in filling an available empty seat. In Figure 10-2, overpricing loses a great deal of revenue while saving only a small amount of cost. Moreover, overpricing can decrease net profits from albums, concessions, and future ticket sales. In contrast, underpricing is usually a less costly mistake. Only total revenue from current ticket sales decreases, though by a large amount (Q_c times the amount of underpricing). In all, the rational seller, facing uncertain demand, may well prefer to underprice rather than overprice tickets, thus increasing the probability of scalping.

In the real world, it is generally advisable for the monopolist to begin selling tickets well in advance of the event. In terms of marketing, advance sales can make purchases more convenient, decrease buyer congestion problems, and allow early customers to plan their lives better by assuring them seats. In the interval between the purchase of advance tickets and the event, demand can be strongly affected by changing circumstances. The expected quality of a football game, for instance, may change sharply as weather forecasts are modified or players sustain or recover from injuries.

Adding the time element and the additional uncertainty created by changing conditions and information greatly complicates the analysis. We do not presume to investigate thoroughly the vast array of potential situations. Instead, we will briefly mention a number of possibilities that would tend to increase the likelihood of scalping in the real world.

If conditions turn out much better than expected, advance buyers may find scalping profitable. This is particularly true if the official seller is risk averse and prefers to sell a large number of advance tickets at well below the expected profit-maximizing price, in case the adverse contingency arises. A ticket seller may have other reasons for charging low prices for advance sales. For example, real-world capital markets being far from perfect, she may simply have an immediate need for cash.

Advance sales provide consumers with improved information about probable attendance. For many events, total attendance affects the utility an individual derives from the performance. A rock concert with tens of thousands attending is a happening; the same concert before five hundred may be a bust. There are, in other words, externalities in purchase. Your buying decisions affect my enjoyment of the event. If the externalities are positive-- as in the example above-- by changing expectations about actual attendance, high advance sales may increase demand, making a sellout and scalping even more likely.[2]

It is possible to extend the argument further. Consumers often gain utility from the envy of others. Once it becomes clear that the event will sell out and that excess demand exists, the expected utility from attending may be enhanced. Demand is again expanded, increasing still further the likelihood and profitability of scalping.

EFFICIENCY EFFECTS

Begin with the normal assumptions of the competitive model, but assume a monopolistic ticket seller, who, for one of the reasons mentioned above, has set price at P_*, below P_c, so that excess demand exists ($Q_* - Q_c$ in Figure 10-3). Tickets are sold on a first-come, first-served basis. For the moment, we assume that transferability is impossible; there is no scalping.

Equilibrium is reached in this market by waiting. Though demand uncertainty was a principal reason the monopolist might price below P_c, we assume, for simplicity, that each individual buyer has complete and costless information about potential queues. No one makes a mistake by waiting, or not waiting, in line. In

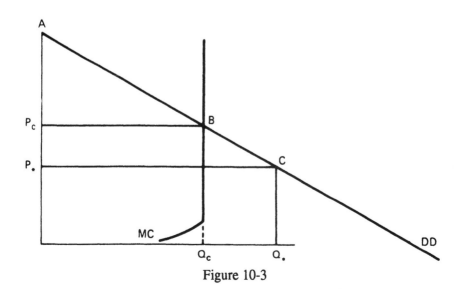

Figure 10-3

equilibrium, the total costs for the marginal individual, P_*, plus her time costs, will be equal to (or possibly less than, if there is discontinuity) the total value she receives from the event. Neglecting income effects, as we do throughout the analysis, and assuming the arena is filled, this total cost per person must be less than or equal to P_c.

With queuing and nontransferability, an individual i will purchase a ticket as long as her dollar benefit from the event, U_i, minus her time costs, t_i, are greater than or equal to the purchase price, P_*. $U_i \geq P_* + t_i$; we assume no one enjoys waiting in line, so $t_i \geq 0$. The individuals who may buy tickets are those on the demand curve from A to C in Figure 10-3. No one below C will attend the event since $U_i < P_*$. While those people from B to C receive lower dollar utility from the event than do those from A to B, if they have very low waiting costs they may be the ones to purchase tickets. When compared to an ideal market, there is inefficiency because some wrong people (from B to C) may be attending the event, and because any waiting can be considered a deadweight loss. Waiting generally creates costs for the consumer without providing any benefit to the seller or to society.

The inefficiencies caused by waiting are due to the fact that no well-defined property rights exist for the underpriced tickets. Some of the available monopoly rent is dissipated as buyers use resources to establish claims to such rights.[3] In the case at hand, time is employed in queuing to gain the right to purchase a ticket. Efficiency would be increased if cheaper methods for assigning property rights were employed. Since tickets are assumed to be nontransferable, it is also very important to assign the rights to the correct people.

If the property rights for access to tickets are arbitrarily assigned, then permitting the transferability of tickets will increase economic efficiency. Assuming no transaction costs for scalping, then customers A to B will attend the concert, which is the competitive result. Any costs in assigning property rights may be considered a deadweight loss. And any transaction costs in reselling tickets or property rights may prevent some of those with the highest dollar utility from viewing the event. For example, individuals B to C who receive property rights may prefer to attend the concert rather than resell their tickets should there be large costs associated with this transaction.

When property rights are established by queuing, contrasting situations of ticket transferability versus nontransferability becomes a more difficult exercise. Here we examine only a few simple possibilities but show that allowing scalping can actually decrease economic efficiency. While the addition of markets generally enhances well-being, in this instance the negative externalities caused by waiting in line prevent such a facile conclusion.

The main efficiency problems caused by queuing and nontransferability are (1) that the "wrong" people may attend the event (those from B to C) and (2) that there will be a deadweight loss from waiting. Queuing combined with transferability lessens or eliminates the former inefficiency but may increase the latter. Transferability, if there are no transaction costs, ensures that individuals A to B will wind up with the tickets. Transferability generally means that the total *time* spent queuing will increase; the total *cost* of queuing may be either higher or lower.

Without scalping, only individuals A to C are interested in waiting in line for tickets. Transferability makes potential waiters out of the entire population. Whether this increases or decreases the total cost of queuing depends on the situation. It would be necessary to know something about the time costs of the entire population A to Z and the specific time costs associated with each individual A to C.

Many assumptions are possible. We assume that an individual's waiting costs are constant over time and that there are no other transaction costs in buying or reselling the tickets. Then, permitting scalping, and given no restrictions on how many tickets a single customer may purchase, theoretically a one-person line will emerge. This person can be expected to buy all the tickets for price P_*. She then becomes the monopolist and can resell the tickets, making a minimum monetary profit of $(P_c - P_*)Q_c$. She is the one in the entire population with the lowest time costs. If others' time costs were nearly as inexpensive, their competition would force her to arrive so early and wait so long that most of his surplus would be dissipated.

Limiting sales of tickets to, say, one per customer would normally decrease the waste (still assuming no transaction costs). Given our assumptions, a line of Q_c people with the lowest time costs will form instantaneously some time before ticket sales begin. Since all have complete information about the queue, no one will arrive sooner or wait longer. With no transactions costs, box office sales are also instantaneous. Thus, everyone will wait the same amount of time. The cost of waiting to the individual among those who value time most highly will not exceed $P_c - P_*$, the monetary gain from reselling the ticket. The surplus is dissipated only for the marginal individual. For all others, who value their time less highly, the benefits of possessing the ticket exceed their cost of waiting.

Nontransferability of tickets makes it quite unlikely that the total cost of waiting will reach $(P_c - P_*)Q_c$. Not only would all those in line need to have identical time costs, but the line would have to be composed entirely of individuals A to B. Given differing time costs, the surplus can only be dissipated at the margin. In such circumstances, the total waiting costs are less than under conditions of transferability and unlimited sales per customer, and they may be less (or more) than such costs with transferability and one-to-a-customer sales.

Let us elaborate, comparing one-to-a-customer sales with and without transferability. It might seem that by allowing tickets to be transferred, the number of potential waiters would be increased and waiting costs decreased. Individuals A to B could hire waiters who placed low values on time. If an individual in A to B had formerly waited herself, and now purchases the waiting services of others, doesn't her voluntary entrance into the transaction previously prohibited prove that she is now better off? The answer is no.

Let us assume that there are at least Q_c individuals C to Z with lower time costs than anyone in A to B. Their willingness to wait in line for long periods increases the cost to individuals A to B of waiting themselves. The length of the wait increases, and to get a ticket, individuals A to B are forced to hire waiters at the competitive rate, which is $(P_c - P_*)$. This price turns out to be the highest any one of them could possibly have paid (in terms of waiting costs) under conditions of nontransferability, with only individuals A to C interested in waiting.

Without transferability, individuals A to C with low time costs would gain some of the potentially available monopoly rent $(P_c - P_*) Q_c$. With transferability, it is individuals C to Z who wait. They wait longer but at a lower cost per minute. The cost to the marginal waiter among them is $P_c - P_*$. Others with lower time costs now receive some of the benefits of the monopoly rent. Whether the total costs of waiting would be more or less with or without transferability depends principally on the variability of time costs for those who wait in populations A to C and in populations A to Z.

In the real world, we often observe games and concerts that will eventually sell out not doing so immediately upon the opening of sales or within the first few days or even weeks. To explain this phenomenon, let us assume that buyers vary about when they make the final decision to attend the event and about when it is convenient to purchase tickets. We also assume that there are transaction costs to every sale and higher costs when buyers are forced to enter the market at inconvenient times. In such circumstances, we can easily imagine that lifting the prohibition against scalping could make society worse off. With scalping there is a huge population in the market for buying the limited number of tickets, and we may find long early lines where none previously existed. The increased number of individuals who can conveniently buy tickets the first day of sales causes congestion and a deadweight waiting loss. Also, some of the individuals A to B who prefer purchases on the second or third day now find themselves induced to make early decisions and perhaps arrive at the box office and wait in line at an inconvenient hour. Scalping increases not only the waiting and inconvenience but also the number of transactions and, thus, normal transaction costs. The total welfare of society is diminished. Though pure scalpers are made better off, many individuals from A to B are now much poorer, since they pay higher monetary prices for tickets or wait in lines at times that are, for them, inconvenient.

DISTRIBUTIONAL EFFECTS

Consider a situation with perfect buyer information and excess demand, with tickets limited one to a customer and sold on a first-come, first-served basis. Allowing the transferability of tickets clearly benefits individuals C to Z with low time costs, permitting them to sell their time and earn a surplus. On the other hand, scalping may hurt some individuals A to C who had low time costs relative to others in that grouping but not relative to the entire population. They do not wait themselves, and if they desire tickets, they must pay a larger premium in dollar terms than it would have cost in waiting time were scalping impossible. However, some individuals A to B with high time costs, who would not formerly have attended the event, are better off with scalping. And some individuals B to C with low time costs are better off if their waiting costs are increased by less than the added gain to be derived from reselling their tickets.

In general, scalping benefits some people C to Z and can either improve or worsen the position of particular individuals A to C. Up to this point, our analysis depicted scalping as having little effect on the profits of event producers. In the real world, of course, scalping may influence the timing and transaction costs of sales and the type of people attending the event and, thus, the demand for concessions and other complementary items. But given our assumptions thus far, total ticket revenue for producers remains unaffected by scalping. We now consider a situation in which scalping can seemingly decrease ticket revenues, in which original sellers can profitably tie or bundle together different events.[4]

We assume perfect information. The seller produces a series of events, such as a season of football games. For simplicity we assume that there are two games, and stadium capacity is two. Marginal cost is zero up to two seats per game and infinite beyond that. The four individuals with the highest reservation prices for the events are given below:

	Reservation Prices	
	Game 1	*Game 2*
Individual Alpha	$10	$ 1
Beta	9	6
Gamma	6	7
Delta	2	10

Pricing independently for each game, the profit-maximizing seller, unable to identify individuals, charges $9 for game 1, and $7 for game 2. Alpha and Beta attend the first game, Gamma and Delta the second. Total revenue is $32.

Let the seller bundle her products, offering the option of season tickets. Assuming the nontransferability of tickets, her optimal strategy is to provide season passes for $15, individual game tickets for $10. Beta purchases the season pass, and Alpha and Delta the tickets for individual games. Total revenue is $35; bundling is profitable.

	P_1	P_2	Season Pass	Total Revenue
Single Game Seats Only	$ 9$_{A,B}$	$ 7$_{C,D}$	-	$32
Season Tickets Included	10$_A$	10$_D$	15_B$	35

Now allow scalping, at zero transaction costs. Individuals have an incentive to purchase two season tickets for $15. Epsilon (she is no fool) could resell them as single game passes for $32, making a $2 profit. With two season tickets being sold, total revenue for the event producer falls to $30. Scalping decreases the seller's prospective profits. She thus has an incentive to oppose scalping and perhaps to make tickets nontransferable.

CONCLUSION

The strategy of ticket pricing is an intriguing subject. The first half of this chapter focused on only one aspect of this topic, explaining why, under conditions of uncertainty, tickets tend to be underpriced rather than overpriced. We argued that high attendance not only increases demand for complementary items but also improves the seller's reputation for the future. Moreover, high advance sales can increase the likelihood of an exciting evening, favorably influencing other potential ticket buyers.

To simplify the analysis, the economic effects of scalping were examined under the assumption of perfect (buyer) information. This ignored the general uncertainty that may have given rise to the underpricing in the first place. But a fundamental conclusion was derived, that even under conditions of perfect information but excess demand, scalping might not prove socially beneficial. When tickets are underpriced and sold to competitive buyers on a first-come, first-served basis, scalping may increase waiting costs and decrease wellbeing.

FOR DISCUSSION

1. This chapter argues that allowing scalping might sometimes prove detrimental to society. Cite other examples in which preventing the formation of certain markets could be the correct policy. Relate to the theory of the second best.

2. What do you think is the principal reason that many localities outlaw scalping? Is the scalper a nuisance? Are counterfeit tickets a problem? What pressure group might benefit from making scalping illegal? Explain.

3. If scalping is effectively prohibited, can a case be made for also banning transferability? Should student athletic-participation cards be transferable? Why or why not?

4. Do consumers have a notion of a "just price"? Would fans be outraged if World Series tickets were priced ten times higher than the regular season entry fee? Do

pennant winners underprice their series tickets to protect goodwill? (How can you tell if tickets are underpriced?) Is rationing by waiting a more equitable method than rationing by price? Explain.

5. Cite some circumstances or events where audience satisfaction is positively correlated with attendance. In such situations, would spectators really subsidize others to attend? Could this be arranged practically?

NOTES TO CHAPTER 10

1. "Stones Loom, Tickets Boom," *Rolling Stone*, June 19, 1975, p. 15.
2. Gary S. Becker, "A Note on Restaurant Pricing and Other Examples of Social Influences on Price," *Journal of Political Economy* 99 (1991): 1109-16.
3. Yoram Barzel, "A Theory of Rationing by Waiting," *Journal of Labor and Economics* 17 (April 1974): 73-95.
4. William James Adams and Janet Yellen, "Commodity Bundling and the Burden of Monopoly," *Quarterly Journal of Economics* 90 (August 1976): 475-98.

III SPILLOVER PROBLEMS

INTRODUCTION

The three chapters in this section-- insurance, crime, and externalities-- demonstrate the usefulness of microeconomics in explaining phenomena as diverse as the rapid rise of health care costs and the need for international regulations to limit the killing of whales. A common thread in these chapters, as in those on fashion and social forces, is the concept of spillover effects--that people who are not voluntary parties to a decision may nonetheless bear part of its costs or benefits.

Insurance protects individuals and institutions against financial losses but, unfortunately, also tends to exacerbate the problems insured against. Car insurance increases the number and severity of automobile accidents; strike insurance promotes management intransigence; fire insurance encourages arson. Chapter 11 explores this moral hazard problem of insurance.

Criminals can impose large costs on their victims and on others in society. Chapter 12 describes the real economic costs of theft and the effects of maintaining the illegality of so-called victimless crimes.

All spillovers can be subsumed under the broad concept of externalities, which is described and discussed in Chapter 13. Collective or public goods, such as flood control or national defense, are rightfully studied under the general externality heading. The public goods problem is that many worthwhile services may not be provided by decentralized decisionmaking. Aesop furnishes one of the earliest literary examples of a public goods-externality-spillover problem:

An old cat, says Aesop, was in a fair way to kill all the mice in the barn. One day the mice met to talk about the great harm she was doing them. Each one told of some plan by which to keep out of her way. "Do as I say," said an old gray mouse that was thought to be very wise. "Do as I say. Hang a bell to the cat's neck. Then, when we hear it ring, we shall know that she is coming and can scamper out of her way." "Good! good!" said all the other mice; and one ran to get the bell. "Now which of you will hang this bell on the cat's neck?" said the old gray mouse. "Not I! not I!" said all the mice together. And they scampered away to their holes.

11 INSURANCE

There is an old vaudeville song, sung by a poor man, that argues that money doesn't mean a thing to a person's mental state. After all, "a man with seven million is as happy as a man who has eight." An economist would agree with the spirit of that verse. In economic jargon, since the law of diminishing marginal utility holds for most goods and combinations of goods, it also holds for money. As money income increases, each new dollar adds something to utility, but total utility grows at a slower and slower rate. The extra amounts of goods, services, leisure, or security that can be bought with the additional money contribute less and less to satisfaction.

The diminishing marginal utility of money means that individuals will tend to be risk averters. Given the option of taking a large, actuarially fair bet versus not gambling at all, most people will choose not to gamble. Who would bet her entire income, double or nothing, on the flip of a coin? While it is sometimes enjoyable to make small bets, few people are willing to stake significant portions of their wealth on a game of pure chance.

Risk aversion makes people willing to pay something to reduce the risk of loss; the larger the potential loss, the more they will pay. Consider a situation in which an individual owns a house valued at $100,000. Ninety-nine other individuals own similar houses, and it is known that one of these 100 homes will be totally destroyed this year. When the year ends, each homeowner has a 99 percent chance of having a $100,000 house and a 1 percent chance of having nothing. Assume that there is no danger of personal injury. Rather than face the possibility of large loss, most individuals would prefer to enter into some risk-spreading arrangement. Each could agree to pay $1,000 into a pot, with the $100,000 going to that unlucky individual whose house has been destroyed. Everyone would thus convert the 1 percent chance of a $100,000 loss into a certain, but much smaller, loss of $1,000. If the homeowners were true risk averters, they would be willing to pay somewhat more than the $1,000. There thus may be room for a profit-making insurance company to exist, the expenses and profit of which can be met out of the higher premiums.

An insurance contract can be considered an exchange of today's money for the guarantee of larger amounts to be returned in the future if some unfortunate contingency occurs. The purpose of insurance is to reduce risk by converting large uncertain losses into smaller but certain premiums. Since insurance entails administrative expenses, it doesn't make sense to insure against minor losses. These are better handled through savings.[1]

While insurance usually covers against large losses, the insurance company itself may not be taking on great risks because what is somewhat unpredictable for the individual is often highly predictable for the group. The homeowner does not know which particular houses will be destroyed this year, but the insurance company can estimate the percentages relatively accurately. Generally speaking, spreading the risk reduces it. For the insurance company, the larger the number of policies, the less the risk if the occurrence of the adverse events are largely independent. However, when the occurrences are positively correlated, increasing the number of policies may actually increase the insurer's risk. For example, it may not be wise for a single company to insure more and more homes in any particular valley against flood or more and more San Franciscans against earthquake damage.

Interdependent contingencies constitute just one of the problems that worry insurance companies. Two others, of great interest to the economist, are termed "adverse selection" and "moral hazard."

ADVERSE SELECTION

A health insurance company is, in effect, betting with each policyholder that she will not get sick. The insurer can get excellent average data on what percentage of a large group of similar individuals is likely to become ill. But each individual may know more about her own particular susceptibilities than an insurance company can easily find out. For example, the individual usually has better information about her own family's medical history.

Since insurance premiums tend to reflect the average level of risk for any category, those people within groupings whose individual risks are greater than the average are likely to be attracted by the good bargain the insurance represents. Conversely, those who know that their own risk is below the average are less likely to purchase the insurance. The worse risks tend to buy insurance, while the better risks do not. An example of this phenomenon of adverse selection occurs with pregnancy insurance. Those who intend not to have children are less attracted to the policy; those planning a family tend to enroll. The insuring of primarily high-risk families forces premiums to rise, which further reduces the number of insureds.

Why does a new car lose so much of its value in the first few months of ownership? An explanation is that adverse selection exists in the market for used cars. While buyers may be able to discover the average quality of specific make/model cars on the market, any potential seller should know a great deal more about the quality of her own particular automobile. Product information is asymmetrically distributed in the market, but here the sellers know more than the buyers. At any given market price for a specific make/model, those potential sellers with cars of lower quality will be more attracted into the market, and those with higher quality cars will be less likely to enter. Adverse selection occurs. The average quality of cars in the market falls, and so does price. The market may become a market for "lemons."[2]

Several methods are used to deal with the problem of adverse selection. Insurers can try to gain more information about the potential purchaser, by, for example, requiring medical tests before issuing health or life insurance. They can make narrower and narrower groupings for different classes of insurance, lessening the variance within each group and, thus, the magnitude of the adverse selection problem. Ideally, each buyer could be put in a separate category representing her particular risk.

The adverse selection problem is that relatively too few low-risk (high-quality) individuals become insured. Fixed and compulsory coverage, as is required of some aspects of automobile insurance, solves the problem. In voluntary plans, it helps if the cost of insurance is kept low. Group plans tend to be less expensive because of lower administrative and selling costs. The income tax laws also promote group insurance: rather than the individual paying for coverage out of already-taxed take-home pay, the employer is allowed to pay for coverage tax free. This decreased cost makes it more likely that low-risk individuals will purchase group insurance.

MORAL HAZARD

A second major problem faced by insurers is that having insurance often changes the individual's incentives and decisions. This is the "moral hazard" problem. The term does not usually imply moral perfidy, although it may, as when an arsonist burns down a building for the insurance. Instead, the phrase generally denotes rational economic behavior when prices change. The problem for society is that private rational choices are not always socially rational.

Owning insurance influences a person's behavior in two principal ways: ex ante, it makes the individual less careful in avoiding or preventing the danger, thus increasing the likelihood that the catastrophe will occur; ex post, it increases the insured's demand for replacement and repair goods and services.

Consider the example of home fire protection. A rational individual should ask herself how much fire protection apparatus she should buy and how safe against fire she should make her house. The economist's answer is that the homeowner should buy an additional unit of fire protection (e.g., thicker walls, less flammable fabrics, better fire extinguishers) as long as the extra benefit is greater than the extra cost. The individual's demand for fire protection will be downward sloping: the lower the price,

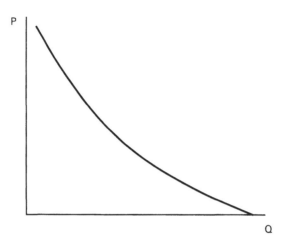

Figure 11-1

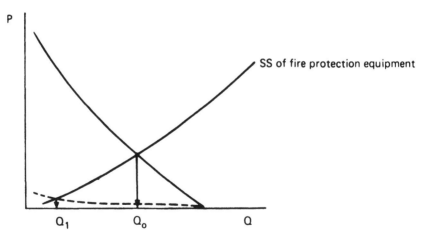

Q_1 = the postinsurance amount of protection actually bought

Q_0 = the preinsurance optimal purchases of fire protection

Figure 11-2

the more she will demand. As price falls, she will increase her purchases and her protection (Figure 11.1).[3]

What is the effect of owning home fire insurance? The insurance, by decreasing the individual's loss from fire, will decrease her demand for fire protection. Assume for simplicity that the only danger is property damage and that the fire creates no inconvenience. If the insurance pays for the entire loss, a fire destroying an individual's home affects her only to the extent that it may raise everyone's premiums. Therefore, the demand for fire protection equipment falls. In the initial example of the 100 homeowners, it falls by 99 percent. If we begin from a position of optimality, insurance means that there will be too little concern for fire protection and too many fires.

If there are no fire externalities (e.g., other houses burning), then the marginal social benefit of preventing a $100,000 home from burning down is $100,000. Without insurance, the extra benefit to the homeowner from avoiding a fire is also $100,000. But with insurance, this figure drops to $1,000. The owner now receives only one one-hundredth of the benefit from protecting her own home. The other ninety-nine insureds receive the rest. From the social perspective, each individual has an incentive to purchase too few safety options (Figure 11-2).

Consider an owner who could buy a device that would decrease the chance her home would burn down from 1 percent to 0.25 percent. Without insurance, she would pay up to $750 for the device (more if she is risk averse), or 0.75 of 1 percent multiplied by $100,000. With complete insurance, the device is worth only about $7.50, or 0.75 of 1 percent multiplied by $1,000. The risk-neutral individual will not buy the device if it costs more than this, and too many homes may burn down.

The existence of insurance increases the likelihood that the insured-against event will occur. This is the ex ante moral hazard problem. Contact lens insurance reduces the cost of carelessness. Unemployment insurance permits the worker to be more choosy and take more time in selecting a new job. The availability of flood insurance induces more people to locate in flood-prone areas.

It is not only policyholder behavior that may be modified. The ultimate beneficiaries of insurance, for example, may be encouraged to commit criminal acts. Ransom insurance can promote kidnapping by assuring terrorists that funds will be readily available to meet their ransom demands. And not surprisingly, life insurance recipients are often prime suspects in murder cases.

The ex post moral hazard problem is that insurance leads individuals to demand more and higher quality goods and services for replacement or repair. If we begin with perfect competition, then insurance causes a divergence from the Pareto optimal solution. We will discuss hospital services since that is one area in which insurance has caused severe efficiency losses in recent years.

Consider a simple insurance plan that will pay 80 percent of all medical fees. Without insurance, an individual has some demand curve for medical care; the higher the price, the less she demands. However, once she becomes insured, she pays only

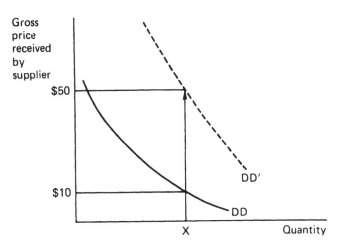

Figure 11-3

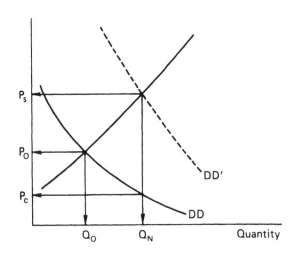

Q_O = old (equilibrium) quantity
Q_N = new quantity

P_O = old (equilibrium) price
P_s = new price received by suppliers
P_c = new price paid by customers

Figure 11-4

one-fifth of the total or gross price. Given this fall in price, she will demand more and higher quality services.

The effect is much like an 80 percent subsidy. If we think about the subsidy going directly to the patient, this will shift her demand curve upward by fivefold. Without insurance, if the price per unit of health care were $10 per unit, she would demand X units. Now the price can be $50, the insurer will provide $40, the insured will pay $10 and still demand the same X units (Figure 11-3).

Begin with a perfectly competitive market. Then add this 80 percent insurance plan for all buyers. Equilibrium price received by suppliers rises and quantity increases (Figure 11-4). This new market price will not be five times higher (unless supply is perfectly inelastic or demand perfectly elastic). Nor will quantity typically increase by anything near fivefold. Indeed, there is no change in equilibrium quantity if demand or supply is perfectly inelastic.

An alternative and equivalent approach is to have the supply curve fall by fivefold when the 80 percent insurance coverage is introduced (Figure 11-5). In this case it is easiest to suppose that the insurance is paid directly to the producer. Note that net price paid by the patient rather than gross price received by the supplier is on the vertical axis. Without insurance, when the net price paid by patients is $60, only Y units are supplied. With insurance, the consumer need only pay $12; the insurer will contribute $48; the producer will receive the same $60 and will supply Y units. Adding the market demand curve, we find that the equilibrium net price falls with insurance and quantity increases (Figure 11-6).

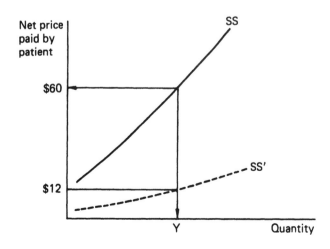

Figure 11-5

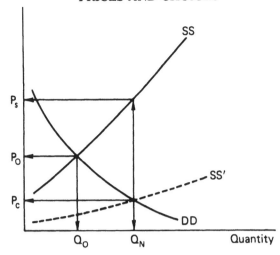

Q_O = old (equilibrium) quantity
Q_N = new quantity

P_O = old (equilibrium) price
P_s = new price received by suppliers
P_c = new price paid by customers

Figure 11-6

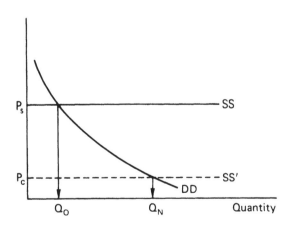

Q_O = old amount purchased by the individual
Q_N = new amount purchased

P_s = market price
P_c = price paid by the individual

Figure 11-7

Begin again with a perfectly competitive market and no insurance. Each individual buyer, as a price taker, faces a horizontal supply curve. Now assume that only a single small purchaser becomes insured (with the 80% coverage). Market price is unaffected, but the price faced by this lone individual falls fivefold. This situation is most easily depicted by a downshift in the supply curve. The individual's purchases increase, as shown in Figure 11-7.

In the health care field, the rapid increase in private and government insurance coverage has caused a pronounced increase in demand and prices. The increase in coverage has increased demand, and since long-run supply has not been highly elastic, prices have shot up dramatically. Between 1950 and 1980, direct hospital payments by the patient fell precipitously, from 30 to 10 percent. During the same thirty years, as the consumer price index rose by 278 percent, hospital charges increased by over 1,400 percent.[4] Whenever possible, patients demanded not only more medical care but also care of higher quality. To make matters worse, the skyrocketing medical prices forced more individuals to seek more complete medical coverage, thus exacerbating the moral hazard problem.

Consider a perfectly competitive world, and add health insurance. The insurance acts like a subsidy and, with any elasticity in demand and supply curves, causes individuals to consume too much medical care. Any individual is not sufficiently motivated to restrain her own use since while she receives the total benefit (assuming, for simplicity, that there are no externalities), the cost is spread over others. The new demand (or supply) curves do not reflect marginal social benefit (or marginal social cost). And price, quantity, and quality of services consumed are too high from the viewpoint of society. There is allocative inefficiency. Society could be better off if fewer resources were devoted to health care, leaving more available for other areas.

As insurance coverage increases, patients become more interested in quality and less interested in price. If out-of-pocket costs fall to zero, they desire even the smallest quality improvement, virtually irrespective of cost. Product innovations (quality increasing) are rewarded by individual consumers; process innovations (cost-cutting measures) are not. The patient has little incentive to shop around for the best bargain. The innovative energies of suppliers are thus channeled somewhat inappropriately. While the quality of medicine improves over time, the cost of care also keeps rising.[5]

There are a variety of measures designed to alleviate the problems of moral hazard. One is simply to limit the amount of insurance coverage, such as having copayments, deductibles, or maximum limits.

Copayments and deductibles help increase precaution and decrease overuse. Copayment means that insurance covers less than 100 percent of all expenses. In other words, the insured is forced to pay a fraction of all costs. This fraction (20% in our medical care example) should be low enough to avoid financial calamity but large enough to reduce the moral hazard problem. Deductibles are equivalent to 100 percent copayment (or 0% insurance) for small repairs. For example, the first $100 or $200 of car repairs must often be paid by the insured. A principal purpose of deductibles is to avoid the administrative cost of small claims, but they also provide a financial incentive that encourages precaution, though not one that inhibits demand once the deductible limit has been passed.

Feature rating, underwriting criteria, and experience rating can all help limit moral hazard ex ante. The premium structure can provide useful information about safety precautions as well as financial incentives to take them. For example, the fact that automobile insurers give discounts for a Chapman Lok suggests to automobile owners that the device is effective in decreasing theft and rewards them financially for purchasing it.

Underwriting criteria can also be used to increase safety. The insurance company can simply refuse to write the policy unless precautions are taken. Industrial fire insurers, for example, carefully inspect the production process and the premises and may require significant modifications (e.g., a sprinkler system) before granting coverage.

Experience rating is another method for promoting carefulness. Premiums are raised for policyholders with past problems and lowered for those with proven safety records. Workers compensation, for example, gives large manufacturing concerns an incentive to reduce reported injuries since a record of few claims is rewarded with lower insurance costs.

Indemnities provide a method that virtually eliminates the ex post problem of overuse. Instead of covering a certain percentage of costs, indemnity insurance provides a fixed-sum payment for loss. While indemnities usually cover losses where replacement is difficult or impossible (e.g., loss of life), they could be used to protect against a variety of risks. Their major limitation is that when damage and replacement expenses are variable, a fixed, lump-sum payment generally leads to over- or underinsurance.

Careful monitoring of replacement and repair expenses is another method by which insurers seek to control the ex post moral hazard problem. So too are prepayment schemes, such as those used by health maintenance organizations (HMOs). In HMOs the client pays an insurance premium and can receive reimbursement should she become ill. But instead of cash, payment is in kind. It is the supplier who receives a type of fixed indemnity payment, which gives her an incentive to provide efficient, though perhaps less extensive, service.

Private insurers have enormous economic power in the United States. In the mid-1980s they collected over $200 billion per year in premiums, owned some $1 trillion in assets, and employed 2 million workers. A question of serious policy importance is under what circumstances these companies have both the incentive and the ability, either individually or collectively, actually to limit the moral hazard problem.[6]

CONCLUSION

The law of diminishing marginal utility holds not only for most goods but also for money, income, and wealth. Thus, there is a demand for insurance against large losses, even though administrative expenses may be high. Of course, some large risks cannot be insured against; the prime examples concern events over which the potential insureds have great control, such as business failure. Those businesses seeking such insurance would know they had a high likelihood of failure and, once insured, would have much less incentive for success. These are the problems of adverse selection and moral hazard.

Adverse selection and moral hazard create problems for insurers and for society. Adverse selection is caused by the buyer's greater knowledge of whether or not the unwanted contingency is likely to occur. If inadequate information forces insurance companies to group lower and higher risks together, the lower have less incentive to purchase coverage. Such individuals, though they may want insurance, find the price too high. The dynamics of the situation could worsen the problem as insurers are forced to raise premiums, driving even higher risk purchasers out of the market.

The problems of moral hazard are caused by the changed prices faced by the insureds. Insurance against catastrophe makes people (rationally) more careless, increasing the likelihood that the catastrophe will occur. And insurance that pays for replacement or repair increases demand for such products and services. These moral hazard effects not only create problems for the insurer but also reduce economic efficiency.

FOR DISCUSSION

1. If people are generally risk averse, why do so many gamble? Does it ever make sense to match quarters? Why or why not?

2. The adverse selection problem occurs in the market for insurance and for used cars. Give another example of a market where adverse selection may exist.

3. Does a single insurance company have much of an incentive to promote safety? Does the insurance industry? Explain.

4. Since a fire at one's house may damage other homes, will individual decisionmaking lead to the optimal amount of private fire protection? Does insurance ameliorate or aggravate the problem?

5. "Not enough houses burn down." Could this statement ever be true? Can houses ever be too well protected against fire?

6. "Auto insurers have discovered that people settle for smaller amounts in cash than in repair services, because they always want the smashed left door to look as good as new if somebody else pays for it, but are often happy to get it banged back into workable shape for $50 if they can pocket $100 in cash."[7] Comment. Relate to moral hazard.

7. I am planning to open a fixed-price "All-You-Can-Eat" restaurant. Will I encounter adverse selection or moral hazard problems? Explain.

8. In medical malpractice cases, the higher the limits of the defendent's insurance policy, the higher the amount of damages awarded by the jury.[8] Relate to moral hazard.

9. Explain the major differences between the market for health insurance and the market for property insurance.

10. Carefully explain the inefficiencies caused by adverse selection.

11. Employers' contributions to group health insurance plans are not taxable as personal income. What are the reasons for and effects of this tax policy?

NOTES TO CHAPTER 11

1. For every dollar put into a Blue Cross health insurance plan, approximately 93¢ is returned to policyholders. The rest, plus interest, represents administrative expense and profit, or the loading factor. Automobile insurance returns about 62¢ on the dollar, homeowners insurance 58¢, rental car insurance 20¢, and flight insurance 10¢. Andrew Tobias, *The Invisible Bankers Everything the Insurance Industry Never Wanted You to Know* (New York: Simon & Schuster, 1982).
2. George Akerlof, "The Market for 'Lemons': Quality Uncertainty and the Market Mechanism," *Quarterly Journal of Economics* 84 (August 1970): 488-501.
3. "Price Critical for Smoke Alarms," *Chain Store Age*, General Marketing Edition (December 1983): 51.
4. Health Insurance Associations of America, *Source Book of Health Insurance Data* (Washington, DC: Health Insurance Associations, 1981-82), p. 64; U.S. Department of Health and Human Services, *Health Care Financing Review* (Washington, DC: Government Printing Office, September 1982), p. 24.

5. David Hemenway, Herb Sherman, Gilbert Mudge, Margaret Flatley, Nancy Lindsay, and Lee Goldman, "Benefits of Experience: Treating Coronary Artery Disease," *Medical Care* 24, no. 5 (February 1986): 125-33.

6. David Hemenway, "Private Insurance as an Alternative to Protective Regulation," *Policy Studies Journal* 15, no. 3 (March 1987): 415-40.

7. Thomas C. Schelling, "Medical Care Guarantees: Economics of Choice," in Institute of Medicine, *Implications of Guaranteeing Medical Care* (Washington, DC: National Academy of Sciences, 1975), p. 28.

8. Patricia M. Danzon, *Medical Malpractice: Theory, Evidence and Public Policy* (Cambridge, MA: Harvard University Press, 1985).

12 CRIME

Have you ever broken the law? There are many ways to do it. To name but a few crimes, there is murder, assault, rape, robbery, burglary, larceny, arson, manslaughter, kidnapping, and hijacking; there is extortion, embezzlement, fraud, forgery, counterfeiting, bribery, perjury, and plagiarism,; there is adultery, bigamy, incest, indecent exposure, prostitution, and obscenity; there is smuggling, espionage, desertion, and treason; there is vagrancy, truancy, drunkenness, and disorderly conduct; there is impersonating an officer, violating parole, and breaking out of prison; there is unlawful assembly, obstructing justice, and inciting to riot; there is hunting, driving, or practicing without a license; there is speeding, double-parking, hitchhiking, and jaywalking; there is gambling, loan-sharking, and dealing in drugs; there are housing code violations, blue law violations, and discrimination; there is child abuse, tax and draft evasion, suicide, sale of stolen goods, aiding and abetting a fugitive, illegal immigration, insider dealing, smoking in an elevator, and vandalism.

Most of us have committed offenses that could land us in jail. One suggestive though nonrandom self-report survey of 1,000 adult males found that 64 percent were unarrested felons, having engaged in such activities as grand larceny (13 percent), auto theft (26 percent), assault (49 percent), and burglary (17 percent). Of lesser crimes, 84 percent of respondents admitted to malicious mischief, 85 percent to disorderly conduct, 57 percent to tax evasion, and 36 percent to criminal libel. A typical adult male had committed some eighteen offenses![1] More recent self-report studies indicate that well over 70% of adolescents aged 12-19 have already exhibited delinquent behavior and could be arrested.[2]

Although many of us have committed crimes, only a small portion of us have been arrested or imprisoned. It is thus probably incorrect to draw a sharp distinction between "them" (the criminals) and "us" (the good guys). Of course, the high recidivism rate for serious crimes such as robbery indicates that some of us commit more serious crimes than do others.

Economists postulate that criminals are rational decision-makers. The economist assumes that an individual who steals does so largely because he has different opportunities and perceives different costs and benefits than one who doesn't. Believing that criminals are not fundamentally different than other people, economists include both the criminals' and their victims' utility when considering the welfare effects of crime.

Economists are able to bring a variety of insights and analytical tools to the study of the complex phenomenon called crime. Public finance economists are trained to analyze the optimal allocation of resources-- among various enforcement tools, among different locational districts, among various crimes, and between law enforcement and other activities. Industrial organization economists can discuss the black market for illegal goods and services, the relationship between market size and theft, why some crimes are organized while others are not, and why some legitimate industries are more susceptible than others to incursions by organized crime. Fraud, deception, and swindling can be analyzed, as can other white-collar crimes such as violations of the antitrust or pollution control laws. Labor economists can investigate racketeering, the effects of unemployment and labor-force participation on crime, and the problem of the released offender. All the subdisciplines of economics can contribute to our understanding of crime, including economic history (e.g., the effects of prohibition), urban economics (e.g.,city size and crime), international economics (e.g., smuggling), and radical economics (capitalism and class struggle as part of the problem).

The economist is trained to analyze myriad issues in criminology. Th's essay examines two: the economic costs of theft and the economics of black markets.

THE COSTS OF THEFT

When most people discuss the costs of theft, they emphasize the amount stolen. To an economist, this amount merely represents a transfer of wealth. If Peter takes $15 from Paul, Paul is $15 poorer, but Peter is $15 richer. There are clearly issues of equity, ethics, and morality involved, but in terms of efficiency, we cannot conclude that the before-theft situation is (Pareto) superior to the after-theft result. If Paul is sweet, kind, virtuous, and perhaps poor, while Peter is rich and horrid, we may be justifiably angered by the theft. But if we refuse to make interpersonal comparisons, as is normal in welfare economics, we cannot rank the two situations. Moreover, there is no way to further redistribute wealth to make *both* prefer that the theft had or had not occurred. Therefore, at first blush, one might conclude that there are no *efficiency* problems with theft.

On further reflection, however, there appear to be a number of potentially large efficiency losses associated with stealing. Let us abstract from the immense possible disutility caused by physical harm, or the fear of harm that may accompany theft, and consider situations in which there is no meeting or communication between thief and victim (or bystanders) and no fear of future physical harm.

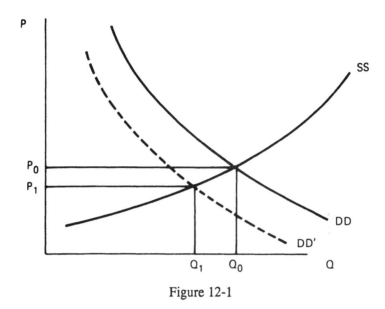

Figure 12-1

One efficiency problem caused by theft is this: if property rights cannot be easily safeguarded, less than the optimal amount of property will be produced. Figure 12-1 gives the demand and supply curves for bicycles in a competitive market, with theft impossible. Given perfect competition, $P_0 Q_0$ represents equilibrium price and quantity as well as the optimal amount of bicycle production and purchases given the initial distribution of income. Now let bicycles be stolen from users. The demand curve will shift down to DD' in the diagram. (If bikes are stolen from suppliers, the supply curve will shift up.) The expected utility of the bicycle for purchasers is now less since they may lose the bike to thieves. The new equilibrium $P_1 Q_1$ is not optimal, for P_1 understates the true value of bicycles-the value or utility of the bicycle for the thief is not included. If the thief were required to purchase the bike, the price would truly represent the marginal social benefit of the last bicycle provided. But with theft in this market, too few bicycles are produced and consumed. The more likely bicycles are of being stolen, the more the demand curve shifts down, the fewer bikes are produced, and the greater the allocative inefficiency.

A social cost of theft is that both the thief and the potential victim use resources to gain or maintain control over property. Both parties use capital and labor in the struggle to secure property rights. In a broad sense, this struggle may be called a "transaction cost." The thief spends time and money in the attempt to steal (buying wire cutters), and the legitimate property owner expends resources to prevent the theft (buying locks). These costs may escalate as a type of technological arms race unfolds. A bank may purchase more and more complicated and sophisticated safes, forcing safecrackers to invest further in safecracking equipment and education.

A related cost of theft is that it forces changes in decisions, lifestyles, and perceptions. A bank may not be able to open at the most convenient times or locations if this unduly encourages theft. A bike owner may find it too risky to leave his bike in certain locations and may sometimes be reluctant to use it at all. Crimes can be most destructive if they alter attitudes unfavorably. People may become distrustful and less likely to emote goodwill and compassion; they may be less willing to aid· strangers. Some of the community spirit that helps keep crime low and the quality of life high may be lost.

BLACK MARKETS

For a variety of reasons, many transactions between willing participants are or have been outlawed. The loaning of money at usury rates is banned in most states. So is the selling of cigarettes to minors and the hiring of illegal immigrants. Dope, prostitution, gambling, and pornography are also illegal, as is the exchange of contraband or stolen goods. At times in the United States, the sale of liquor, gold, abortions, contraceptives, and ration coupons has violated the law.

It is policy that creates black markets. We currently forbid certain narcotics but not tobacco, gambling on football but not on the stock market, extramarital sex but not gluttony.[3] Here we examine some of the major economic consequences of the illegality of marijuana.

With no government interference, the market for marijuana might approximate the model of perfect competition. There could be many small manufacturers, wholesalers and retailers, easy entry, and good information about prices and product quality. Figure 12-2 shows the free market demand and supply curves for this substance.

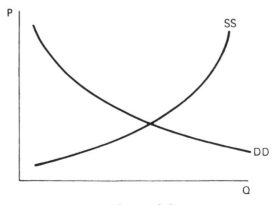

Figure 12-2

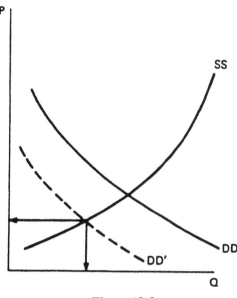

Figure 12-3

Suppose now that the government makes marijuana *consumption* illegal for all its citizens. It slaps a large fine on any citizen smoking or otherwise consuming marijuana; selling marijuana is still permitted (perhaps because sales to foreign tourists are considered desirable). What is the effect on price and quantity consumed?

A citizen's demand now becomes wrong and risky. The simple fact that the good is now illegal will probably decrease most people's desire for the weed, though it may increase a few people's demand. The risk of being caught and fined decreases virtually everyone's demand. The demand curve thus falls. At the same market price, less is demanded; alternatively, a lower price is required for consumption to remain the same. As shown in Figure 12-3, equilibrium price and quantity have decreased.

Now consider an alternative enforcement scheme. Possession and consumption are permitted, but growing and selling are prohibited. There are now higher costs of production: the cost of paying fines, of bribing the police, and of producing and selling in less efficient ways but ones that decrease the likelihood of detection. The supply curve shifts up and to the left. At any market price, less will be supplied; suppliers now require a higher price to supply the same amount. Figure 12-4 shows the effect on equilibrium price and quantity. Market price rises as quantity falls. Outlawing a commodity generally decreases output, but depending on the enforcement scheme, market price can either rise or fall.

An enforcement policy directed at the supply side decreases information availability. Advertising is made exceedingly difficult; brand names are hard to establish; liability or fraud suits may be impossible. The lack of buyer information tends to increase price and quality variation among sellers. It also tends to decrease

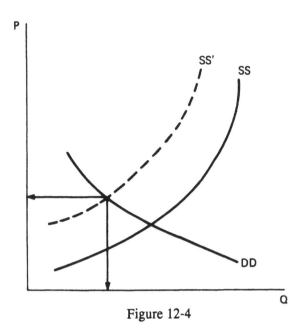

Figure 12-4

average quality by increasing the likelihood of successful adulteration. Illegality also decreases quality by forcing suppliers to use less detectable methods. This can be most readily perceived in the case of prostitution, where the possibility of discovery by police makes it less profitable for sellers to invest heavily in plush surroundings.

What are the costs and benefits of keeping marijuana illegal? The principal benefit is that it decreases consumption. This benefits those who favor the law. They derive utility from having others not smoke. The user himself may benefit if the law helps him in his desire to avoid and resist the temptation. If marijuana were addictive or associated with other social problems-theft, poor driving, assault, insulting behavior, inability to support one's family, heroin addiction-the benefits would be larger and more apparent.

The costs of illegality include a higher price and lower quality for those who want to consume, law enforcement expenditures and costs (including jail sentences), and increased disrespect for the law. The costs (and benefits) of making desired transactions illegal are probably larger for many other commodities: making abortions illegal decreases their quality, thus mutilating more women; the illegality of prostitution decreases its quality, increasing the likelihood of venereal disease and the robbery of clients; rising heroin prices due to illegality increase the need for addicts to steal to feed their habit; liquor and gambling bans helped establish organized crime. The magnitude of these costs, combined with a belief that the individual is generally the best person to know what is good for himself, leads many economists to advocate the decriminalization of many of the so-called victimless crimes.

FOR DISCUSSION

1. "People seldom plant apple trees where passers-by can easily take apples even if the value of the apples to society would exceed the costs" (Alchian and Allen, *Exchange and Production,* 1969, p. 244). Comment. Relate to the costs of theft.

2. Why do many buses require exact change? Is this a cost of theft?

3. The thief and the potential victim are struggling over property rights. Compare this to the situation in which goods are underpriced and distributed on a first-come, first-served basis. (See Chapter 10.)

4. What would be the effect if, instead of outlawing pot, the government granted a monopoly to a particular seller? What if the monopoly were granted annually and given to that firm willing to pay the government the most money for the right to produce and sell?

5. Blackmail is a (somewhat) willing transaction between a seller and a particular prospective buyer. Why is it illegal? What would be the economic effects of legalizing it?

6. Why is it illegal to sell your vote?

7. Are some crimes more likely to involve calculating cost-benefit analysis than others? Are safecrackers, armed robbers and terrorists any more or less rational than vandals, shoplifters and joyriders?

8. The fewer people that are out walking the street at night, the less safe it is to be walking around at night. Will the optimal number of people go out at night?

9. On the average, ex-convicts are less reliable than other employees. But hiring ex-cons reduces their likelihood of returning to a life of crime; it reduces the recidivism rate. Will the free market provide jobs for the right number of ex-cons? Would governmental policies be helpful?

NOTES TO CHAPTER 12

1. James S. Wallerstein and Clement J. Wyle, "Our Law-Abiding Law-Breakers," in *Probation* (New York: National Probation Association, 1947); see also Charles R. Tittle and Wayne J. Villemez, "Social Class and Criminality," *Social Forces* 56 (December 1977): 474-502.

2. Many study results are summarized in Jeffrey Fagan, Jospeh G. Weis and Yu-Teh Cheng, "Delinquency and Substance Abuse Among Inner City Students," *Journal of Drug Issues* 20 (1990): 351-402. See also Jay R. Williams and Martin Gold, "From Delinquent Behavior to Official Delinquency," *Social Problems* 20 (Fall 1972): 213.

3. Thomas C. Schelling, "Economics and Criminal Enterprise," in *Choice and Consequence* (Cambridge, MA: Harvard University Press): pp. 158-178.

OTHER SOURCES

Alchian, Armen A., and William R. Allen. *Exchange and Production*. Belmont, CA: Wadsworth Publishing Company, 1969, chapter 12.

Cornish, Derek B., and Ronald V. Clarke, eds. *The Reasoning Criminal: Rational Choice Perspectives on Offending*. New York: Springer-Verlag, 1986.

Hellman, Daryl. *The Economics of Crime*. New York: St. Martin's Press, 1980.

Rogers, A.J. *The Economics of Crime*. Hinsdale, IL: The Dryden Press, 1973, chapter 4.

Tullock, Gordon. "The Welfare Costs of Tariffs, Monopolies and Theft." *Western Economic Journal* 5 (June 1967): 228-31.

13 EXTERNALITIES

As chairperson of the Arrangements Committee, you are responsible for the organization and success of the class party. Your conception of a successful party is one at which everyone consumes large quantities of alcohol, but you also want to be assured that proceeds from the party will just cover costs. How do you go about pricing drinks?

A cash bar, where people pay by the drink, is one possibility. A much superior alternative from your perspective is for the class as a group to agree to share alcoholic costs equally. After the party, the total cost of drinks will be divided by class size, and all will pay an equal assessment. This arrangement covers costs, and it also increases consumption.

Let us examine a simple numerical example. There are fifty students in the class. Drinks are homogeneous (for instance, beer) and cost the committee 50¢ per glass. A typical individual's demand curve for drinks is given in Figure 13-1. The higher the price she pays for a drink, the less she consumes. At a cash bar, with drinks priced at 50¢, she buys Q_o.

Now consider the alternative arrangement. Each member of the class has agreed to share all alcoholic costs equally. An individual deciding whether or not to have another drink realizes that the cost to her is only 1¢. The forty-nine other members of the class each bear a 1¢ cost for her drink. In Figure 13-1, the marginal private cost curve has fallen to 1¢. A rational individual consumes Q_1, consuming more as long as the extra utility or benefit to her is greater than 1¢. The underpricing has caused her to increase her consumption.

A similar situation occurs in many localities with the pricing of another liquid-tap water. A community demand curve for such fresh water is given in Figure 13-2. There are costs to the community of supplying water to each household: the cost of purifying and transporting the water, as well as the possible cost of decreased swimming and boating pleasures if lakes are turned into reservoirs. The marginal social cost is given by MSC in Figure 13-2.

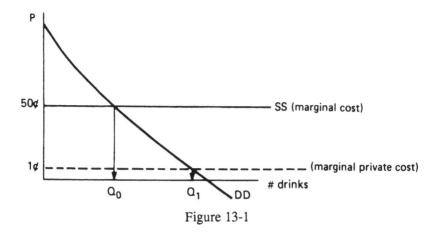

Figure 13-1

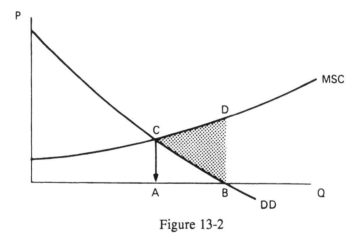

Figure 13-2

With marginal cost pricing, A units of water are consumed. But many localities do not charge the user anything for water. The costs are instead borne by the entire community, via taxes. If the community is large, any individual will perceive the cost to herself of consuming another unit of water as being virtually zero. Individuals will become wasteful of water, leaving the tap on, not fixing leaky faucets, and so forth. Consumption increases to B, past the point where the marginal benefit from an additional unit of water exceeds the marginal cost.

Figure 13-2 gives a measure of the efficiency costs of this underpricing and overconsumption. Ignoring income effects, the extra benefit of consuming B rather than A units is given by the area within triangle ABC; the extra cost is given by quadrangle ABDC. The social cost of overconsumption is therefore represented by the shaded triangle BCD.

In both of these examples, there are externalities; the individual consumer does not bear the full cost of her consumption. The marginal private cost of another drink of water or beer is unequal to the marginal social cost. Decisionmakers do not take sufficient account of the costs they impose on others. Their decisions are not optimal from the viewpoint of society.

The problem of pollution is similar. The cost of pouring impurities into the air or water is usually not fully borne by the polluter. The polluter imposes costs on others, but these costs are not sufficiently represented in the polluter's cost/benefit calculus. The private cost-- the negative price for producing this "bad"-- is not large enough. Hence, acting rationally, following her own self-interest, the decisionmaker tends to overpollute.

In equilibrium, perfect competition ensures that the amount produced or consumed of each commodity for every decisionmaker is at a level where the marginal private benefit = (price) = marginal private cost. An externality occurs when the marginal *social* benefit is unequal to the marginal private benefit, or the marginal *social* cost is unequal to the marginal private cost. For example, if you play the jukebox, this may enhance (or detract from) others' pleasure; if you catch the flu, you may infect others; if you attend the basketball game, it may increase fan excitement; if you remodel your home, it may boost neighborhood land values.

There are also external effects when a new product decreases the profits of firms in competing industries or changed preferences decrease the demand for one product and increase it for another. But these are pecuniary externalities, externalities that affect others not directly but through the price system. Pecuniary externalities are not discussed here, for they do not prevent perfect competition from achieving Pareto optimality in long-run equilibrium.

Direct externalities cause nonoptimal amounts of goods or bads to be produced and consumed. One could view this as a pricing problem; production or consumption of the commodity is at a level where marginal social benefit $\neq$ price, and/or marginal social cost $\neq$ price. Economists thus often favor "internalizing" the externality as a method for correcting the inefficiency. This means charging the decisionmaker with the costs she imposes on others or rewarding her with the benefits.

Assume, for example, that Figure 13-3 gives the demand and supply schedules for competitively produced studded snow tires. The supply curve represents the marginal cost in terms of real resources used (land, labor, and capital) to produce another snow tire. The demand represents the extra utility of another snow tire to the next highest bidder. In a world of perfect competition and no externalities, $P_o Q_o$ represents not only equilibrium price/quantity but also the Pareto optimal result for the given distribution of resources. However, studded snow tires create externalities. They ruin roads, which creates additional costs for others: less comfortable rides, shorter auto life, and increased taxes for road paving and repair. We might say that the supply curve does not include all the costs of another studded snow tire. People rationally following their own self-interest buy too many.

Let us make a heroic simplification and assume that each studded snow tire creates the same extra cost, $10 per tire. The externality could then be easily internalized by requiring buyers of studded tires to pay the cost they impose on society. An excise tax of $10 per tire would shift up the supply curve to reflect marginal social cost. Equilibrium price would then equate marginal social benefit and marginal social cost and decrease output to the optimal level. Note that the externality problem would not arise if each individual drove only on her own property. Then any damage done would be borne entirely by the decisionmaker, and marginal private cost would be equivalent to marginal social cost.

PROPERTY RIGHTS

The absence of well-defined and easily enforceable individual property rights is one of the fundamental causes of externalities. In the city water example, imagine a number of fresh ponds from which residents gather water. The water is owned by the public collectively, and it is distributed on a first-come, first-served basis at zero price. As population and demand grow, a point is reached where the marginal social cost exceeds zero. One citizen's drawing of water forces others to do without or to trudge to more and more distant ponds. There is overconsumption. In order to achieve efficiency, government must begin marginal cost pricing. If there are large numbers of small ponds, private ownership of each by competitive water suppliers could achieve the same result automatically. Each tiny supplier would face a horizontal demand curve and would profit maximize by producing where $P = MC$.

Efficiency problems will also occur if particular oil fields are under multiple ownership and control. Under law, the oil belongs to the firm that brings it to the

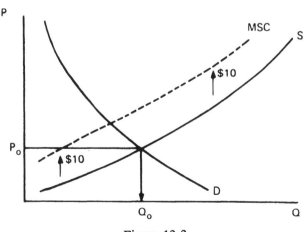

Figure 13-3

surface. While there is a maximum efficient pumping rate, this will usually be exceeded, since it does not pay for any individual firm to exercise restraint while its neighbors capture more than their share of the resource. Competition for the oil in any particular field leads to too many holes being drilled and too rapid pumping, resulting in a loss of natural pressure and a greatly reduced total oil yield. The problem may be decreased by government regulation, but unitized management of each field eliminates the inefficiency without government interference. If there are large numbers of oil fields, unitized management also allows the existence of a competitive oil market.

The rule of capture also applies to common fishing areas, leading to the killing of too many and too small fish. The problem is that no one owns the fish while they are in the water, and a single fisherman does not bear the full cost he imposes on society. Killing fish increases the cost to other fishermen by decreasing the current and future numbers of fish available. Without some common enforceable agreement, an individual fisherman has little incentive to refrain from catching fish, even relatively young fish, in order to increase next year's yield. He has no guarantee that others will also refrain or that his own action will have more than a negligible effect. His restraint benefits all fishermen, but he himself receives only a small portion of the benefit. But all fishermen would be better off if all exercised restraint.

The situation can be depicted by a prisoner's dilemma game (see the Appendix). Any individual fisherman profits depend in part on the actions of other fishermen. Each individual acting purely in his own interest will disregard the effects of his actions on other fishermen. He wishes others would exercise restraint, but his own dominant strategy is not to. If all act in their own self-interest, they will reach a dominated outcome. All would be better off if all exercised restraint, but each has an incentive to cheat. They would thus like some method to help them collectively achieve the preferable result (Figure 13-4).

	(Others)	
	Restraint	No Restraint
Restraint	(8) 8	(10) 2
No Restraint	(2) 10	(5) 5

Figure 13-4

Theoretically, there are a variety of methods to eliminate the problem of overfishing, including catch limits, taxes to internalize the externality, or attempts at unified management, especially for nonmigratory fish such as salmon, cod, and haddock. The usual method of making fishing vessels technologically inefficient seems less desirable. Virginia oystermen, for example, are required to employ cumbersome twenty-foot tongs to raise oysters laboriously from public waters instead of using efficient dredges towed by motor boats. In Maryland dredges can be used if they are towed by sailboat, except on Monday and Tuesday, when motorized pusher-boats are permitted.

Why may whales, buffalo, deer, alligators, lions, and hawks be in some danger of extinction while pigs, camels, horses, goats, cats, and goldfish are not? The fundamental explanation seems to be the absence, or presence, of property rights. There is great difficulty in owning, domesticating, and breeding the former animals. They are wild. Ownership is determined by the rule of capture-- a type of first-come, first-served arrangement. A nineteenth-century American hunter had little incentive to refrain from killing buffalo; if he didn't kill them, someone else would. Too many buffalo were destroyed, virtually eliminating them from the American scene. The prisoner's dilemma model is applicable here. Individual hunters did not take into account the costs they imposed on others, especially the Indians.

On the other hand, there is little need to worry about the extinction of pigs. Pigs are privately owned. An owner receives virtually all the direct benefits and costs when a pig is destroyed. He has no incentive to kill her own pigs wantonly, and no one else is allowed to. If the pig population were to fall suddenly (because of disease), then ceteris paribus, the value of each pig would increase, creating an incentive for farms to try to increase pig production.

PUBLIC GOODS

The examples so far have focused on rival goods, where one person's consumption of a particular item eliminates the possibility for others to consume it. Pork is a rival good; if one person owns and eats the meat, another cannot also eat it. By contrast, public goods are nonrival goods. Enjoyment by one individual in no way detracts from use or enjoyment by others. Flood control, military defense, and lighthouse signals are common examples. While individual demand curves for rival goods are added horizontally to obtain market demand, individual demand curves for public goods should be added vertically. For example, if the one hundred million households that would be protected by an increase in defense spending would be willing to pay $10 for another unit of missile defense, this unit is worth at least $1 billion (100 million x $10) and should be produced if it costs less than this amount.

A second aspect of pure public goods is that noncontributors cannot be excluded from the benefits. Thus, individuals have no material incentive to pay for the public good unless compelled to. This is the "free rider" problem and it is the reason that public goods are provided publicly rather than by private entrepreneurs. No one has an incentive to pay for a dam if he will receive its protection whether or not he contributes financially to its construction and maintenance. The prisoner's dilemma game illustrates the problem. Each person has a dominant strategy not to contribute but wishes everyone else would contribute. All could be better off if all, rather than none, contributed. The typical solution is to agree collectively to require everyone to contribute through taxes.

Private decisionmaking will not provide the optimal amount of public goods. However, there are often methods of making the goods less public by devising ways of excluding noncontributors, of eliminating the free riders. Thus, a lighthouse could send out only coded signals on selected frequencies, with only financial supporters having knowledge of these. Defense against crime in the streets (police protection) could be provided only for those with special badges indicating voluntary contribution to the defense program. But such methods eliminate only the free rider aspect of public goods, not their nonrivalry. Their nonrival nature means the marginal cost of providing the service to another individual is zero, and hence any exclusion, even if possible, is inefficient. However, if the service is to be profitably provided by private organizations, some sort of exclusion is usually necessary.

The classic western movie *High Noon* is a drama built around the public goods-free rider problem. Gary Cooper as sheriff learns that an outlaw leader he sent to jail has been released and will arrive on the twelve o'clock train to be met by his terrorist gang. Coop seeks aid from the townsfolk, but while each desires defense-- "so that decent women and children can walk the streets"-- this benefit will be available to anyone whether or not he stands with Cooper at high noon to face the outlaws' guns. The townsfolk, given little time to collectively mobilize, end up hiding. The one early volunteer quickly deserts when he learns that there is no one else willing to help; his likelihood of dying has become too high. Cooper also has great incentive to leave town: his term as sheriff expires the next day; his Quaker bride threatens to leave him; the townsfolk have deserted him; and his chance of survival is low-- all of which make his decision to stay and his ultimate victory the more heroic and incredible.

PERVASIVENESS

Economist Tom Schelling tells of the time his two-year-old son, looking out the window, asked his father, "Why are all the other houses on the outside, when ours is on the inside?" While microeconomics usually focuses on situations in which all nonpecuniary costs and benefits are internalized, real-world situations almost always involve interesting and important externalities. Social interaction, for example, is virtually all "externality." If you are not Robinson Crusoe, almost everything you do affects others in positive or negative ways. A smile, a friendly hello, a pat on the back brings utility to others; how you eat, what you wear, with whom you associate matters to other people. Chapters 4 and 5 on fashion and social forces discuss some of these externalities.

Most of society's laws can be viewed as attempts to channel private behavior so as to promote the public interest. Fines for walking on the grass, littering, and double parking try to internalize the disutility such actions can impose on others. Prohibitions against murder and assault have the clear purpose of deterring conduct that can cause enormous unhappiness to others.

Many of society's customs and codes of ethics are also designed to help make the invisible hand work. The social rules concerning reciprocity in gift and social exchange promote beneficial transactions while maintaining part of their spontaneity and voluntarism. Such conventions as the handshake, the bow, and the "excuse me" keep interactions friendly. The golden rule is a prime example of a code of conduct that, if followed, would make everyone better off.

CONCLUSION

An externality is defined as an action that brings direct benefits or costs to others, but these do not sufficiently enter into the utility calculus of the decisionmaker. There are probably some externalities in most actions you take, including washing the dishes, wearing new clothes, walking the dog, driving a car, or having a child. The importance of the externality depends on a large number of factors.

Where there are externalities, private decisionmaking may not lead to the social optimal. From the social perspective, too much or too little of an activity will be undertaken. A variety of methods can improve the situation, including the changing of ownership patterns, taxes and subsidies, regulations, laws, social sanctions, and moral imperatives. Which, if any, is most appropriate depends on the specific situation.

FOR DISCUSSION

1. Is it proper to force people to get polio inoculations?

2. What is the rationale for government allocation of the radio spectrum?

3. What is the reasoning behind urban renewal? Why won't individual owners improve their property to gain higher rents? Why don't individual families have the responsibility of maintaining their own cemetery plots in large graveyards?

4. Why do we need zoning laws?

5. Are people more careless with library books than with their own books? In public parks than in their own backyards? Why?

6. How do communes get people to work their fair share?

7. After all the talk about democracy, why do so few people vote in the United States?

8. Why weren't the buffalo wiped out by the Native Americans before the advent of Europeans?

9. Will private decisionmaking lead to the optimal population size?

SOURCES

Hardin, Garrett. "The Tragedy of the Commons." *Science* 162 (December, 1968): 1243-48.

Olson, Mancur, *The Logic of Collective Action* (Cambridge, MA: Harvard University Press, 1965).

Schelling, Thomas C. "On the Ecology of Micromotives." *The Public Interest*, no. 25 (Fall 1971): 59-98.

IV QUALITY

INTRODUCTION

The Lioness and the Vixen:

> A lioness and a vixen were talking together about their young, as mothers will, and saying how healthy and well groomed they were, and what beautiful coats they had, and how they were the image of their parents. "My litter of cubs is a joy to see," said the Fox; and then she added, rather maliciously, "but I notice you never have more than one." "No," said the Lioness grimly, "but that one's a lion."

Quality, not quantity

While the importance of product quality is undisputed, as late as the 1970s it was correct to conclude that "what economists study are quantities, not qualities,"[1] and that "quality is a topic which economists, by and large, have swept under the rug."[2] In recent years, there has been a reawakening of professional economic interest in quality issues. This section contains five chapters dealing with this vital topic.

Chapter 14 examines the issue of quality assessment. It presents a taxonomy of approaches for determining quality and illustrates them with evaluations of nursing-home care. Although all approaches have limitations and are not necessarily consistent within or among themselves, they can provide useful insights concerning relative quality levels.

The following chapter highlights the fact that optimal quality is different from maximum quality. It then discusses five factors that can affect average quality: buyer information, excess demand, legality, licensing, and insurance. Examples are provided from various industries, but a goal throughout is to relate these factors to the quality of services provided in one market-- the market for health care.

Chapter 16 examines voluntary standards, particularly quality standards, discussing their importance in our economy, who writes them, and where they are likely to arise. The emphasis is on the relationship between market structure and standards creation.

The final chapter deals with a related topic: grading-- not the grading of students by teachers, but the grading of products, usually by governmental agents. It describes important economic effects of grading and helps explain why some goods are graded while others are not.

NOTES TO INTRODUCTION

1. C. S. Bell, "Discussion," in National Academy of Engineering, ed., *Product Quality, Performance and Cost* (Washington, DC: National Academy of Engineering, 1972), p. 39.
2. E. S. Maynes, "The Concept and Measurement of Product Quality," in N. E. Terleckyj, ed., *Household Production and Competition* (New York: National Bureau of Economic Research, 1975), p. 529.

14 QUALITY ASSESSMENT

There is no theoretically correct way for society to assess the quality of a good or service. This is because individual tastes differ, so that even fully informed individuals will not rank goods identically. The problem is similar to the general impossibility of constructing a consistent social welfare function.[1]

In an article on health care, researchers analyzed a supposed paradox.[2] Looking at patient surveys, they discovered that most individuals believe there is a crisis in terms of the quality of medical care, yet the majority also believe that their own medical care is reasonably good. The researchers argued that "most people apparently see other people's care as generally worse than their own. This is by definition an incorrect assessment as we are dealing with a national sample." Thus, the researchers concluded that people must generally be misinformed. Their reasoning seems to go along these lines: more than half the people in society cannot be above median height. If more than half believe they are taller than the median, some must be wrong.

The paradox can be explained in other ways. A simple one is to recognize that while there is virtual unanimity about how height should be measured, there is no such agreement concerning the way to assess quality. People's tastes differ, so that even if two individuals had complete information, they could easily disagree about relative quality rankings. Indeed, if buyers are well informed, they will tend to purchase items that rate high in their own particular quality ordering. Thus, there need be nothing fatuous about most individuals believing that the car they continue to buy, the toothpaste they continue to use, or the physician they continue to see is above average quality-- in terms of their own personal but reasonable rating scheme. It would certainly not be surprising to discover that 90 percent of dog owners believe that their dog is above the median in terms of being a wonderful pet.

Quality has many aspects. This multidimensionality provides two reasons why individual quality rankings may differ. The first reason is that people may disagree about the ratings of any one of the various components of quality. This is especially likely when subjective evaluation is required. A second reason tastes may differ is that individuals may put different weights on the various quality dimensions. They may not even agree on what aspects deserve any weight at all.

Consider the difficulty of agreeing on the current quality rankings of air passenger service among the various airline companies. There are some relatively objective performance measures, such as accident rates, delays, lost baggage, and so forth. Even assuming that these are reliable indicators of current and future service and that they are the only quality dimensions that matter, different purchasers may rate the airlines differently. Indeed, a single buyer may vary his rankings depending on his specific need. And there are, of course, many subjective aspects of air service quality about which unanimity is unlikely, such as the taste of the food, the comfort of the seats, and the helpfulness of the flight attendants.

Although there is no ideal method for society to measure quality, policy decisions must be made and, often, quality evaluated. As a nation, for example, we are vitally interested in the quality of our food, housing, education, health care, and so forth. Much government regulation-- from automobile inspection to building codes to doctors' licenses-- is designed to ensure minimum levels of quality. This requires some assessment of product or service quality.

One area in which quality assessment has received a great deal of attention is the health care field. Health analysts have delineated three main approaches for measuring quality: structural, process, and outcome evaluation.[3] This chapter presents a somewhat different and more "economic" taxonomy of approaches the use of (1) market variables, (2) survey results, (3) output variables, and (4) input variables. Each approach is described in turn. The final section discusses the four approaches with respect to measuring the quality of a particular service the care provided by nursing-home facilities.

THE MARKET APPROACH

In trying to judge product quality, an economist naturally looks toward the market. The fact that the price of a Mercedes is four times that of a Hyundai indicates a perceived quality difference between these two automobiles. That Baltimore Orioles star shortstop Cal Ripken Jr. earns three times as much as his brother, second-baseman Billy Ripken, says something significant about their respective playing abilities. Demand or price can often provide a useful proxy for quality, particularly since market information is generally inexpensive to collect. One possible virtue of the market approach is that it eliminates the difficult problem of creating explicit weighting schemes for product attributes and individual preferences.

What do demand comparisons tell us about relative product quality? They may suggest something, but a number of points must be recognized. First, demand is affected by many factors, some of which we might want to exclude from the concept of product quality. This year's demand for Toyota automobiles, for example, depends in part on the location of retail outlets, the current stock of existing Toyotas, and expectations about next year's Toyota price. Second, demand will change if other economic variables change, such as the prices of complements and substitutes and the distribution of income. Finally, if there is less than perfect product information, demand may not reflect people's true tastes or preferences.

Relative prices tell us even less about quality than does demand. This is because prices are affected not only by demand but also by relative scarcity (supply). For example, if the cost of making modern chairs decreases, the price of modern chairs will tend to fall. The price of antique chairs will thus appear higher by comparison. Such relative price movements would occur in competitive markets even though the intrinsic nature of the chairs was unchanged and preferences remained stable.

Two strains in the economics literature on quality are especially relevant to the discussion. The first concerns the hedonic approach to consumer demand theory.[4] Quality is recognized as multidimensional, but all product dimensions ("characteristics") are assumed to be objective and scalar-- there is unanimity in the ranking of products along every particular quality dimension. The principal application of this approach is to account for quality changes in the construction of price indices.

The goal of the hedonic method is to disaggregate the price of a commodity into implicit prices for its various components or characteristics. In so doing, the hedonic approach accepts the "quality" rankings of products as provided by the market. The statistical procedure used is multiple regression, applied to cross-sectional data in a single market. The independent variables are the commodity characteristics. These are either quantifiable (e.g., horsepower, length, and weight of automobiles) or dummy variables (e.g., automatic transmission? power steering? power brakes?). The dependent variable is the price of each differentiated product. The regression coefficients on the independent variables allow the determination of their implicit prices. One hedonic analysis of automobile prices indicated that an increase of ten units of horsepower, ceteris paribus, would result in a 1.2 percent increase in the price of a car. Since vehicle horsepower had risen during the period studied, some of the automobile price increases over time were attributed to increased quality rather than pure inflation.[5]

A second strain in the economic literature is the empirical testing of the extent to which price is actually an indicator of quality. The quality measures are usually provided by expert raters, typically *Consumer Reports* magazine. A main conclusion of this research is that the relationship between price and quality is positive but rather weak.[6]

The low correlation between price and quality is not surprising. First, Consumers Union's determination of quality may not be the best or the most appropriate one. Second, as argued above, many factors other than quality affect price. For example, even physically identical products in a single market may have different prices, not only if information about them is incomplete, but also if there is discrimination or if the market is not in equilibrium. Physically identical products in distinct markets may sell at different prices for a variety of additional reasons, including transportation costs, resource immobility, and monopolistic restrictions, as well as taxes, tariffs, and other government regulations.

Extending the hedonic approach, one could use multivariate analysis to try to isolate the effect on price of many of these extraneous factors. Thus, in explaining price variations among automobiles, variables such as taxes, transport costs, tariffs, and monopoly measures could be regressed on price, and any residual price differences might be attributed to differences in quality. While there are many empirical difficulties with using the hedonic approach, the fundamental problems with using market data remain theoretical. Since notions of quality vary across individuals and among uses, some weighting of preferences is necessary. The market implicitly weights preferences by effective demand and, thus, largely by income and wealth. One can certainly question such a weighting procedure for determining quality.

QUESTIONNAIRE RESULTS

A direct approach to determining quality is to ask people-- buyers, sellers, independent experts (e.g., Consumers Union)-- to define and assess quality. Economists are often distrustful of this interview method for eliciting information. Like behavioral psychologists, they prefer inferring beliefs from observed behavior. Instead of asking people for their opinions, economists prefer to watch them reveal their preferences by actual conduct in the marketplace.

There are many practical problems with eliciting opinions through the survey technique. Respondents may have reasons for hiding their true beliefs. They may not understand their own motives or their own actions; they may, for example, unconsciously try to please the interviewer. If the situation is not "real," they have less incentive to search for relevant information and may not think seriously enough about the question. Many people surveyed may simply fail to respond.

A variety of techniques are available to ameliorate such problems. An economist would suggest turning opinions into actions. Instead of asking, "Do you prefer this dishwashing liquid over that one?" it is sometimes possible to force actual choices by, for example, saying, "I will give you a dishwashing liquid; do you want brand X or brand Y?" This approach is similar to using market data and has some of the same limitations. For example, there may be poor product information, or recipients may select on characteristics not considered to be quality aspects (e.g., prestige).

One could go a step further. Rather than asking people about prospective choices, one could question them about product quality *after* purchase and use. This approach might help correct for poor choices caused by temptation or inadequate information. However, even this won't work for "credence" goods-- goods the quality of which cannot be sufficiently evaluated even after use (e.g., vitamins). An additional difficulty is that buying and owning the product may alter the individual's tastes and preferences. Since a poor decision reflects badly on the buyer's shrewdness and rationality, he may not only overstate his degree of satisfaction but may actually increase his subjective evaluation of the product's attributes. This reduces the cognitive dissonance caused by a potentially bad choice.[7] Conversely, if "the grass is always greener on the other side of the fence," the purchaser may modify his preferences in a manner that increases the attractiveness of rejected alternatives while decreasing that of the selected product.

Since buyers have different tastes, in order to assess overall or aggregate quality, the questionnaire approach requires an explicit weighting scheme for individual preferences. For patient satisfaction measures, for example, it must be decided whom to include, whether their opinions should be given equal weight, and whether and how to allow for intensity of preference.

It is not only buyers or users whose opinion can be elicited. Independent experts, for example, can provide information that is useful-- particularly when users are ill suited to judge product quality (e.g., infant day care, old-age homes, insane asylums). An excellent way to assess hospital quality, for instance, may be to ask doctors, or perhaps better still, watch where they admit their loved ones. This latter technique observes actual market behavior and thus tends to be preferred by economists.

Both the market and the described questionnaire approach for assessing quality could be said to use "implicit criteria." Items are rated, but the reasons for the ratings need not be completely delineated or even fully understood. The next two approaches-- output and input measures-- employ explicit criteria. One could argue that the individual judgments from the questionnaire and even the market approach rely (implicitly) on these output or input measures.

OUTPUT MEASURES

A third method of judging quality is to use output measures, or performance characteristics. Products generally have many aspects, some of which are objectively measurable, others of which are not. The output or performance approach to measuring quality must of necessity focus on the former. This procedure is thus not very helpful in assessing the quality of items the principal characteristics of which cannot be measured objectively-- for example, a painting, a novel, or a sonata.

To use the output approach, one should carefully describe which aspects are being excluded from consideration. It is also necessary to explicitly weight those characteristics that are being measured.

One area in which output measures are currently used to rank products by quality is commodity grading. Grading is rarely so precise as to require an explicit scoring system. Generally, some principal characteristic determines the grade (e.g., color for apples, taste for butter). Additionally, any of a variety of imperfections may lower the grade (e.g., texture, color, or salt defects for butter). It is primarily in special contests to determine which manufacturer's product is best that explicit scoring systems are used (e.g., butter flavor may receive a 45% weight, salt 15%, color 15%).

Rather than using grades, most mandatory regulations employ a pass/fail approach to quality. These regulations specify minimum characteristics. There are usually no weightings or tradeoffs; to pass, each specific attribute must meet the prescribed minimum.

A voluntary method by which many products are currently ranked is through interfirm quality standards. Such standards are probably used, in one manner or another, in the majority of industrial transactions in the United States; they also form the basis for many of our mandatory regulations. Over 400 nonprofit organizations-- including the American Society for Testing and Materials, the Society of Automotive Engineers, the American Petroleum Institute, the National Fire Protection Association, and Underwriters' Laboratories-- write standards in the United States. Many organizations use the consensus method of standards creation. This works best when a wide spectrum of experts is involved. It is a kind of survey method of determining quality, but instead of deciding directly that product A is superior to product B, the focus is more basic-- agreeing on how to define, measure, and test aspects of product quality.[8]

INPUT MEASURES

In an ideal world, quality standards would specify desired levels of performance. Compared to output criteria, input measures are clearly a "second-best" method for judging quality. Inputs are not always good proxies for output. The amount of time a worker spends on the job may not be highly correlated with production. The number of doctors and hospital beds per capita may not be a good indicator of the quality of medical care provided. A school with a large library and a low student-to-teacher ratio may still give a low-quality education.

An economic rationale for preferring outcome indicators to either structure or process measures is that they are more likely to allow for and promote beneficial diversity and innovation. An economics textbook sums up the conventional wisdom as applied to the medicalcare field:

> Although outcome measures have been difficult to develop, emphasizing even primitive outcome measures in the monitoring process would speed the development of improved measures and allow greater flexibility in the use of medical inputs to achieve those outcomes. Measuring quality in terms of inputs used or through the credentials of licensed personnel increases the costs of providing care . . . and would inhibit innovation in the provision of medical care.[9]

While output measures are theoretically preferred, in the real world, input measures are generally used. Standards for judging the quality of medical care, for example, normally employ structural and process criteria. Standards for plywood may specify the number of plies required. Standards for concrete precisely describe the entire production process.

Design or input criteria are used for a variety of reasons. Good input standards are usually easier to write, administer, and enforce. There are also special explanations for why input measures dominate evaluations in fields such as health care. One concerns the distinction between output measures that can be determined before the fact and those judgments that must be made after the fact.

In the building area, performance is judged by testing materials and model structures before construction begins. No one advocates waiting decades or even centuries before determining whether an innovative structure is sufficiently durable or nonflammable. A principal problem in building regulation is creating ex ante laboratory experiments that can simulate long-term actual use.

In health care, it is more difficult to create good ex ante output measures. Judging the quality of health services by output measures thus requires a greater reliance on actual outcome. This makes the output approach less valuable, since we may have to wait until patients deteriorate or die before determining the quality of care provided. The use of intermediate performance standards, or "proxy outcomes," can reduce this problem. For example, if the goal is to prevent stroke, and high blood pressure is known to be a contributing cause, an increase in blood pressure could be considered a poor intermediate or proxy outcome.

An additional problem with using the outcome approach for health care evaluation is that while the architect and builder can be held responsible for the soundness of the structure, the medical provider cannot be held similarly accountable for the health of the patient. Factors such as heredity, lifestyle, and patient compliance determine particular health outcomes, and these are largely outside the control of the medical practitioner. In order to use the output approach to quality assessment, we must statistically control for these other influences. Unfortunately, we normally have neither the knowledge nor the ability to do so.[10]

Because of the problems connected with outcome evaluations, some health analysts have argued for the possible primacy of process measures.[11] It seems some combination of input and output, as well as market and survey approaches, might be most appropriate. No approach is ideal; nor are the approaches completely consistent with each other. But they all can provide important clues about the quality of services provided.

Nursing-Home Quality

The four approaches to assessing quality-- market, survey, output, and input measures-- have all been employed in a variety of areas. Here we give examples of their use in evaluating the quality of nursing-home care.

If buyers were rational and well informed, we might agree that a successful, competitive, high-priced nursing home was probably providing high-quality care. Popularity might be a better indicator of quality here than it is in the case of novels or TV shows. But some firms have market power; prices charged public patients are regulated; and many residents are neither rational nor knowledgeable. There is often excess demand (by public patients); patients are not mobile; and the choice of nursing homes is often made by third parties.

Yet, the market still may provide some clues about quality. Prospective patients and their agents are not completely ignorant. There are many private patients willing to pay high prices for high-quality care. Fully subsidized patients will also try to get into the better facilities. Since immediate entry is not always necessary, long waiting lists for some homes but not for others may indicate a perceived quality difference.

While the market approach has rarely been used for assessing the quality of nursing-home care, it has been advocated. Anderson, for example, proposes market "choice as a proxy for quality."[12] She argues that "a public objective should be the availability of choices and sufficient information, so that older persons, their families, and the professionals working with them can select health care programs appropriate to their personal needs, as defined personally and professionally. Quality could then be individually defined and sought."

Market variables have also been employed, both directly and indirectly, in assessing the quality of nursing home care. Kosberg and Tobin used total treatment resources per patient as their proxy for the quality of care delivered. This variable is closely related to average cost, and hence, to price. As they concluded: "As to the extent of treatment resources within nursing homes, 'you get what you pay for'; nursing homes which were rich in treatment resources were expensive homes."[13] Greene and Monahan used a composite index including direct patient expenditures as well as R.N. nursing hours as their measure of quality.[14] Independent variables included the room rate ("the more one pays in basic charges, the more one gets in basic services") as well as the occupancy rate. Interestingly, they found occupancy to be negatively correlated with quality, arguing that better homes were better able to select the cream of the applicants, holding out longer for more desirable patients.

The questionnaire approach has occasionally been used to assess the quality of nursing-home care. Taietz had knowledgeable professionals rate three homes on quality. He then interviewed the residents and found that, indeed, their self-assessed level of satisfaction was greatest in the home judged to be of highest quality. He also discovered, however, that the characteristics that made the home best from the viewpoint of the outside professionals were not, in many cases, the ones that made it the happiest environment for the patients.[15]

Linn had six social workers knowledgeable in the area rate forty community nursing homes on a five-point scale. She then correlated these ratings with seventy-one input measures from each home and found "a remarkably high agreement between the two sources of evaluation."[16]

Kayser-Jones interviewed residents to compare the quality of care in a Scottish and a U.S. nursing home. Scottish residents saw their physicians more frequently and were more satisfied with their care.[17] Stein et al. had patients and staff rate the same nursing homes in terms of social climate. Staff ratings were significantly more favorable.[18]

Nursing-home output has many dimensions, and many important aspects of quality are difficult to quantify. Still, a few analysts have constructed and used outcome measures of nursing-home care. Linn et al. focused on the patients' physical capabilities and overall mental state.[19] They examined 1,000 men who went directly from a VA hospital to a community nursing home. They determined the functional status of these patients (1) at admission to a home and (2) six months later. Functional status was assessed in terms of the degree of assistance needed in areas such as eating, dressing, toileting, bathing, and ambulation, as well as degree of mental depression. From this information, each patient was classified as having deteriorated, improved, or stayed the same.

Since the men had different prognoses at the time of hospital discharge, Linn et al. had asked each patient's physician to predict, given optimal nursing-home care, whether the patient should be expected to deteriorate or improve. They then compared the actual change in functional status with those predictions to assess the quality of care in each home.

Shaughnessy et al. used change in patient status (e.g., stabilization of bowel incontinence) and discharge to independent living to compare the care in nursing homes versus swing-bed hospitals.[20] They cross-validated their findings with questionnaires of experienced nurses and physicians, who overwhelmingly agreed that swing-bed hospitals were better for patients with rehabilitation potential.

Because nursing homes are homes, providing living accommodations, activities, support systems, and so forth as well as health care, it is sometimes difficult to distinguish between input and (proxy) outcome measures. Activities offered, for example, is clearly an input. Activities actually engaged in, on the other hand, has elements of both.

Gottesman focused on psychosocial aspects of nursing-home living.[21] He reported on the results from two twelve-hour observations made of more than 1,000 residents in forty nursing homes. For each patient, simple counts were made of the number of specific activities engaged in-such as TV watching-as well as social and medical interactions. While Gottesman did not construct a composite index of quality, he determined the percentage of residents engaging in each specific activity or interaction and correlated these with nursing home characteristics such as size and ownership type.

Most assessments of nursing-home care focus on unambiguous inputs.[22] Quality regulations almost exclusively use structural and process criteria. In Massachusetts, for example, regulations required that a team of inspectors evaluate homes on 627 items, virtually all of which are classifiable as inputs.

Analysts have also typically rated homes using input criteria. Holmberg and Anderson assessed homes on measures such as registered nurses per patient and patients per bathroom. They did not present an overall rating for each facility but compared proprietary with nonproprietary homes on every measure.[23]

Levey et al. did develop an overall quality rating of homes derived from information provided in state inspection reports.[24] They selected a number of crucial variables, which were weighted by a panel of consultants according to their importance. Thus, having sprinklers was weighted at 6 percent of the total score, employing a qualified therapist at 5 percent. The scores were used to determine if homes had improved in quality over time.[25]

CONCLUSION

Of the four approaches for measuring nursing-home quality, no one way is always preferable to the others. To an economist, which approach (or combination of approaches) is most appropriate depends on the costs and benefits of each. This in turn depends on a variety of factors. For example, in areas where there are many well-informed private patients and little excess demand, market data might be especially illuminating. The market approach might also be appealing since statistics on prices and waiting lists often can be gathered inexpensively. If a number of recognized independent experts are available with specific detailed knowledge of the homes in question, then the survey approach might prove best. If input-oriented but well-designed inspection reports have recently been compiled by reliable and competent surveyors, then using that information might make most sense.

One factor that is crucial to the choice of approaches is the purpose of the evaluation. If, for example, the purpose is to close a few seriously deficient facilities, then legal requirements may limit the worth of the market and survey approaches and possibly even the output approach. In this instance, the focus of the input approach should be on determining and documenting the problems of the poorest facilities rather than on precisely ranking the better homes. On the other hand, market, survey, and output criteria might possibly give the affluent consumer better information about where among a few select homes to place a beloved aunt.

In general, of course, using a variety of approaches should provide more and better information about quality. This is particularly true since all the approaches have both theoretical and practical limitations. For example, among other problems, the market approach may overweight the preferences of the rich. Survey evaluations may be superficial and impressionistic. There are usually too few objective output measures to accurately gauge overall quality. And input variables are often poor proxies for what really concerns us. While more approaches are thus usually better, an economist would emphasize that the benefit of some additional information is not always worth the added cost.

FOR DISCUSSION

1. How is the quality of business schools typically assessed? Is this a reasonable approach? What is the purpose of ranking the schools?

2. When Los Angeles Dodger star Fernando Valenzuela received a contract for a million dollars per year for his pitching services, Steve Carlton, the league's most consistent and, previously, its highest paid pitcher, immediately demanded to renegotiate his contract with the Philadelphia Phillies. He told them to take money off the third year of his contract but to make sure he received more than a million this year. Why was Carlton so insistent on raising his current salary over the one-million-dollar mark?

3. Why do employers try to prevent workers from knowing each other's wages? What does this have to do with quality assessment?

4. If the demand for make/model A is greater than the demand for make/model B at all prices (where price of A = price of B), is this an indication that A is judged superior to B? When might it not be?

5. Why are economists so distrustful of the questionnaire approach? Would an executive questionnaire be a good way to determine the goals of the corporation?

6. In the building area, while performance standards are preferable, design standards are normally used. Who benefits from the use of design criteria? Who is hurt?

7. Suppose there are fewer Toyota "lemons" than Cadillac "lemons." Does this make Toyota a higher quality car?

NOTES TO CHAPTER 14

1. K. J. Arrow, *Social Choices and Individual Values* (New York: Wiley, 1951).
2. R. M. Anderson, G. V. Fleming, and T. F. Champney, "Exploring a Paradox Belief in a Crisis and General Satisfaction with Medical Care," *Milbank Memorial Fund Quarterly* 60, no. 2 (Spring 1982): 329-51.
3. A. Donabedian, "Evaluating the Quality of Medical Care," *Milbank Memorial Fund Quarterly* 44, no. 2 (Spring 1966): 166-206.
4. K. Lancaster, *Consumer Demand: A New Approach* (New York Columbia University Press, 1971).
5. Z. Griliches, ed., *Price Indexes and Quality Change* (Cambridge, MA: Harvard University Press, 1971), pp. 55-69.

6. C. Hjorth-Andersen, "Quality Indicators: In Theory and in Fact," *European Economic Review* 35, (1991): 1491-505; R. J. Sutton and P. C. Riesz, "The Effect of Product Visibility Upon the Relationship between Price and Quality," *Journal of Consumer Policy* 3, no. 2 (1979): 145-50.

7. L. Festinger, *A Theory of Cognitive Dissonance* (Stanford, CA: Stanford University Press, 1957).

8. D. Hemenway, *Industrywide Voluntary Product Standards* (Cambridge, MA: Ballinger Publishing Company, 1975).

9. P. Feldstein, *Health Care Economics*, Third Edition (New York: John Wiley & Sons, 1988), p. 327.

10. For a more complete economic analysis of the output versus input issue in both health and non-health care areas, see D. Hemenway, "Performance vs. Design Standards," NBS/GSC 80-287 (Springfield, VA: National Bureau of Standards, National Technical Information Service, 1980). For an excellent discussion of quality assurance approaches in health care, see R. H. Palmer and R. H. Nesson, "A Review of Methods for Ambulatory Medical Care Evaluations," *Medical Care* 20 (1982): 758-81. For a specific illustration, see S. Wilner et al., "A Comparison of the Quality of Maternity Care Between an HMO and Fee-for-service Practice," *New England Journal of Medicine* 304 (1981): 784-87.

11. W. E. McAuliffe, "Measuring the Quality of Medical Care: Process versus Outcome," *Milbank Memorial Fund Quarterly* 57, no. 1 (Winter 1979): 118-52.

12. N. N. Anderson, "Approaches to Improving the Quality of Long-term Care for Older Persons," *The Gerontologist* 14 (December 1974): 519-24.

13. J. I. Kosberg and S. S. Tobin, "Variability among Nursing Homes," *The Gerontologist* 12, part I (Autumn 1972): 214-19.

14. V. L. Greene and D. J. Monahan, "Structural and Operational Factors Affecting Quality of Patient Care in Nursing Homes," *Public Policy* 29, no. 4 (Fall 1981): 399-415.

15. P. Taietz, "Administrative Practices and Person Adjustment in Homes for the Aged," Cornell Experiment Station Bulletin #899 (January 1953): 1-39.

16. M. W. Linn, "Predicting Quality of Patient Care in Nursing Homes," *The Gerontologist* 14 (June 1974) 225-27.

17. J. S. Kayser-Jones, "Institutional Structures: Catalysts or Barriers to Quality Care for the Institutionalized Aged in Scotland and the United States," *Social Science and Medicine* 16 (1982): 935-44.

18. S. Stein, M. W. Linn and E. M. Stein, "Patients and Staff Assess Social Climate of Different Quality Nursing Homes," *Comprehensive Gerontology*, Section B 1, no. 1 (March 1987): 41-6.

19. M. W. Linn, L. Gurel, and B. S. Linn, "Patient Outcome as a Measure of Quality of Nursing Home Care," *American Journal of Public Health* 67, no. 4 (April 1977): 337-44.

20. P. W. Shaughnessy, R. E. Schlenker and A. M. Kramer, "Quality of Long-Term Care in Nursing Homes and Swing-Bed Hospitals," *Health Services Research* 25, no. 1 (April 1990, Part I): 65-96.

21. L. E. Gottesman, "Nursing Home Performance as Related to Resident Traits, Ownership, Size and Source of Payment," *American Journal of Public Health* 63, no. 3 (March 1974): 269-76.

22. A. L. Siu, "The Quality of Medical Care Received by Older Persons," *Journal of the American Geriatric Society* 35 (1987): 1084-91.

23. R. H. Holmberg and N. N. Anderson, "Implications of Ownership for Nursing Home Care," *Medical Care* 6, no. 4 (July-August 1968): 300-307.

24. S. Levey et al., "An Appraisal of Nursing Home Care," *Journal of Gerontology* 28, no. 2 (1973): 222-28.

25. For a similar, more sophisticated approach, see D. H. Gustafson, F.C. Sainfort, R. Van Konigsveld and D. R. Zimmerman, "The Quality Assessment Index for Measuring Nursing Home Quality," *Health Services Research* 25, no. 1 (April 1990, Part I): 97-127.

15 DETERMINANTS OF QUALITY

OPTIMAL QUALITY

One of the key concepts in microeconomics is opportunity cost. For an economist, the real cost of anything is its opportunity cost-- the cost of not doing something else. The fundamental precept in economics is that resources are scarce; society cannot have everything it wants. For every specific thing that is produced, there will be fewer raw materials, capital, labor, land and time available to produce other things. The cost of building a hospital, for instance, is the forgone opportunity of using the land for other purposes, such as a playground, of not using the labor to build something else, such as a bridge.

Individuals have finite resources. The cost of buying a shirt is that the buyer no longer has the purchasing power to buy other goods and services. The primary cost of reading this chapter is the time that could have been spent in other pursuits. (Opportunity costs are often measured in dollar terms simply because money provides a common denominator for aggregation.)

A second basic microeconomic concept is marginal analysis. Many options are not "all or nothing"; that is, most policy issues do not require "either/or" decisions. These options can be usefully analyzed by looking at the margin, considering whether to do a little more, and if so, perhaps even a little more than that. The controversy over national defense expenditures, for example, is not typically a debate about whether we should have a reasonably strong military. Most people believe that we should. Instead, the issue is a marginal one-- are the extra benefits from each additional dollar we spend worth the extra cost?

How might the concepts of opportunity cost and marginal analysis be applied to the topic of quality? Economists are trained to think in terms of optimal levels. The quality of a product or service might be too low; a less recognized problem is that it could be too high. Nursing homes can be made too safe against fire; hospitals can be made too sanitary; and physicians can be required to be too well trained. The extra benefit of decreasing the chance of dying in a nursing home fire by .0001 percent may not be worth the extra cost-- the opportunity cost of doing something else worthwhile with our scarce resources. The notion that quality can be too high is sometimes a difficult one to accept. During wartime, members of Congress often say things like, "We want the best available equipment for our troops in the field." That doesn't sound unreasonable. They certainly don't want to go around saying, "We want second-rate equipment for our troops." Yet, in a world of limited resources, we cannot have the best in every area. Striving for it in one field may lead us far from the overall optimum.

Even the Pentagon has a finite budget. Assume that during the Korean War the army had $1 million to spend on tanks for every 10,000 infantry soldiers. It might have been able to buy a cheap tank for $5,000 and thus purchase 200 of them, a somewhat better tank for $10,000 and purchase 100, a pretty good tank for $50,000 and purchase 20, an excellent tank for $100,000 and purchase 10, or a fantastic $1 million tank. But in the last case, the army could have only one such tank for every 10,000 soldiers. It is not certain that the extra benefit from making the tank better is worth the extra cost. In this simple example, the opportunity cost is fewer available tanks.

Economists often make points graphically. Assume that our interest is in determining the optimal quality of laboratory tests. On the horizontal axis of Figure 15-1 are levels of quality; moves to the right go through levels of higher and higher reliability. On the vertical axis are benefits or costs, measured conveniently in dollars. The benefit and cost curves should be read from the horizontal to the vertical axis. The slopes are positive because additional reliability brings additional benefits, but at an added cost. The optimal quality level, from an economic viewpoint, is not where total benefits are maximized (point A), or where total benefits and total costs are equal (point B), but where the difference between total benefits and total costs is greatest (point C). This is where marginal benefit equals marginal cost.

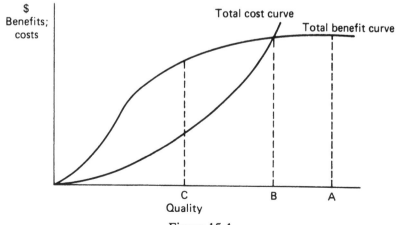

Figure 15-1

FACTORS AFFECTING QUALITY

Many factors can influence the quality of goods and services supplied in the market. This chapter discusses a few: buyer information, excess demand, legality, licensing, and insurance. Examples come from a variety of industries, but the emphasis throughout is on the implications for the quality of care provided in the medical marketplace.

Consumer Information

One way economists categorize goods (and aspects of goods) is by designating them search, experience, or credence goods.[1] Consumers are able to judge the quality of search goods by inspection before they buy (e.g., apples). The quality of experience goods, on the other hand, can be assessed only after purchase. For example, one may be able to determine whether a new car is a lemon only after driving it for some period of time. But even after use, the quality of credence goods, such as vitamins, cannot be evaluated completely.

Some aspects of medical care have credence characteristics. Many diseases are self-limiting; others may not respond to the best known treatments. It may be impossible for the patient to determine accurately the quality of a physician's services not only before but even after treatment. In health care, consumers also have difficulty obtaining useful information from other sources. Advertising, for example, has long been inhibited. And information on physicians' medical school performance or reputation among their peers is not readily available.

The fact that health care consumers have poor-quality information means that they cannot easily reward high-quality nor punish low quality providers. In other words, the incentives given to practitioners are not optimal and tend to lower the overall quality level of services provided.

When buyers have difficulty judging quality before purchase, they rely heavily on the reputation of the supplier. For experience characteristics, brand-name goods can be purchased with some security because it is in the interest of the supplier to protect its reputation. It pays for the firm to spend large amounts of energy and resources to ensure adequate quality control. Consider a simple model in which a product defect is reported by a consumer to ten acquaintances. If there are many small sellers, few of the ten will be likely purchasers of that brand. On the other hand, if the seller is large, several of the ten will be actual or potential buyers, and they may reduce their consumption. Additionally, the more prominent the firm, the more likely the defect will be a topic of interesting conversation; it might even be newsworthy. While major brands are not always of superior quality, they are rarely markedly inferior. The major manufacturer has more to lose and thus a stronger incentive to eliminate product defects.

In the past few years, American health care has seen the proliferation of a new type of health care institution: the chain-owned, walk-in clinic. These typically charge low prices and enhance accessibility. Established hospitals and physicians claim the clinics provide low quality care. They scornfully call them "Docs in the Box" or "McDocs." Yet, as with McDonalds, there is some assurance that the quality of services provided at chain-owned clinics will not be exceedingly low. McDonalds spends large amounts of resources on quality control. It is, likewise, in the interest of health-care chains to ensure that a few bad physicians or clinics do not ruin their image. Reputational considerations make it likely they will exert strong oversight over individual practitioners.[2]

Excess Demand

A regulated price set at a level different than the market clearing price will create a disequilibrium. If price is set too low, the amount demanded will be greater than the amount willingly supplied; there will be excess demand. When tough rent control regulations are imposed on competitive housing markets, excess demand is created. One effect is that market forces tend to push up the real price consumers pay. Prospective tenants often give key money to building superintendents and financial rewards to individuals who can find them an apartment.

Excess demand can also lead to a decline in quality. Under rent control, apartments in New York and Paris have deteriorated badly. Landlords have lost much of their economic incentive to maintain or upgrade their buildings. Excess demand ensures that tenants willing to pay the rent control price can be found, whether or not the apartment is in good condition. One foreign scholar observed: "Next to bombing, rent control seems in many cases to be the most efficient technique so far known for destroying cities, as the housing situation in New York City demonstrates."[3]

Socialist economies are often chronic shortage economies; there is general excess demand for most consumer goods. Goods and services are rationed not only by price but also by waiting in line. Whom you know also matters; it is not unusual to discover that your physician-prescribed drug is unavailable-- unless you happen to have a pharmacist for a friend. The chronic excess demand for final goods leads to quality deterioration. Producers have little incentive to provide quality control since consumers will buy whatever is available.[4]

In the United States, there is excess demand by public patients for nursing-home care. Government has given poor patients the right to such care, but low reimbursement rates and Certificate of Need constraints have prevented providers from supplying the required number of beds. The excess demand creates a major disincentive to provide quality care. Indeed, research suggests that the low quality care given in nursing homes is best explained by the effect of excess demand on quality.[5]

Legality

Government prohibition of goods or services increases the cost of production, decreases the quantity purchased, and lowers product quality. Examples include alcohol during prohibition and marijuana, cocaine, and prostitution today.

There are two principal reasons that quality falls with illegality. The first concerns information. When a commodity is outlawed, it is hard to establish well-known brand reputations. Advertising becomes covert or nonexistent. Potential buyers have difficulty gathering credible quality information; it is not easy to comparison shop. Moreover, disgruntled purchasers cannot sue for defective merchandise. A second problem is that the commodity must be manufactured and supplied surreptitiously. Production and distribution costs increase, and quality falls.

Prior to 1945, prostitution was legal in France, and over 150 licensed brothels were in operation. Prostitution could be practiced in beautiful houses and pleasant surroundings. Moreover, the French government made weekly medical inspections for venereal disease. After the war, however, prostitution was declared illegal, and the amount of prostitution decreased. Many women left the business. Service ambience declined, and V.D. skyrocketed. Although there was less prostitution, venereal disease became more common.[6]

In the United States, when abortions became legal in the early 1970s, the number performed increased dramatically. And so did the quality of the operations. In part this was because purchasers could obtain better quality information. More importantly, abortions could now be performed openly. Previously, many pregnancy terminations had been done by unlicensed abortionists, with inadequate equipment, often in unsanitary conditions. The services of licensed physicians have now driven the unqualified practitioners out of this market. Government inspection and review of doctors and hospitals helps to ensure quality. While the number of abortions has increased since legalization, mortality and morbidity due to abortion have plummeted.[7]

Licensing

The public interest rationale for licensing is to ensure quality when buyers have poor product-quality information. Economists, however, have not been particularly fond of licensing. Perhaps we are jealous because there is no licensing in our profession. Thus, even those with little training can not only call themselves economists but also hold powerful public positions that should require great economic expertise.

A large number of services are currently licensed by many states, including medicine, law, mine management, veterinary medicine, public accounting, funeral direction, barbering, beauty culture, horseshoeing, tree surgery, private detective work, surveying, falconry, ferret breeding and real estate sales. A major problem with licensing is that it is often used to restrict entry rather than to ensure quality. The demand for licensing usually comes not from consumers but from suppliers. Licensing boards are also controlled by providers. This certainly has been the general experience in medicine.

If the primary purpose of medical licensure is to improve quality, we should expect to see difficult re-examination and frequent license revocations. Instead, re-examination is rare, and licenses are removed only for the most objectionable conduct.

To the extent that licensure is used to restrict entry, it generally raises prices. If consumers are paying for their own health care-- which many still are, especially for physicians' services-- high prices may cause them to seek help elsewhere, possibly from less expensive unlicensed providers, or to rely on self-care. Thus, even if licensure increases the average quality of physicians, it might decrease the overall quality of health care actually received.[8]

There are indications that licensure in other areas, by limiting service, may, on balance, have harmed the consumer. The risk of infection from rabies and brucellosis is higher where there are strict limits on veterinary practice. And accidental electrocutions occur much more frequently in states with restrictive licensure rules for electricians.[9]

There is little solid evidence regarding the effects of physician licensure on the quality of medical care. There exists, however, some interesting information concerning the consequences of licensure in a similarly structured market-- the market for television repairs. In 1973 the Federal Trade Commission (FTC) examined TV repairers in three major cities: Washington, D.C.; New Orleans; and San Francisco. In the District of Columbia there were no regulations; the market for TV repair was free and open. In New Orleans, licensure laws required a passing grade on a competency exam. Although San Francisco had no entry restrictions, a state laboratory conducted active monitoring for quality.

To test the effects of licensure regulations, the FTC prepared a large number of "doctored" television sets, sets that were in perfect condition save for one specific problem: each had a burned-out horizontal oscillating tube. Then, to discover whether consumers in the three test cities were being charged for unnecessary parts or services, the FTC requested repairs on these sets. In the District of Columbia, which had no licensure regulations, "parts fraud" was evident in 48 percent of the sets repaired: either unnecessary work was done, or work was charged but not done. In New Orleans, which did regulate the TV repair market, there was "parts fraud" in 50 percent of the cases. Moreover, licensing caused prices to be higher for the services rendered. On the other hand, only 20 percent of the repairers in San Francisco charged for unnecessary parts or services.[10]

While the FTC study was not a controlled experiment, it does suggest that when consumers have little knowledge, the free market, as in the District of Columbia, does not work very well. Licensure laws as existed in New Orleans, however, did not seem to improve the situation. It was in San Francisco, with its consumer-oriented state inspector, that the market appeared to be working best.

Insurance

Economists divide technological advances into process innovations and product innovations. Process innovations lower the cost of production, decreasing the real resources-land, labor, capital, raw materials-needed to produce a given product. Product innovations improve the quality of the product or service. If an insurance company is paying the bill, individual consumers do not care about process innovations. They do not search for efficient, low-priced sellers. Instead, their concern is solely for quality.

In regard to health care, where third parties currently pay more than 90 percent of the hospital care provided in the United States, individual patients may not be overly concerned about the financial implications of their medical-care decisions. They can request the best hospital care available with little regard to cost.

In most other markets, however, buyers will demand increases in quality as long as the extra benefits from them are greater than the extra cost. For hospital care, insurance has significantly decreased the cost to the individual patient; often the marginal dollar price is effectively zero. In this situation, the patient wants any improvement in quality, virtually independent of cost. Until recently, third parties in the United States were generally willing to pay for these improvements, giving suppliers a strong incentive to provide them.

The quality of U.S. medical care has improved dramatically over the post-war period. Economists believe that insurance has provided an important impetus for increased quality, both in terms of employing the best current technology and, over time, in devising improved methods for treatment. The problem, from an economic perspective, is that the marginal benefit from the added quality may not have been worth the additional cost in terms of forgone opportunities. If some of the resources had been devoted to other things, such as highway safety, fire safety, or occupational health, many more lives probably could have been saved. The cost-plus insurance reimbursement system distorted the incentives not only of consumers but also of suppliers: it overly rewarded product innovators and high-cost providers while actually giving financial disincentives to process innovation and efficient production.[11] As illustrated by Figure 15-1, insurance tended to push us toward point A, and perhaps beyond.

CONCLUSION

The quality of goods and services provided in the market are affected by a large number of variables: technology, training, tastes, income, liability, complaints, and so forth. This chapter discussed five factors as they influence the quality of medical care: buyer information, excess demand, legality, licensing, and insurance. Poor patient information, excess demand, and illegality tend to reduce quality levels. Licensing has potentially mixed effects. Insurance coverage, particularly the cost-plus type of reimbursement common in the 1960s and 1970s, leads to increased quality. The optimal level of quality, of course, is not necessarily the highest level.

There has been much recent discussion and concern about the quality of health care in the United States. This is reflected in the rapid increase in risk-management and quality-assurance programs, as well as the rising prominence of Peer Review Organizations (PROs). Somewhat paradoxically, economists continue to complain about America's "Cadillac Medicine." It is believed that too many resources are being devoted to high-technology, high-quality health care. In response to such complaints, providers often stress the improvements made in the quality of care over the last fifty years. While costs may have increased, diseases that previously could not be cured can now be treated successfully. Can such conflicting perceptions about health-care quality be reconciled?

Economists divide efficiency into three categories: technical, allocative, and dynamic. To be technically efficient, we are maximizing the bang for the buck. (This phrase comes from the military. The Russians try to maximize the rubble for the ruble.) For any given amount of resources devoted to a certain area, we get the most for our money. Allocative efficiency asks: Are we spending the optimal amount of resources on that particular area? Since resources are scarce, the more we give to one industry, the less is available for producing other goods and services. The time element is crucial for dynamic efficiency. Over time, are we learning to produce improved products and services at lower real resource costs?

Quality may be usefully divided into similar categories. Risk-management programs are primarily concerned with quality in a technical sense. The goal is to improve quality without devoting more resources to health care. When discussing Cadillac medicine, economists focus on quality in an allocative sense. Some believe that 13 percent of our GNP may be too much to be spending on medical care. We might do better to spend more on occupational safety, nutrition, education, and housing. Discussions of improved medical care over time emphasize the dynamic aspects of quality. The issue is not so much the competence of current practitioners but the benefits of past medical discoveries.

As a society, we can have good or bad performance in different quality categories. They are affected by different factors. For example, PROs focus on technical, not allocative or dynamic, quality. Insurance is blamed by economists for allocative quality problems. Dynamic quality is partly determined by the size of government subsidies to basic medical research. While dynamic considerations have only been touched on in this chapter, in some sense this dimension of quality is the most important. Expanding medical knowledge will permit a mediocre physician in 2050 to cure ailments that defy the most expert practitioners today.

FOR DISCUSSION

1. Describe the expected effect on average product quality of (a) rapidly increasing demand; (b) excess supply; (c) excise taxes; (d) quotas.

2. What is the effect of quantity on quality? Discuss with respect to congestion; to fashion; to learning-by-doing.

3. What is the effect of consumer education on the product quality of final goods?

4. Suppose few buyers are ever expected to make repeat purchases. How will this fact affect product quality? How might sellers try to assure purchasers that the product is reliable?

5. How much effort will counterfeiters of brand-name products spend on quality control?

6. What is the role of product quality information on the firm's "make-or-buy" decision?

7. When is average product quality the crucial consideration? When might the variance in product quality be more important?

8. How important are formal consumer complaints in maintaining product quality? Which consumers are likely to complain? For what type of products?

9. Ford reports that satisfied customers tell eight people; those dissatisfied complain to twenty-two. How might this fact affect Ford's quality control expenditures?

NOTES TO CHAPTER 15

1. P. Nelson, "Information and Consumer Behavior," *Journal of Political Economy* 78 (1970): 311-29.
2. C. L. Parks, S. B. Cashman, D. Hemenway et al., "Quality of Care in a Chain of Walk-In Centers," *Quality Review Bulletin* 17 (April 1991): 120-25.
3. A. Linbeck. *The Political Economy of the New Left* (New York: Harper & Row, 1971), p. 39.
4. J. Kornai, *The Economics of Shortage* (New York: Elsevier, 1981).
5. J. A. Nyman, "Excess Demand, the Percentage of Medicaid Patients, and the Quality of Nursing Home Care," *Journal of Human Resources* 23 (1988): 76-91.

6. D. C. North and R. L. Miller, *The Economics of Public Issues*, 5th ed. (New York: Harper & Row, 1980), pp. 10-18.

7. C. Tietze, *Induced Abortion* (New York: Population Council, 1979).

8. P. Feldstein, *Health Care Economics* (New York: John Wiley & Sons, 1988), pp. 369-74.

9. S. Carrol and R. Gaston, "Occupational Licensing and the Quality of Service An Overview." *Law and Human Behavior* 7 (1983): 139-46.

10. J. Phelan, "Regulation of the Television Repair Industry in Louisiana and California: A Case Study" (Report to Federal Trade Commission, 1974).

11. D. Hemenway et al., "Benefits of Experience: Treating Coronary Artery Disease," *Medical Care* 24 (1986): 125-33.

16 VOLUNTARY STANDARDS

In February 1904 a great blaze broke out in downtown Baltimore. The fire became so serious that help was solicited from surrounding communities. Washington, D.C. fire engines reached the scene within three hours, and additional units later arrived from as far afield as Annapolis, Wilmington, Chester, York, Altoona, Harrisburg, Philadelphia, and New York. Unfortunately, most of these units proved to be of little assistance, for their hoses would not fit Baltimore hydrants. Though there was never a shortage of water, many fire-fighting units had to stand by, virtually helpless, as the fire raged for over thirty hours, destroying more than 1,500 buildings and all the electric light, telephone, telegraph, and power facilities in an area of seventy city blocks.[1]

The need for uniform screw threads had long been recognized in industrial societies. In 1864 William Sellers read a paper before the Franklin Institute in which he argued: "In this country no organized attempt has as yet been made to establish any system [of screw threads], each manufacturer having adopted whatever his judgment may have dictated as the best, or as most convenient for himself, but . . . so radical a defect should be allowed to exist no longer."[2] The standard proposed by Sellers was gradually adopted in North America. That the system did not completely pervade the American economy is illustrated by the Baltimore tragedy and by the fact that as late as 1964, fire fighters in a county contiguous to Baltimore were still being confronted with two types of hydrants, one with the national thread standard and the other with the Baltimore steamer thread.

Even with the adoption of a standard screw thread in America, the problem was not entirely resolved. Major difficulties continued to occur internationally due to differing national standards. During World War II, for example, many damaged American tanks in North Africa remained immobilized simply because British

This chapter is based on David Hemenway, *Industrywide Voluntary Product Standards* (Cambridge, MA: Ballinger Publishing Company. 1975).

fasteners could not be used to repair them.[3] It was not until 1948 that a uniform screw thread agreement was signed by the United States, Canada, and Britain. There is now an International Screw Thread Standard, though it is not universally followed.[4]

The screw thread standard of the nineteenth century was perhaps the first modern industrial standard established for public, as distinct from private, use. Intensive efforts at industrywide product standardization really began in the early twentieth century. Some early examples of successful standardization were the 1921 reduction in the varieties of paving brick from sixty-six different sizes to eleven, the rigid definitions of "manganese steel" and "nickel steel," and the 1914 Boiler Code for safety. Such industrywide voluntary product standards are the topic of this chapter.

A distinction should be made between two types of product standards-- standards of quality and standards for uniformity. For this latter type of standard, the issue is not one of "better" or "worse" but rather of sameness or uniformity. Screw thread standards, for example, are basically dimensional standards. It is not crucial to the performance of a screw whether the grooves are at a 55°, 60°, or 50° angle. However, it can be extremely important that the angle be the same for all screws.

The railroad track gauge standard provides an example of an early and important standard for uniformity. It makes little difference whether the standard distance between tracks is 7 feet, as on the original Great Western Railroad, 5'6" as in South America, or 3'6" as in South Africa. It does matter, however, whether or not there is a uniform national standard. Following England's lead, the United States chose 4'8½" as its standard gauge, and most of our northern railroads had switched to this gauge by the time of the Civil War. Combined with a system of interchangeable brakes and couplings, this made possible the interchangeability of rolling stock among virtually all roads throughout the Union. Australia, on the other hand, through most of the twentieth century never adopted a uniform standard. Thus when cargoes are transferred, inconvenient and costly reloading or special undertrucks are required.[5]

While the lack of standards can cause problems, the existence of uniformity standards may also cause problems by impeding improvement-- often to a wider or superior standard for uniformity. The informal standardization of the typewriter keyboard, for example, permits the interchangeability of typists and of machines. But the current QWERTY keyboard is far from the best. The present keyboard was designed in 1873 with the purpose of keeping keys used together as far apart as possible since the key return mechanism worked quite slowly. But clashing type bars are no longer a problem, and other keyboards have been proven markedly superior. Yet acting individually, society has been unable to change to a better system, even though a single focal-point alternative, the Dvorak system, has been available for over half a century.[6]

Other examples of standards for uniformity include those for record sizes and record-player speeds (33, 45, and 78 RPM), bed sizes (king, queen, double, twin) and electric lamp sockets (the Edison base). A principal benefit of such standards is that they allow for the interchangeability of the products of different manufacturers. This tends to widen markets and decrease entry barriers.[7]

A second type of product standard, and the focus of this chapter, are quality standards. Quality standards are typically minimum rather than maximum standards. They divide products into categories of better (meeting the standard) and worse (not meeting the standard), superior and inferior. Examples of quality standards include standards of identity (such as the mandatory USDA standards that "peanut butter" must contain at least 90 percent peanuts by weight, that "orange drink" must consist of at least 10 percent orange juice), safety standards (such as industrywide voluntary standards for such products as power tools and stepladders), and standard specifications (such as the cement and concrete standards, which not only specify the proportions of constituent materials but also provide strict guidelines controlling the mixing, transporting, placing, and curing of the concrete).

Formal quality standards are written by a wide variety of trade associations (e.g., the Aerospace Industries Association), engineering societies (e.g., the Institute of Electrical and Electronics Engineers), and other nonprofit organizations (e.g., the National Fire Protection Association, Underwriters' Laboratories). Standards are critical to the American economy. Voluntary product standards, for example, are used in a large percentage of industrial transactions.

The importance of voluntary standards is underscored by the fact that many are made mandatory by local, state, and federal authorities. The National Electric Code, despite minor modifications at the local level, accounts for the vast majority of U.S. electrical safety regulations. The Society of Automotive Engineers (SAE) technical standards are widely used by both the Federal Aviation Administration and the National Highway Traffic Safety Administration as a basis for establishing standards. Most Occupational Safety and Health standards were initially voluntary standards. And the American Society of Mechanical Engineers (ASME) Boiler and Pressure Vessel Code has been adopted by most states and by Canada. In an antitrust suit against ASME, a judge ruled in 1982 that:

> ASME wields great power in the Nation's economy. Its codes and standards influence the policies of numerous states and cities, and, as has been said about 'so-called voluntary standards' generally, its interpretations of its guidelines 'may result in economic prosperity or economic failure, for a number of businesses of all sizes through the country,' as well as entire segments of an industry.[8]

STANDARD SPECIFICATIONS

Buyers can obtain information on product quality in a variety of ways. Personal experience, advice from friends, advertisements, warranties, brand reputation, the Consumers Union, and so on, may all provide a certain amount of information. A common method by which large buyers secure product-quality information is the careful specification of desired characteristics. When General Motors wants a cleaner for a dirty painted wall, does it send an employee out to purchase an off-the-shelf product in a grocery store? Not at all. It orders a "painted surface cleanser" by specification. Specifications and brand names are substitutes for industrial buyers and are used in varying degrees. Specifications are often preferable because they invite competitive bidding. Less reliance needs to be placed on the integrity of an individual seller, and the risk is smaller that quality will change with subsequent purchases. The precise details of the specification help eliminate much of the fuzziness in exchange. A buyer receiving an inferior product can frequently claim breach of contract rather than merely registering a complaint. However, when it is costly to write specifications (e.g., to cover intangible quality aspects such as "workmanship"), purchase description is often made by brand name.

Specifications generally make sense only for large purchasers. For a small buyer, such as a final consumer, the original cost of specification-- learning what aspects are crucial, writing the specification, and perhaps even testing the product-- proves too great. In the real world, this high fixed cost of specification means, in effect, that there are economies of scale in buying. The large purchaser gets better information and thus a better product for its money.

Standard specifications provide a related method for securing product quality information. Standard specifications are merely particular specifications used by a number of different buyers. Generally they are formal standards, created for the particular purpose of becoming industrywide standards and written by representatives from a variety of firms and institutions.

When available, standard specifications have some definite advantages for buyers. Since they are usually created by the consensus of diverse and knowledgeable parties, they should be reasonably good and can be used with some security. The buyer is saved the expense of writing her own specification and of gaining detailed knowledge about all the relevant aspects of quality. These have been reduced to one: the product does or does not meet the standard. Most importantly, standard specifications serve a coordinating function, providing a focal point for purchase. The fact that others purchase by standards can benefit the buyer. For one thing, as standards become widely known, the negotiation burden should be reduced and misunderstandings and disputes decreased. Additionally, ordering by standards promotes price competition, since sellers are already producing such varieties. Conversely, it takes time-- and risk-- to quote on unusual specifications, and fewer sellers are willing to compete for the order. Buying by standards also allows potential scale-production economies, permits quick delivery, and ensures future availability. All these factors effectively lower price. Furthermore, because standard items have been purchased by a large number and variety of users, information about them is great and can be obtained through observation, personal contacts, trade journals, and other sources.

On the other hand, standards may be more costly to write than specifications since they require some consensus. Or they may be expensive to purchase from a standards writing organization. Since they are employed for different purposes, standard specifications can sometimes be too general or not perfectly suitable for a particular use. Additionally, technological change can decrease the value of a standard. The buyer often needs information on the current "quality" of the standard itself before she confidently can use it for making purchases.

INCENTIVE TO CREATE STANDARDS

Buyers

Buyers generally have less knowledge about product quality than do sellers, and usually want to learn more. Standard specifications provide one means by which they can. Whether or not these standards exist often depends on whether or not buyers are able to convert their desires into an effective demand. Large or organized purchasers generally can. Small, disorganized ones cannot. Two crucial factors determining the usefulness and existence of voluntary industrywide standards in various markets are the number of buyers and the size of their purchases.[9]

As a standardizing society official asserts:

> The strongest impetus for the development of a particular standard is that exercised by users who demand solution to some problem which has vexed them in the market place. Users who are organized in their own industry organization have become most powerful in this respect and through threats of writing their own standard, frequently push manufacturers into efforts they might not otherwise undertake....
>
> It is an obvious axiom that manufacturers are exceedingly reluctant to relinquish any flexibility that they might exercise in the production of their products. By contrast, users are most strenuous in their demands for the maximum degree of standardization to eliminate work for themselves.[10]

Standard specifications for steel were written in the early twentieth century, not by the steel companies but by the automobile companies, through the Society of Automotive Engineers (SAE). The establishment of standards for alloy steel was a major mission of the SAE but was met with bitter opposition.

The rule of the 1910 steel salesperson was "special brands, secret processes and mysterious ingredients"[11]-- combined with high prices and delays in delivery. Established steel manufacturers were reluctant to relinquish brand advantages; they saw little benefit from providing detailed product information to buyers and helping them coordinate their purchases. The general attitude of the steel industry was perhaps typified by the sarcastic comment of a steel spring executive: "I say it is none of your business if I make my springs of pot metal. What is it to you, if they carry a car and never break."[12]

But SAE standard specifications were written for steel and supported by the automobile manufacturers, who were able to impose them on suppliers. Standard specifications were soon widely used by automobile companies when purchasing from the steel, rubber, petroleum, and machine-product industries. The collection of SAE standards-- the SAE handbook-- quickly became the "bible" of the automotive engineer. SAE standards for oil were also written over protests from the producing industry. In the 1920s, after much research and experimentation, the SAE was able to create a system for the determination of motor-oil viscosity, a system of far greater precision and accuracy than the then-current arbitrary seller designation of "light," "medium," or "heavy." While some refineries worked with the society to help formulate the standards, others opposed any labeling of their cans or barrels. They believed such ratings would only decrease the value of their carefully built reputations, "detracting from the individuality of the brand."[13]

The petroleum industry itself writes standards through its trade association, the American Petroleum Institute, but these standards concern products purchased by the industry (e.g., specifications for steel-plug valves with flanged ends or recommended practices for electrical installations in petroleum refineries). The API says:

> All of our standards are written from the point of view of a consuming industry.... Our motive simply is to provide uniform performance requirements to the widest possible range of suppliers, while maintaining the level of operational efficiency, safety and durability suited to the needs of any and all companies engaged in petroleum operations.[14]

Overall, the large majority of quality standards in the United States are for producers' goods rather than for final products. Unlike the large corporate buyer, the small, inexpert, and unorganized consumer generally has no way of effectuating her desire for standards, save through the political process. Voluntary quality standards arise for final goods mainly in areas where their existence benefits producers or sellers.

Sellers

The principal impetus for standardization usually comes from buyers. Established sellers, on the other hand, often want to preserve product-differentiation advantages and thus oppose the creation of minimum standards. Without sufficient buyer pressure to counter these strong vested interests, few industrywide quality standards will arise. As the National Industrial Conference Board (NICB) concluded in its 1929 survey of standards:

> Whenever extensively exploited trade or brand names or patent rights are involved, standardization has made little headway. The object of trade and brand names is

to build up goodwill and lift goods out of competition. The object of standards and specifications is primarily to eliminate superficial differences and to center attention on price. Manufacturers do not want to sacrifice a trade advantage based upon goodwill secured through the popularization of a trade or brand name by admitting that their product is made according to a specification followed by the entire trade.[15]

While small sellers or potential entrants might gain from the information that standards provide to buyers, without strong buyer support their power is rarely enough to create effective standards. Even if most sellers are indifferent rather than opposed to standardization, there is little reason to expect that minimum industrywide standards will somehow spontaneously arise. The "natural" order of things is usually for there to be no standards, for creation often takes time, energy, expense, and cooperation.

There are, of course, occasions when most sellers actually favor standardization. This section examines some instances when sellers have the incentive to create quality standards.

Expected Governmental Action. A prime motive for sellers to produce their own minimum standards is to thwart anticipated government interference. A classic example concerns the Code of the Comics Magazine Association of America. The effect of mass media upon juvenile delinquency was a major public issue in 1954. The voluntary comics code was adopted in that year as the basis for the industry's program of self-regulation. The industry was assuring parents and legislators that its house was now in order-- it guaranteed that high standards of decency and morality would be followed by those large majority of comic books bearing the Code Seal of Approval.[16]

Voluntary standardization efforts may make sense even when mandatory standards are expected. This is because the existence of a voluntary standard can significantly affect the subsequent government regulations. The issues involved in standardization are often so technical that government may not have the in-house experts necessary to independently determine an appropriate standard. Since the writing of a good standard entails some cost, government is likely to be receptive to any existing consensus standard, especially when written by a broad spectrum of interests to whom the government itself might reasonably turn for technical assistance. Many government standards were thus originally voluntary standards, accepted as mandatory without substantial modifications. The industry, if its consensus standard is accepted as law, can be assured that the standard is technically sound,[17] not generally detrimental to the entire industry, and perhaps especially beneficial to those who dominated the creation process.

Quality Improvements. Buyers can sometimes discern average product quality within an industry but not the quality of a particular item. An individual seller may find it too costly to distinguish its product; the sellers may be too small and potential customers too scattered for major attempts at product differentiation to prove profitable.

In such circumstances, an individual seller has little incentive to upgrade her product since benefits accrue to the industry as a whole. Indeed, the individual incentive of any seller may be to decrease quality and cut costs. As a group, however, producers sometimes have a strong desire to raise average quality and thus a powerful motive to create minimum industrywide product standards.

An illustrative case study is provided by the experience of Japanese export industries in the postwar period. Before World War II, cheap Japanese goods had flooded world markets and were generally known for their low quality. After the war, Japan decided that it must alter that reputation if its goods were to compete in the expanding markets for high-quality items. While an individual manufacturer might have had little incentive to upgrade its product, collectively the incentive was strong.[18]

In 1949 the Japanese government, with domestic manufacturers' blessings, enacted its comprehensive export standards and inspection law, perhaps the first of its kind in the world. A substantial percentage of all Japanese exports are covered by this law. Manufacturers whose goods have passed the many detailed quality standards are licensed to affix the JIS (Japanese Industrial Standard) seal of approval on their products. Part of the rapid increase in Japanese exports in the post-war period is credited to this guarantee of product quality.[19]

Significantly, most products bearing the JIS mark are produced by small- or medium-sized firms. These are the firms expected to have the most difficulty in distinguishing their products. By acting collectively, in this case under governmental auspices, these companies were able to achieve the scale economies in guaranteeing product quality that is already possessed by the large scale enterprise. And national standards probably made good sense for Japanese exports since "averaging" externalities may also occur between industries (e.g., one bad Japanese product may have made Americans leery of buying completely different Japanese products).[20]

Risk Reduction. Sellers may favor standards when their absence increases the risk of costly misunderstandings and disputes. At the turn of the century, the growth of the electric industry was being retarded by frequent and expensive litigation caused by the lack of generally accepted measurement and minimum-quality standards.[21] In 1905 the National Bureau of Standards reported "numerous cases of dispute regarding the quality of construction materials,"[22] due to the inadequacy of standardization in the building materials industries. In such cases, there is some incentive for sellers to cooperate together to create industrywide measurement and quality standards.

Manufacturers sometimes find standards useful in reducing the risk of liability suits.[23] A single producer's argument that her product is neither unsafe nor unsound is much more persuasive if it can be shown that the item meets current industrywide quality standards. While the standard itself is generally held inadmissible, most courts permit testimony about the provisions of a standard as evidence of the prevailing practices in an industry.[24] With respect to major safety codes, sellers and insurance companies have been known to take the position that contracts do not require repair of even major defects unless they are discovered by the specific inspection techniques laid down by the code.[25]

Sellers may also find that standards tend to increase industry stability. The measurement standards of the Association of Home Appliance Manufacturers, for example, identify those aspects of quality upon which competition will focus.[26] Early measurement and testing standards in the farm machinery industry performed a similar function.[27] Standards tend to make life easier for the manufacturer; they can reduce risk and uncertainty by making quality competition somewhat more predictable. This potential benefit from standards is most likely to be recognized by oligopolists, whose profits can be noticeably affected by the actions of specific rivals.

Complements. Sellers like complements to be both inexpensive and of high quality, for this increases the demand for their product. Industrywide quality standards can help in both respects for they reduce buyer information costs, coordinate demand, and help limit adulteration. Standards for complements may be especially beneficial to sellers by identifying and reducing the number of "substandard" items that might reduce overall consumer utility, and that could even injure seller reputation if consumers cannot properly assess the cause of malfunctions or other problems.

Automotive products provide classic examples of items manufactured and sold to the consumer by varying industries but used conjointly in the final product. Automobile manufacturers have an incentive to help ensure that consumers receive excellent information about complementary products such as brake fluid and oil. They also have a mutual interest with the gasoline industry to engage in cooperative research to help adapt the fuel to the engine, the engine to the fuel.[28]

Gas and gas appliances are conjointly used complements, and gas utilities have provided the impetus behind the standardization of gas appliances.[29] The American Gas Association, representing the vast majority of gas distribution and transmission companies, has long "been concerned about the safety and durability of gas-utilizing appliances, since they are the medium through which our product is sold."[30] The AGA has been involved in the formal standards program for gas appliances and accessories since 1925, sponsoring the writing of safety, durability, and performance standards. Substantial governmental concern over the safety aspects of appliances provided further impetus for the standardization program. Currently, AGA-sponsored safety standards are mandatory in many areas, having been adopted as law by local authorities.

Anticompetitive Motives. Sellers may use standards to decrease competition, by limiting competition among established firms or by handicapping particular rivals or potential entrants. Standards can limit both price and quality competition among existing firms by facilitating implicit oligopolistic coordination or even explicit price-fixing and restrictive withholding agreements. Standards not only tend to coordinate buyer demand but can also coordinate sellers' price and product policies.

Standards attacked by antitrust authorities as integral parts of price-fixing agreements have typically been uniformity standards rather than quality standards.[31] However, quality standards have been involved in antitrust action, concerning restrictive withholding arrangements. In the *Standard Sanitary* case, for example, it was held that standards had helped to illegally eliminate inferior "seconds" from the market.[32] In the *Carpet Manufacturers* consent decree, agreements to make only the standard item were specifically prohibited as tending to limit competition.[33] And in the famous *Trenton Potteries* case, the defendant association was charged with seeking to exclude second-grade pottery from the market.[34] In general, under the U.S. antitrust laws, agreements to withhold, along with price-fixing agreements, have been treated as per se illegal.

Standards can also be used to handicap rivals or exclude them from the market. Standards have the greatest exclusionary impact when a seal of approval gains importance in a market or when, as frequently occurs in the construction business, the standard becomes codified into law. The potential for exclusion is significantly increased when the standard is based on design or material requirements, rather than on performance criteria. Thus wrought brass doorknobs were effectively barred from certain markets because HUD adopted standards requiring doorknobs of cast brass.[35] Plastic products were similarly denied access to markets when construction codes were written exclusively for more traditional materials, such as iron, steel, and glass.[36]

It is probably in the area of international trade that the exclusionary effect of standards can be most pronounced. Where standards are international, such as in cinematography, international exchange is facilitated.[37] In other areas, however, such as electrical equipment and color TV, differences in national standards can create high barriers for foreign producers to overcome.[38] While exporters may favor international standardization, domestic producers desiring protection usually prefer unique national standards that handicap foreign sellers. Until quite recently, for example, the Japanese standard for baseball bats effectively excluded bats manufactured in the United States.[39]

CONCLUSION

Uniform standards for screw threads, track gauges, and bumper heights may not simply emerge from the competitive process. Neither may many beneficial quality standards. Standardization typically requires *collective* action. There is thus no *market* mechanism to automatically ensure the creation of many useful standards. For example, both advocates and critics of nuclear power agree that lack of standardization has hurt the U.S. nuclear industry. The U.S. is the only major nuclear country in which virtually every nuclear plant is largely custom-built.[40]

Even when beneficial quality standards are created, there is no reason to expect that they will be set at optimal levels. For standards writing generally involves negotiation, bargaining, and compromise among a variety of interests. Such a political process tends to produce workable, rather than economically ideal, standards.

The nonprofit organizations that write standards are typically dominated by the very large-scale firms. Small business is often underrepresented in the standardization process. Whereas the cost of sending representatives to standardization meetings is largely independent of firm size, the absolute benefit (or cost) from any particular standard is generally related to sales. In other words, the large firm internalizes more of the collective benefit from standards than does the individual small company. The numerous small firms generally find it difficult to harmonize their somewhat conflicting interests, and singly, any individual concern may correctly conclude that it cannot substantially influence the standards-writing process. For consumers, labor, and the general public interest, which internally lack the requisite technical expertise, the problems of securing adequate representation on the standardizing committees are even more substantial. The domination by big business over the formal standards-writing process gives them great power in determining not only what standards are created but what exactly those standards will say.

This chapter examined the incentives for standardization, looking at the relationship between market structure and the desire and ability to create standards. Buyers are the prime beneficiaries of standards and provide the main impetus for their creation. However, only when buyers are large do they generally have the ability to write and use voluntary standards.

Sellers possessing product-differentiation advantages typically oppose the creation of quality standards. There are reasons, of course, for producers to favor standards: to forestall or help shape government regulations, to limit adulteration, or to reduce uncertainty. They may also promote standards for complementary products or employ standards for anticompetitive purposes.

From a social viewpoint, standards can have beneficial or deleterious effects. Many standards have elements of both. Some performance standards, for instance, can decrease search costs, minimize brand distinctions, and lower entry barriers. Design standards, on the other hand, sometimes raise barriers and impede innovation.[41]

Oligopolistic firms typically have little difficulty collaborating to create standards (if they so desire).[42] These standards are most likely to be socially beneficial if they deal, not with the firms' own output, but with the items they purchase or the goods produced by complementary industries.

FOR DISCUSSION

1. Under what circumstances is product adulteration likely? For what product characteristics?

2. Performance standards are generally considered preferable to design standards. Why, then, do prescriptive (design) standards still predominate?

3. How can standards test for product durability?

4. Underwriters' Laboratories, one of the premier testing and certification labs in the country, has effective monopoly power in many product areas. What would be the benefits and problems of increased competition in the testing and certification of products?

5. When is it socially desirable to eliminate all "seconds" from the market?

6. Contrast voluntary and mandatory standards. When are mandatory standards preferable? What will be the real-world differences between standards written by private and public bodies?

7. Voluntary standard setting can be one approach to industry self-regulation. Describe and discuss other methods.

8. The typewriter keyboard is an implicit standard-for-uniformity. Describe two other implicit uniformity standards.

NOTES TO CHAPTER 16

1. Rexmond C. Cochrane, *Measures for Progress* (Washington, DC: National Bureau of Standards, 1966), p. 84.
2. *Dictionary of American Biography*, 1935 ed., s.v. "William Sellers."
3. H. W. Robb, "Significance of Company and National Standards to Industrial Management," in Dickson Reck, ed., *National Standards in a Modern Economy* (New York: Harper & Row, 1956), p. 296.
4. Robert F. Legget, *Standards in Canada* (Ottawa: Economic Council of Canada, 1970), pp. 56-60; Edward R. Weidlein and Vera Reck, "A Million Years of Standards" in Reck, ed., *National Standards*.
5. American Standards Association, "Throughout History with Standards," (n.d., Pamphlet), p. 1.
6. Paul David, "CLIO and the Economics of QWERTY," *American Economic Review: Papers and Proceedings* 75, no. 2 (May 1985): 332-37.

7. For useful analyses of the economics of uniformity standards, see Joseph Farrell and Garth Saloner, "Standardization, Compatibility and Innovation," *Rand Journal of Economics* 16, no. 1 (Spring 1985): 70-83 and Michael Katz and Carl Shapiro, "Network Externalities, Competition and Compatibility," *American Economic Review* 75, no. 3 (June 1985): 424-40.

8. *American Society of Mechanical Engineers* v. *Hydrolevel Corporation*, 456 U.S. 556, 570 (1982).

9. Donald L. Lecraw, "Some Economic Effects of Standards," *Applied Economics* 16, no. 4 (1984): 507-22.

10. Manufacturers Standardization Society of the Valve and Fittings Industry, letter to author, August 9, 1972.

11. John K. Barnes, "The Men Who 'Standardized' Automobile Parts," *The World's Work*, June 1921, p. 206.

12. George V. Thompson, "Intercompany Technical Standardization in the Early American Automobile Industry," *Journal of Economic History* 14 (Winter 1954): 15-16.

13. "Refiners Should Play Ball with S.A.E.," *SAE Journal* (June 1928): 673.

14. Wallace N. Seward, "Publications and Materials" (Washington, DC: American Petroleum Institute, 1972), p. 51.

15. National Industrial Conference Board, *Industrial Standardization* (New York: National Industrial Conference Board, 1929), p. 260.

16. Leonard Darvin, Code Authority Comics Magazine Association of America, letter to author, July 6, 1972.

17. A comparative advantage of voluntary versus government-created standards is the technical expertise of the private sector. Ross Cheit, *Setting Safety Standards: Regulation in the Public and Private Sectors* (Berkeley, CA: University of California Press, 1990).

18. Lol C. Verman, *Standardization: A New Discipline* (Hamden, CT: Shoe String Press, 1973), p. 272.

19. Charles Sharpston, "Standardization," Monograph #12 (New York: United Nations Industrial Development Organization, 1967), p. 20; Donald L. Lecraw, "Japanese Standards: A Barrier to Trade?" in H. Landis Gabel, *Product Standardization and Competitive Strategy* (New York: North-Holland, 1987), pp. 29-46.

20. Shih-Chien Chang and Robert Masson, "Domestic Industrial Structure and Expert Quality," *International Economic Review* 29, no. 2 (May 1988): 261-69.

21. Cochrane, *Measures for Progress*, p. 38.

22. National Bureau of Standards, "Annual Report," 1906, p. 15.

23. Standards sometimes increase liability (e.g., "upgrading" a safety standard can leave existing products more vulnerable to suits). Cheit, *Setting Safety Standards*, pp. 190-91.

24. Marian P. Opala, "The Anatomy of Private Standards-Making Process: The Operating Procedures of the USA Standards Institute," *Oklahoma Law Review* 22 (February 1969): 64, 68.

25. H. G. Rickover, "Who Protects the Public?" *Materials Evaluation*, (December 1968): 27-29.

26. Michael Hunt, "Trade Associations and Self-Regulation: Major Home Appliances," in Richard Caves and Marc Roberts, eds., *Regulating the Product: Quality and Variety* (Cambridge, MA: Ballinger Publishing Company, 1975), pp. 39-55.

27. Robert Kudrle, "Regulation and Self-Regulation in the Farm Machinery Industry," in Caves and Roberts, eds., *Regulating the Product*, pp. 57-73.

28. "The Birth of Cooperative Research," *SAE Journal* (February 1955): 63; "Cooperative Fuel Research and Its Results," *SAE Journal* (August 1929): 171.

29. Frank E. Hodgdon, American Gas Association Laboratories, letter to author, August 14, 1972.

30. American Gas Association, comments in response to a Federal Trade Commission inquiry with respect to private testing and certification programs (Arlington, VA, 1972, Mimeographed), p. 1.

31. E.g., *Milk and Ice Cream Can Institute v. FTC*, 152 F.2d 478, 480 (9th Cir. 1946); *Bond Crown and Cork Company v. FTC*, 176 F.2d 974 (4th Cir. 1949); *C-O-Two Fire Equipment Co. v. United States*, 197 F.2d 489 (9th Cir. 1952) *Cert. denied*, 344 U.S. 892 (1952).

32. *Standard Sanitary Manufacturing Co. v. United States*, 226 U.S. 20 (1912).

33. *United States v. Institute of Carpet Manufacturers*, 1940-43 Trade Cases, 56, 097 (S.D.N.Y. 1941).

34. *United States v. Trenton Potteries Co.*, 273 U.S. 392, 398 (1927).

35. Hearings before the House Small Business Committee on the Rural and Urban Problems of Small Businessmen, 91st Cong., 2nd sess., (1970), pp. 47-53.

36. The first model code group to approve ABS plumbing pipe did not do so until 18 years after it was invented and 8 years after it was in widespread use in mobile homes. Michael Goldberg, "Standards, Public Welfare Defenses, and the Antitrust Laws," *Business Lawyer* 42 (May 1987): 629-74.

37. Organization for European Economic Cooperation, *Some Aspects of Standardization in the United States and Europe* (Paris: OEEC, 1953), pp. 61-62. See also C.S. McCamy, "A Half-Century of Photographic Standardization" (Washington, DC: National Bureau of Standards, 1967).

38. "Technology and World Trade," Misc. Publication 284 (Washington, DC: National Bureau of Standards, 1967), p. 48; Jacques Pelkmans and Rita Beuter, "Standardization and Competitiveness: Private and Public Strategies in the EC Color TV Industry," in H. Landis Gabel, *Product Standardization and Competitive Strategy*, pp. 171-215.

39. Donald L. Lecraw, "Japanese Standards: A Barrier to Trade?" in H. Landis Gabel, *Product Standardization and Competitive Strategy*, pp. 29-46.

40. John L. Campbell. *Collapse of an Industry: Nuclear Power and Contradictions of U.S. Policy* (Ithica, NY: Cornell University Press, 1988).

41. David Hemenway, "Performance vs. Design Standards," NBS/GRC 80287 (Springfield, VA: National Bureau of Standards, National Technical Information Service, 1980), pp. 5-8.

42. David Garvin, "Can Industry Self-Regulation Work?" *California Management Review* 25, no. 4 (Summer 1983): 44-45; Albert Link, "Market Structure and Voluntary Product Standards," *Applied Economics* 15 (1983): 399.

17 GRADES

Classification and grading of goods are often mentioned together. Classification generally refers to the dividing of a commodity into lots that have uniform characteristics, without implying either superior or inferior groupings. Thus, wheat is sometimes classified by variety, honey by color, potatoes by size, and beef by sex. Within classifications, grading is often performed, categorizing the commodity according to quality. Grades for honey include "fancy" and "standard"; beef is graded as "prime," "choice," "select" and "standard."

There are many potentially competitive repercussions from the grading of goods and services. This chapter discusses some of the principal effects of grading, especially with respect to scale advantages, and tries in general to explain why grading occurs where it does.

SOME EFFECTS OF GRADES

The principal economic benefit of grades is in the provision of information on product quality. Grading is one way of supplying such information-- a substitute and sometimes a complement for other methods such as advertising, brand names, and guarantees. Grading differs from these particular alternatives in being an industrywide rather than a firm-specific method of providing information. Products of differing sellers are ranked by the identical grading system.

A common grading system increases the ability of buyers to purchase without personal inspection, thereby facilitating transactions at a distance. Grades can also help to eliminate fraud, expedite the financing of loans to producers and middlemen, and ease the determination of insurance claims.

Grades provide for all buyers the same neat summary appraisal of product quality. Thus, grades not only help to make buyers better informed but also lead them to rank products similarly. Introduction of grades, therefore, tends to eliminate some of the product differentiation advantages of established sellers, making their demand curves more elastic and generally lowering barriers to potential entrants.

There are usually scale advantages in quality assurance. Over some range, the average cost of assuring quality declines as direct assurance expenditures increase. For example, a certain size advertising budget is required to gain access to national TV or to hire the services of well-known independent testing laboratories. Perhaps more important, the average cost of assuring quality also declines for the firm as quantity sold increases. When a particular brand or company has high past and present sales, a potential purchaser finds it easier to obtain "testimonials" from friends, buyer magazines, and so forth and is more likely himself to have had experience with that brand. In other words, quality information about the product is cheaper to obtain. Grades, by providing information to buyers, tend to eliminate some of these scale-differentiation advantages. Grades thus permit the small seller to compete more effectively. One consequence of meat grading, for example, may be to reduce seller concentration in that market.[1]

Many other effects of grading may be mentioned. Grading, for example, may decrease the scale advantages of large-scale *buyers*. Some of the scale economies that exist in purchasing are caused by the fixed costs of obtaining product-quality information. Large firms are often able to employ full-time purchasing agents; they can write their own specifications and buy accordingly. In contrast, smaller concerns and final consumers are forced to rely more heavily on advertising and brand names. Government grading and testing of products provides much quality information and helps eliminate one of the advantages the big purchaser has over the small.

Like any measure, grades may change both perceptions and incentives. Aspects of quality that are heavily weighted in a grading system will tend to be emphasized, while those receiving less weight may tend to be neglected. It is sometimes argued that grades will have the effect of making goods more homogeneous. To the extent that quality is "standardized," this could make oligopolistic coordination easier and cheating on implicit or explicit price-fixing arrangements simpler to detect.[2] It is also claimed that grades could inhibit beneficial technological innovation. Finally, there are the direct costs of grading, which may sometimes be large.

GRADED AND UNGRADED GOODS

Commodities actually graded in the United States include milk, eggs, wool, lumber, mushrooms, soybeans, meat, scrap iron, and diamonds. As should be expected, major brand names are generally not important in such markets, and small firms face few product-differentiation disadvantages. Additionally, graded commodities are often those for which existing firms might have had difficulty in establishing quality assurance advantages and resistance to grading was therefore probably least. A usual feature of currently graded products is that their quality does not predominantly depend on "factory control" procedures but on more unpredictable factors, often on nature. The number of knots in a given piece of lumber, for instance, is a somewhat stochastic variable and is largely independent of the ability or efficiency of the producer.[3]

Graded commodities are probably those for which there was little resistance to grading by established firms. From the social perspective, it might be argued that these were the most desirable candidates for grading. The commodities are often produced by many and scattered firms; thus, grading could provide great assistance to buyers, for a large number of geographically dispersed sellers usually makes search costs high. Grades are also most helpful to purchasers when other information substitutes, such as strong brand identifications, do not exist. And the fact that the commodities were often primary goods made them lend themselves more readily to grading. Their primary nature made it easier to discover some generally agreed upon rank ordering, and their "God-made" property lessened the potential problem that the grades might inhibit major design breakthroughs.

Since grades generally tend to decrease the value of built-up reputation and trade names, firms possessing certain product-differentiation advantages often resist attempts to initiate a grading system. Major paper companies, for example, have long opposed grades for their products. The established firms usually claim that their products are not suitable for grading. Among other things, they argue that the goods possess many noncollinear but highly important product-quality characteristics. Absorbency, softness, and strength are all important aspects of paper towels, and it may depend on use or preference whether an absorbent, weak towel is considered superior to a strong but less absorbent one. Consumers, of course, might still benefit if *each* of the product attributes were graded or if complete grades could be given by product *use*.

A second major argument of those opposed to grading is that grades may focus competition on the wrong areas. Certain characteristics of writing paper, such as appearance, formation, printability, and lack of curl, presently defy accurate measurement. Producers claim that if the setting of definite standards for the measurable characteristics is carried to extremes, this would tend to limit manufacturers in developing some of the unmeasurable characteristics that are often far more important. The argument is that the information provided may prove misleading and that purchasers may actually be made worse off than had they received no grade information at all.

While grading is not practical for all products, for many, grades might provide cheap, useful, and succinct quality information. Commodities currently graded seem ideal for grading, and it is difficult to discover cases in which grading should be stopped. On the other hand, inadequate buyer power combined with the reluctance of established sellers to relinquish brand advantages may combine to prevent the creation of other potentially beneficial grading systems.[4]

CONCLUSION

Where goods are graded, grades written, and products tested by some competent and independent authority, we may expect a number of results. Perhaps the most important is the decrease in certain product-differentiation advantages of established firms. Since there are some scale economies in quality assurance, grades usually make small concerns more competitive and tend to decrease seller concentration. Established firms with brand advantages are therefore generally opposed to grading proposals. From society's viewpoint, whether or not a particular good should be graded is a complex question requiring the comparison of costs and benefits of this form of product information provision with other methods. To answer such a question, an in-depth, case-by-case approach is essential

FOR DISCUSSION

1. Tires are now graded for treadwear, traction and temperature resistance. If you were the CEO of B. F. Goodrich, would you have favored or opposed this federal system for the grading of tires? Explain.

2. Movies are currently rated as G, PG, PG-13, R, or X. Are these grades? Explain. What is the principal industrial organization effect of these ratings?

3. As a consumer, would you want breakfast cereals to be graded? What would be the effect? Would there be more serious problems if computers were graded? What if TV sets had been graded for quality in 1947?

4. Why is it the government that often establishes grades? When can this function be left to the free market? What if a variety of private testing groups each established its own grading system?

5. Is grading generally more useful for consumers' goods or producers' goods? Explain.

6. Do you think grading is more important in developed or less developed countries? Do you expect to find that more of Peru's or the United States' GDP is composed of graded commodities?

7. In Greece, a poor country with more foreign than domestic tourists, the government gives each hotel a quality rating and then sets the appropriate price. The national police inspect hotels to ensure that this price information is conspicuously displayed within each room. Why this governmental interference with the free

market? What are the principal economic effects? What relevance (if any) does this question have to the topic of grades?

NOTES TO CHAPTER 17

1. Willard Williams, E.K. Bowen, and F.C. Genovese, "Economic Effects of U.S. Grades for Beef," U.S. Department of Agriculture Marketing Research Report No. 298 (Washington, DC: Government Printing Office, 1959).
2. Robert Grant, "The Effects of Product Standardization on Competition: Octane Grading of Petrol in the U.K.," in H. Landis Gabel, *Product Standardization and Competitive Strategy* (New York: North-Holland, 1987), pp. 283-301.
3. David Hemenway, *Industrywide Voluntary Product Standards* (Cambridge, MA: Ballinger Publishing Company, 1975), pp. 59-62.
4. Steven Cox, "Consumer Information and Competition in the Synthetic Detergent Industry," *Nebraska Journal of Economics and Business* (Summer 1976): 41-58.

OTHER SOURCES

Bowbrick, Peter, "The Economics of Grades," *Oxford Agrarian Studies* 11 (1982): 65-92.
Cox, Linda J., McMullen, Starr and Garrod, Peter V., "An Analysis of the Use of Grades and Housebrand Labels in the Retail Beef Market," *Western Journal of Agricultural Economics* 15 (1990): 245-253.

V MONOPOLY

INTRODUCTION

After the perfectly competitive model, the theoretical market most analyzed in economics is monopoly. Textbook treatment highlights the allocative efficiency problem caused by monopoly-that under certain very restrictive assumptions a profit-maximizing monopolist produces too little from the viewpoint of society. Chapter 18 takes a different tack; it describes a variety of situations in which monopoly might be socially preferable to increased competition. The aim here is not to defend monopoly but to illustrate how the normative implications of microeconomic theory may be reversed if the assumptions are altered.

At the turn of the century, monopolies were classified as good or bad depending on how they behaved. Chapter 19 describes the old New York ice trust, which acted quite badly. This was a classic monopoly market, characterized by one seller, many buyers, good information, and a homogeneous product but, unfortunately for the trust, easy entry. Chapter 19 gives a glimpse into the seamy side of corporate conduct in 1900 and applies simple microeconomic analysis to this fascinating real-world case study.

18 IS MONOPOLY BAD?

There is no morality in the economic model. Individuals are never depicted as virtuous or wicked, as saints or sinners. People are simply utility maximizers; firms are typically profit maximizers. A competitive firm would behave exactly as a monopolist if placed in that environment, and vice versa. For an economist, the title question of this chapter thus has nothing to do with "good" or "evil." Instead, the issue is one of efficiency: could the elimination of the monopoly result in a Pareto-superior move? In other words, is it possible to make everyone better off (from her own perspective)?

Efficiency is sometimes divided into three components: technical, allocative, and dynamic. Technical efficiency requires that each good be produced as inexpensively as possible; with the given amount of societal resources, it is impossible to produce more of one item without reducing the output of another. Allocative efficiency requires that the optimal mix of goods be produced. Taken together, technical and allocative efficiency achieve Pareto optimality it is impossible to shift input or output levels among various goods and make everyone better off. Dynamic efficiency includes a time element. Over time, are we producing more or better products at the same level of input?

The principal theoretical case against monopoly is that it leads to allocative inefficiency. If a perfectly competitive equilibrium exists in all markets, save one, and that one is controlled by a single-price, profit-maximizing monopolist with high entry barriers, then that industry will produce too little. Price will be greater than marginal cost, and allocative inefficiency will result. Note that this conclusion may not hold if all other markets are not perfectly competitive, or not in equilibrium. Nor does the conclusion hold if the monopolist price discriminates perfectly, nor if entry barriers are negligible. In this latter case, the monopolist is effectively a price taker and cannot raise price above marginal cost without attracting entry.

The monopolist may also be technically inefficient (x-inefficiency). Monopolists often have the ability to make excess profits without ruthlessly cutting costs. In other words, the monopoly often has less need-- compared to a perfect competitor-- to profit-maximize. It probably will not be driven out of business if it does not find its best cost curve. It is sometimes said that "the best monopoly profit is a quiet life." On the other hand, a monopoly may be required for technical efficiency. This is the case of "natural monopoly." If there are continuing economies of scale, industry output is produced most cheaply by a single firm.

It is sometimes argued that a monopolistic industry will be less innovative or progressive than a more competitive one. The monopoly has probably been enjoying excess profits, and "if it ain't broke, don't fix it." The notion again is that monopolists may choose the quiet life. On the other hand, there are famous economists-- most notably Joseph Schumpeter, Harvard's greatest twentieth-century economist and John Kenneth Galbraith, Harvard's tallest twentieth century economist-- who contend that large firms and monopoly power are conducive for rapid technological advance.[1] The arguments are that there are economies of scale in research and development, and that firms with large market shares have more incentive to innovate since they internalize more of the benefits from technological change that accrue to the entire industry.

Since there are few unregulated monopolists in the United States, the relevant empirical evidence concerns the effects of market power on efficiency and contrasts oligopolistic industries with more competitive markets. Virtually all studies show that oligopolists earn higher profits; this is sometimes taken as a sign of allocative inefficiency and sometimes as an indication of rewards to good management for efficient production. In any event, the size of possible losses due to allocative inefficiency is relatively small-- on the order of one to two percent of GDP, or less than one year's growth.[2] The empirical evidence relating market power to technical or dynamic efficiency is even more ambiguous. It does seem that there are some economies of scale to research and development, though not necessarily to innovation. While the evidence is sketchy, most economists probably believe that if technical production economies permit, it is usually better to have more than one seller in the market.

The textbook defense of monopoly typically boils down to economies of scale in production, marketing, or research and development. This chapter provides additional reasons that monopoly might prove beneficial, at least in certain circumstances or in certain respects. At times a monopolistic structure will be compared to oligopoly, at times to a market with many sellers.

THE SECOND BEST

The Theory of the Second Best asks: If some of the conditions for Pareto optimality are not being met, will it still be desirable to fulfill the others? For example, if there are monopolies in some markets, externalities in some, imperfect information, and so forth, can we be sure that making one of these markets more perfectly competitive will increase efficiency? The answer is no.

The Theory of the Second Best-- if there is a variety of problems, fixing one may not improve the situation-- holds in noneconomic as well as economic settings. For example, if the gas stove leaks and the pilot light isn't working, fixing the pilot light alone may make matters worse. Similarly, if the pressure regulator for the furnace is defective, it is not always desirable to fix the oil burner. If a patient has severe, end-stage chronic obstructive lung disease resulting in both a high CO_2 and a low O_2 level in her lungs, giving her oxygen may stop her breathing entirely.[3]

There are many examples from economics. Assume that all markets are perfectly competitive, except one, and there are two problems in that market-large negative externalities are generated by the production process, and the industry is monopolized. In these circumstances, eliminating the monopoly may worsen rather than improve the allocative inefficiency. In Figure 18-1, the ideal output, where marginal social cost (MSC) equals marginal social benefit (represented by the demand curve), is at Q_A. The profit-maximizing monopoly output Q_B is closer to this than is the competitive market output Q_C where too much is produced.

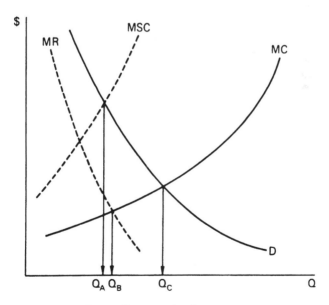

Q_A = Pareto optimal output
Q_B = Monopoly output
Q_C = Competitive market output

Figure 18-1

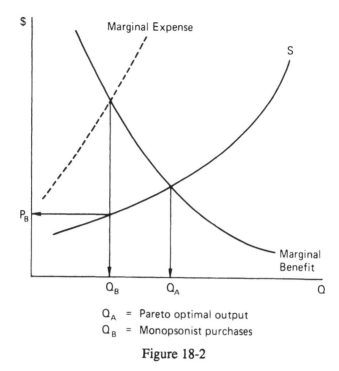

Q_A = Pareto optimal output
Q_B = Monopsonist purchases

Figure 18-2

Or assume all markets are perfectly competitive, except one, and that one is a monopsony-there is only one buyer. Allowing sellers to merge together to form a monopoly might then improve allocative efficiency. In Figure 18-2, the optimal quantity is Q_A, where the marginal benefit curve crosses the supply curve. The monopsonist purchases too little, Q_B, at P_B. Creating a bilateral monopoly can move quantity (and price) toward the optimal level. Many of the examples that follow may be considered types of "Second Best" problems.

EXTERNALITIES

Monopolies may prove beneficial in many situations where externalities exist. There is no official taxonomy for externalities, but two of the kinds discussed below might be labeled "Commons Problems" and "Uniformity Externalities." The absence of well-defined property rights often leads to overconsumption. An example is the commons problem. Competition, combined with the rule of capture, leads to too many and too small fish or wildlife being killed, or to oil being drilled from underground pools at too fast a rate. First-come, first-served allocations, with no restrictions, can result in too many animals or too many campers on a public commons, despoiling the resource for all.

In such situations, the creation of a monopoly means that property rights have effectively been established. There is no "rule of capture": the monopoly legally owns the fish or wildlife. There is no need to kill them before rival firms do. And feeding and nurturing the animals benefits only the monopoly. The externality problem has been eliminated.

Open competition for a free radio spectrum-- a commons-- can create interference and static. Regulation, the public allocation of property rights, solves the externality problem. So would a private monopoly radio or CB system.

In another type of externality situation-when there are uniformity externalities-having a monopoly producer may increase social welfare. For example, beneficial uniformity standards are more easily created by a single firm than by competitive producers. A monopoly railroad has little difficulty ensuring that the track gauges on its various lines are the same size. A monopoly manufacturer of nuts and bolts can easily establish screw thread standards. A monopoly telephone company can guarantee the compatibility of all phone equipment. By contrast, competition may lead to the incompatibility of tracks, fasteners, and telephones, thereby losing the benefits of interconnection and interchangeability.[4]

In general, as a company's share of the market grows, the more formerly external costs will become internalized by the firm. External costs are those imposed on others, including competitors, customers, and bystanders. For example, consider the criminal business of extortion. Racketeers have a collective interest in restricting violence, which could lead to public outrage and police crackdowns against the whole industry. An individual extortionist has less incentive to reduce the violence connected with her own crime. A monopoly syndicate helps internalize part of the externality. The Mob wants to keep the police off the backs of all its members and thus has an incentive to "police" them in order to reduce random violence.[5]

INFORMATION

Competitive firms in an industry often find it difficult to promote the group interest.[6] A monopoly has less trouble; it *is* the industry. The first example below is one of many in this chapter that illustrate this principle; here the situation is one in which imperfect buyer information causes industry externalities. The second example deals with the potential benefits of monopoly when the firm is a product certifier, the provider of a specific type of quality information.

Assume that purchasers in a market cannot determine the quality of any specific good but do know average industry quality. In such circumstances, a small producer typically does better by manufacturing low-cost, low-quality items. A competitive firm that adulterates its product reaps the entire benefit from the reduced cost, but rival suppliers share in the losses caused by buyer recognition of lower average industry quality.[7] Continued adulteration can destroy the market for all producers. A monopoly seller internalizes the "averaging externalities" caused by this imperfect buyer information. The monopolist has no incentive to cut quality below the industry optimum.

A's customers (starting from the left) = .6(150) + 250 + 150 = 490
B's customers (starting from the right) = .6(100) + 250 + 150 = 460

Figure 18-3

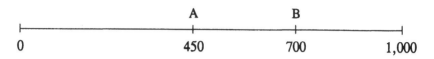

A's customers (starting from the left) = .6(200) + 250 + 125 = 495
B's customers (starting from the right) = .6(100) + 250 + 125 = 435

Figure 18-4

Certain private agencies test and certify aspects of product quality and safety. Two of the more important ones are Underwriters' Laboratories and the American Gas Association. Both have monopoly power. It is not clear that competitive certifiers would be an improvement. Manufacturers whose products are being certified might well seek out the least stringent testing labs. And purchasers, who require certification in part because they lack technical knowledge, might receive less real assurance from the certification. Many certifiers are nonprofit institutions. This organizational structure may help lessen some of the dangers of monopoly power.[8]

DIVERSITY

In the real world, monopolies may sometimes produce too little variety. After all, when the Model T was predominant, Henry Ford supposedly said about his customers: "They can have any color car they want, as long as it's black." Yet situations exist when a monopoly might provide more beneficial diversity than an oligopoly. Suppose that during a specific time slot, potential TV viewers have these preferences: 70 percent want to watch a crime show with car crashes and killings; 20 percent are interested in a serious drama; 10 percent want to see anything in Spanish. Individuals will tune in only if their favorite type of show is being aired. Now assume that there are only three stations or networks, controlled by three competing firms, each striving to maximize its own audience. What kind of programs will be shown? Each will air a crime show, hoping to attract 23 percent or more of the possible audience. In all, 70 percent of the potential viewers will watch TV. Compare this to a monopoly firm that owns the three outlets. It will put on the three different programs and garner 100 percent of the potential audience.

Imagine a beach in summer, 1,000 yards in length, with bathers evenly distributed along it. Bathers want refreshments and will go to the nearest vendor. All will go up to 250 yards, but only 60 percent will go more than that. Assume two competing vendors set up positions. The equilibrium position for these two profit maximizers is next to each other at the center of the beach. In Figure 18-3, let there be one customer every yard. Competitors A and B are located at the 400- and 700-yard markers. Either will gain customers by moving toward the other. For every 50 yards A moves, she gains 25 customers from B and loses (.4) (50) = 20 customers who no longer buy refreshments (Figure 18-4). If both vendors are not at the center, one or both could move and increase its profits. Were these two to combine to form a monopoly partnership, they would locate at the 250- and 750-yard markers, maximizing total industry sales and consumer utility.

DISEQUILIBRIUM

The short-run inefficiencies due to competition are often larger than those caused by monopoly. Competition, for example, may lead to wasteful duplication of hardware or research. Sellers make mistakes about investment decisions since they are uncertain of the future. For competitive firms, an important component of the future-- what other suppliers will do-- is unknown. Even with reasonable information, since competitors do not actively coordinate their policies, selective overinvestment or undersupply is likely in the short run.

Competition among firms may become cutthroat or destructive. High-fixed-cost industries facing cyclical swings in demand are particularly at risk. Competition may become so sharp as to create great instability and destroy efficient firms lacking access to liquid capital. The amount and speed of firm exit may be greater than the optimum.

Firm exit causes many short-run problems. Displaced workers not only lose employment but often suffer a loss of confidence and a lowering of self-esteem. Job loss is associated with anxiety and tension and can lead to increased alcoholism, child abuse, assault, and suicide.[9]

There are other costs of firm failure, including the transaction costs of job search and of the sale of plant and equipment. The company's physical capacity as well as human-capital stock may be enterprise specific and thus lose much of its value. The discontinued firm's suppliers and customers may also feel some loss.

Such problems of business mortality are transitional or short run. Additionally, similar problems may arise by changes within a particular firm. The point to be made here is simply that structural changes-whether long-run improvements or not-are likely to occur more rapidly in competitive than in monopolized industries. And these changes have real economic costs.

IRRATIONALITY

In the real world, individuals may desire items that are deleterious to their well-being. People may purchase more cigarettes, alcohol, pornography, or fatty foods than, at some level, they know is good for them. The issue is not that they are misinformed or underestimate risks; they simply may not be fully able to control their appetites. They are better off consuming less. A higher price, caused by an excise tax or by industry monopolization, might decrease their purchases and increase their utility.

OTHER GOALS

There are many possible social goals other than efficiency: freedom, equality, equity, justice, brotherhood, friendship, and so on. At times a monopoly may prove better than a more competitive marketplace in promoting certain of these values.

The process of competition, for example, may be harmful to individuals and to society. Real-world people, unlike those in the microeconomic model, are not born fully developed, with fixed tastes and preferences. The society and its economic system help mold the person. Economic competition may reward alertness, shrewdness, and efficiency. But it may also increase aggressiveness and acquisitiveness. On the other hand, it is possible that a reduction in competition (e.g., monopoly) might sometimes enhance cooperation, camaraderie, and brotherhood or promote more virtuous behavior.

CONCLUSION

Monopoly may be socially beneficial in a variety of situations. This chapter described a few. The list is not intended to be comprehensive; there are undoubtedly other circumstances in which monopoly has certain advantages. Nor does the chapter purport to defend or praise monopoly. Many of the costs of monopoly-for instance, the social and political problems caused by market power-were not discussed. Instead, the purpose was to examine a broad normative issue in order to help elucidate the assumptions, approach, and uses of microeconomics. Incidentally, the answer to the title question is, of course, "It all depends."

FOR DISCUSSION

1. How empirically might one test for technical inefficiency in a monopolized market?

2. Give additional economic and noneconomic examples of the Theory of the Second Best. Is this a universal principle?

3. Present a useful taxonomy for classifying externalities. Why is it useful?

4. Do you expect to find more advertising in a monopoly or in an oligopolistic market? Explain. When is it better to have more advertising?

5. How much product diversity is optimal?

6. Are markets usually in equilibrium? Under what conditions is it useful to employ equilibrium theory?

7. What social goals, if any, do not easily fit into the efficiency/equity rubric of economic theory? Explain. What does this imply about economic policy prescriptions?

NOTES TO CHAPTER 18

1. Joseph A. Schumpeter, *Capitalism, Socialism and Democracy* (New York: Harper, 1942), pp. 88, 103; John Kenneth Galbraith, *American Capitalism*, revised ed. (Boston: Houghton Mifflin, 1956), pp. 86-87.
2. Douglas F. Greer, *Industrial Organization and Public Policy* (New York: Macmillan, 1980), pp. 462-63.
3. David Hemenway, "The Second Best in Statistics," *Journal of Clinical Epidemiology* 44 (1991): 957-59.
4. David Hemenway, *Industrywide Voluntary Product Standards* (Cambridge, MA: Ballinger Publishing Company, 1975), pp. 19-43; Michael Katz and Carl Shapiro, "Network Externalities, Competition and Compatibility," *American Economic Review* 75 (June 1985): 424-40.
5. Thomas C. Schelling, *Choice and Consequence* (Cambridge, MA: Harvard University Press, 1984), p. 163.
6. Mancur Olson, *The Logic of Collective Action* (Cambridge, MA: Harvard University Press, 1965).
7. George Akerlof, "The Market for 'Lemons': Quality Uncertainty and the Market Mechanism," *Quarterly Journal of Economics* 84 (August 1970): 488-501.

8. David Hemenway, "Standards Systems in Canada, the U.K., West Germany, and Denmark: An Overview," NBS/GCR 79-172, National Bureau of Standards, Office of Engineering Standards, U.S. Department of Commerce, Washington, DC, April 1979.

9. Barry Bluestone and Bennett Harrison, *The Deindustrialization of America* (New York: Basic Books, 1982), chapter 3.

19 THE ICE TRUST

INTRODUCTION

The first great American merger wave had a dramatic effect on the structure of U.S. industry. This early merger movement, culminating in the flurry of consolidations between 1898 and 1902, left an imprint on the American economy that ninety years have not erased. It was during these years that the pattern of concentration characteristic of American business formed and matured.[1] During these four years, 236 important industrial consolidations occurred, with total capital of $6.1 billion.[2] By 1904 the trusts controlled fully 40 percent of the manufacturing capital of the country.[3] It was during this period that U.S. Steel was formed, as were U.S. Rubber, the Tobacco Trust, American Can, U.S. Gypsum, General Electric, International Nickel, International Paper, Allis-Chalmers, United Shoe, United Fruit, Standard Sanitary, National Lead, Pullman Company, National Biscuit Company, the Sugar Trust, International Salt, Western Union, and so forth. Also during this period, a wide variety of less important trusts emerged, including those in bicycles, caramels, grass twine, hominies, chewing gum, buttons, and ice.[4]

This is the story of one of the most fascinating of the lesser trusts, the ice trust, which briefly but spectacularly succeeded in gaining monopoly control over the New York City ice supply. It is the story of Charles W. Morse, tycoon and robber baron, founder and president of the American Ice Company, who ruthlessly ordered prices raised and service cut upon securing his monopoly position. And it is the story of the ensuing public outcry, combined with natural competitive forces, which dethroned the ice trust and quickly sent prices tumbling to pretrust levels.

THE AMERICAN ICE COMPANY

At the turn of the century, the residents of New York City received most of their ice from natural sources, principally cuttings from the Hudson and the Penobscot and Kennebec rivers in Maine. Though the supply of manufactured ice was rapidly increasing in both absolute and relative terms, artificial ice still accounted for less than 15 percent of the city's annual four-million-ton consumption.[5] The reliance upon natural ice resulted in pronounced fluctuations in prices and profits depending upon the vagaries of the climate. Warm winters decreased the supply of ice and increased the cost of harvesting.[6] Warm winters also increased the demand, as did hot summers. The warm weather in 1905-1906, for example, raised the winter sales in New York City 50 percent over the previous winter.[7] The effect of the warm weather in 1905-1906 and 1912-13 is shown clearly in the profits of the American Ice Company. In the former period, net profits jumped from $487,000 in 1904-1905 to over $2 million, falling back to $185,000 the next year. And from $369,000 in 1911-12, annual profits climbed the following year to $1,600,000, dropping to $400,000 in 1913-14.[8]

The American Ice Company was the "ice trust," incorporated in 1899 with Charles W. Morse as president. An independent Maine ice operator, Morse, during the warm New York winter of 1890, had been able to acquire control of the ice-starved New York City Ice Company and Consumers' Ice Company. In 1895 these and other small companies were incorporated into the new Consolidated Ice Company, whose stated objectives were to regulate prices, restrict the amount harvested, and hold down competition.[9] The important Knickerbocker Ice Companies of New York and New Jersey soon joined the alliance.[10] Consolidated thus already had substantial control over the New York market at the time of the formation of the American Ice Company.

Incorporated under the friendly laws of New Jersey, the American Ice Company formally merged Consolidated, Knickerbocker of Maine, and a number of smaller manufacturers and distributors. The combination possessed extensive plants for the housing of ice on the Penobscot, Kennebec, Schuylkill, Susquehanna, and Hudson rivers, Rockland Lake, Croton Lake, and many New Jersey lakes. It also controlled a number of plants for manufacturing artificial ice in New York City, Philadelphia, Camden, Atlantic City, Baltimore, and Washington, D.C. and owned dock facilities and real estate in virtually all of these cities. Moody's listed the number of plants acquired as "about 40," and the proportion of the industry controlled locally as 80 percent.[11]

ELIMINATING COMPETITION

Attaining and, especially, maintaining a monopoly position in ice was not an easy proposition. Ice is a largely homogeneous product, and neither a great deal of capital nor technical expertise was required to enter the natural, or even the artificial, ice business.[12] Not only were entry barriers low, but the market was reasonably large and growing. Total U.S. consumption of ice more than tripled between 1880 and 1914.[13]

The ice trust engaged in a variety of practices designed to limit competition. One device was the restrictive covenant. Managers of acquired companies were required to sign agreements prohibiting them from engaging in the ice business for a period of ten years.[14] These restrictive covenants seem to have been of some importance. In 1902 *Ice and Refrigeration*, a trade journal, reported that the American Ice Company had obtained a permanent injunction from the Supreme Court restraining certain of the ex-dealers from engaging in the retail ice trade.[15] In late 1909 these covenants were attacked under the New York antitrust statute, but this specific charge was dropped since most of the contracts had expired or were shortly due to expire.[16]

The ice trust had other more ruthless ways of crushing competition. One story reported in the *Times* told of the persecution of independent ice dealer W.A. Wynne. The steamer *Norwich* twice smashed all the ice in front of his place of business. The boat was equipped for this very purpose.[17]

The ice trust's alliance with the Tammany city government seems to have played a key role in eliminating stubborn competitors. One ice dealer, Richard Foster, paid over $2,000 a year to the city for his docking privilege. After he refused to sell to Morse, this privilege was revoked and his ice bridge was cut four times by the Dock Department on the excuse that it obstructed snow dumping. When it was learned that there was to be an official inquiry about such treatment, the harassment stopped.[18] Other ice dealers were told to get out of their berths by the Dock Department, which claimed that the spots were needed for something else. They left, only to watch the ice trust move into the vacated berths.[19]

A further method by which the trust attempted to limit competition was by its strict resale rules to its large (lower price) customers.[20] Restaurants, ice-cream saloons, and liquor dealers were all told that if they sold so much as a pound of ice, even in an emergency, in the case of a contract it would be abrogated, and in the case of a cash customer, she would be left out in the cold.[21]

THE PRICE HIKE

In April 1900, a year after its formation, the ice trust arbitrarily doubled its price. For large customers, prices rose from 15¢ to 25¢ per 100 pounds, or $5 per ton. The small consumer was more severely hurt. Here prices rose from 25¢ to 60¢ per 100 pounds, with hints of further advances to come. In addition, households were informed that deliveries would be made only three times a week instead of daily. This was a special hardship since few refrigerators in private homes could hold a two-day supply of ice. The trust also eliminated the 5¢ and 10¢ chunk, the size most convenient for the poor.[22] (This was at a time when the *Times* cost a penny, the *Sunday Times*, 3¢.)

There appears to have been no cost justification for the doubling of prices. While the trust blamed the shortness of supply, *Ice and Refrigeration* refuted the cry of famine. This independent Chicago publication stated: "The much-talked of ice famine apparently exists only in the minds of would-be speculators."[23] The Hudson River crop was only slightly less than normal, and since the previous year's crop had been record breaking (4.3 million tons, or greater than the total New York City ice consumption), there was much left over. Combined with the Maine crop and the manufactured product, there was little shortage in 1900.[24]

Additional evidence attesting to the administered nature of the price rise comes from intercity comparisons. No city had as high a price as New York. In areas where competition existed, prices were little different from previous years. In Buffalo, Boston, Albany, and Bangor, there were no advances. Only in cities like New York and Philadelphia, where the ice trust was strong, did prices increase.[25]

The *Times* claimed that the trust had tried to limit the crop by cutting only fourteen- and twelve-inch ice, whereas ten-inch ice was usually cut, and by leaving much ice unharvested. The trust seems not to have permanently reduced the 1900 supply, however, for when prices returned to their former levels, as they shortly did, no ice shortage occurred in New York City.[26]

PUBLIC OUTCRY

The Tammany Connection

Public outcry against the price hike was strong and clamorous and had its effect. The quickness of the trust's retreat was probably caused by the immense public resentment over the price hike, especially when combined with the subsequent exposure of the trust's shady dealings. The trust did not drop its prices because of a sudden reawakening to its social responsibilities. Instead, the quickness of the price reduction is more explicable in terms of crude jawboning, with the bludgeon of state antitrust action clearly visible. But the responsibility lies with an aroused press and citizenry rather than with an alert and concerned government. Indeed, an important portion of the local government had already embraced the trust.

The public first learned of the connection between Tammany and the ice trust in the spring of 1899. On the day that "Boss" Richard Croker's personal representative, John F. Carroll, was to testify before the State Legislative Investigating Committee (the Mazet Committee), a newspaper ran a story charging that Carroll and others were American Ice Company stockholders. When questioned about it, Carroll refused to testify. "It is a personal matter," he said. "I decline to answer it." Boss Croker then took the stand and also initially declined to respond. It was disclosed, however, that Croker had once owned stock but no longer did. "I turned it over to another person." Q: "Who is that?" A: "In my family, my wife." Croker's wife, it was discovered, owned at least 150 shares, then worth some $40 a share. The family further owned substantial holdings of the Knickerbocker Ice Company of Philadelphia, which had joined the trust.[27] A year later, less than a month after the famed price hike, the mayor of New York, Robert A. Van Wyck, went on a pleasure trip to Maine, accompanied by John Carroll, both as guests of Charles W. Morse, head of the ice trust.[28] The *Times* editorialized, this excursion "cannot escape remark."[29]

Following on the heels of the price advance, a paper's (and people's) crusade began. The *Times* was silent for three weeks but then ran strong editorials against the "hoggish monopoly."[30] The *New York Evening Post* ran articles showing that municipal ice plants could be constructed to produce ice for delivery at 10¢ per 100 pounds.[31] But the most important action was taken by the *New York Journal*, leading newspaper of the Democratic party. It was the *Journal* that strongly asserted that the Tammany Democratic machine held large blocks of ice trust stock, and it was at the instigation of Randolph Hearst himself that the attorney general of New York began an investigation of the company. None of the criminal or civil cases initially brought against the American Ice Company ever amounted to anything, but the exposed facts had a sensational effect.[32]

In June 1900 an official stockholders' list was made public. Mayor Robert Van Wyck was shown to hold 2,660 shares of preferred stock and 3,325 shares of common stock, par value at $100 but selling at $48 in April and falling fast to a record low of $28 on the day after this announcement. It was further disclosed that Morse had let Van Wyck have the stock at "bed-rock price" (half of par) and, in effect, lent him the money with which to buy it![33] (Throughout this trying period there were continual, but false, rumors of the mayor's imminent retirement.)[34]

Another prominent name on the list was the mayor's brother, former judge Augustus Van Wyck, who had unsuccessfully opposed Theodore Roosevelt for governor of New York in 1898 and had been mentioned as a possible vice presidential candidate. It is of interest that Augustus had been touted as the eloquent champion of the movement against the trusts. Wrote the *Independent*: "His utterances against Trust monopolies and exactions are among the most valued campaign documents of his party."[35] The *Independent* felt that the ice scandal might prevent Augustus from being a delegate-at-large at the next convention, though they pointed out that Republican Thurston of Nebraska had recently been elected delegate-at-large upon the platform of denouncing the trusts at the same time that he was defending Standard Oil in court.[36]

Also on the stockholders' list were John Carroll, Boss Crocker's vicegerent, as well as numerous judges and dock commissioners Cram and Murphy. These two officials possessed the principal power to grant or refuse docking facilities to any (ice) firm in New York City. It is estimated that over 50 percent of the property suitable for docking in Manhattan was public or under their control. While Cram had sold his 100 shares of stock, Murphy still possessed his 200, worth close to $10,000 in April 1900.[37]

The scandal had its effect on Tammany. The *Independent* reported that Boss Croker and Carroll turned the Tammany delegation to Bryan and that out-of-city Democrats in New York were preparing to denounce the Ice Company in the coming state convention.[38] At that convention, Tammany did not dare assert itself.[39] In the city the *Times* ran headlines declaring: "Ice Trust's Action Alarms Tammany Men; Rank and File Fear the Effect on Public Sentiment."[40] The Van Wyck brothers were obviously in disfavor. At the subsequent mayoral election, the Tammany candidate was defeated by a "reform mayor," elected by the fusion of all other parties. Interestingly, the major issue was not the ice scandal but the police scandal![41]

The response of the public to the trust's price hike and the Tammany involvement seems to have been substantial. Continually, the *Times* reported that the trust "is talked of everywhere, from the slums to the clubs, in Wall Street, and on street cars. Plans to thwart the combine are considered by the most lowly as well as by the most intelligent."[42] And, in general, the *Times* concluded, the trust is "now loathed by the community."[43]

The Nature of the Product

The public outcry against the trust was largely due to the particular nature of the product. Ice was more a necessity than a luxury in 1900. It was virtually essential for the preservation of foods, and doctors had already documented the relationship between infant mortality and drastic heat or ice shortages-- times when it was difficult for the poor to preserve milk. The poor spent a noticeable part of their income purchasing ice, a product often bought daily, at a price clearly visible. Further, ice seems to have been thought of not only as a vital necessity but also as something of a gift from nature, or a "free good." Wrote the *Times* : "To corner ice is very much like cornering air and water."[45]

It appears quite important that the product monopolized was ice. Wrote the *Outlook*:

> Had Tammany been prime movers in the organization of the wire and steel trust, their constituents would not have cared, for stock-jobbing operations do not really concern them, and the price of wire fences, or even wire nails, is to them a matter of supreme indifference. Had they been prominent in the management of the oil trust, they might incur a slight unpopularity, but even the price of oil concerns but little the voters of a great city to whom gas is the cheaper illuminant. But when the leaders of Tammany Hall became connected with the ice trust, and that trust advanced prices 100%, the wrath of the whole East Side was aroused against the hypocrisy as well as the extortion of its professed defenders.[46]

The sensitivity of the public to substantial increases in the price of ice is amply demonstrated by the outrage during the real shortages in 1906 and 1913. Though high prices during these years were prompted principally by demand and supply conditions (these were very warm winters), antitrust action was either brought or seriously considered in New York; Philadelphia; Washington, D.C.; Boston; Baltimore; and Toledo. Little came of these actions, save in Toledo, where a number of businessmen served thirty-seven days in jail.[47] Between 1906 and 1913 there was a great deal of careful attention given to the possibility of government-owned ice plants. In 1910 the mayor of Schenectady was elected partly on his program for "ice-at-cost." The shortage in 1913 prompted the city of New York to finance the Wentworth Report on municipal ice plants. While quite favorable to the construction of municipal plants, the report indicated that there was then only one in existence in the United States, in Weatherford, Oklahoma![48] With the gradual replacement of manufactured for natural ice, the fluctuations in the supply and price of ice decreased, as did the public clamor for some sort of governmental action.

The Hoggish Monopoly

The clamor raised against the ice trust in 1900 was due not to the fact that it possessed some degree of monopoly power but that it had used that power so arrogantly and brutally. The *Times*, which went out of its way to explain that it was only averse to "bad" trusts, attacked this "hoggish monopoly" that was "holding up" the community.[49] *Gunton's Magazine* (like the *Times* and most economists of the day) was not against trusts in general but was violently opposed to this "bungling burglar" that would bring discredit to its class. "The people," said *Gunton's*, "can be fooled for a while if the fooling is skillfully done, but not when it is bunglingly performed."[50]

The people obviously were not fooled, and their outcry helped secure the trust's quick defeat. Six weeks after the initial price hike, the trust agreed to sell 5¢ pieces but "would make no further concessions." The *Times* strongly denounced this "Public be Damned" attitude.[51] Two weeks later, following the official publication of the Tammany Ice Holdings, prices were quietly slashed from 60¢ to 40¢ per 100 pounds, which the *Times* editors called "a famous victory."[52] Within the week, prices were 25¢ for most sectors of the city as the trust met the price of any independent selling below the 40¢ rate.

In late June the *Times* ran an article under "Ice Plenty and Cheap" (prices still varied from 25¢ to 50¢), which contained this picturesque description of the small ice market:

> Ice was in evidence everywhere on the crowded east side streets. Each block had from one to half a dozen vendors on it, some with huge stores or several tons just from the bridges; others pushed carts which started out with a cake of ice and made journey after journey to the base of supplies as the vendors sold out. Everybody seemed to be buying ice. On stoops and in hallways were women with broods of children and a pitcher of ice-water which was drunk as if it was nectar. Housewives with pans and dishes and cloths left their domestic work to get a chunk of the gelid necessary for 5 or 10¢, and each cart or wagon had its following of children who scrambled for small ice refuse and greedily crushed it.[53]

ENTRY

By November the ice market was glutted.[54] The major cause for the surplus was, as might be expected, the entry of new firms lured by the trust's high prices and profits. Earlier that spring, when prices were high, the *Times* reported the formation of the Empire Ice Company with a manufacturing ice capacity of 600 tons per day and which did "not believe in the exorbitant price which the Trust is asking."[55] The Green Island Ice Company began building a wharf on Sedgwick Street and was expecting to undersell the trust during the summer.[56] The Bronx Consumers Ice Company was incorporated with capital of $100,000, and business purchasers of ice in Brooklyn were seriously considering forming their own "Anti-Trust Ice Company."[57]

The "impetuous rush to form new companies"[58] during "prosperous" times-the perennial fear of the ice industry-seems largely responsible for the oversupply in late 1900. That overentry, or overoptimism of the entrants, was a problem is attested to by company failures large enough to be reported in the *Times*. In the spring of 1901, for example, the Manhattan Ice Company, formed the previous June, employing forty men and serving two thousand customers, toppled.[59] Two years later the People's Co-Op Ice Company, formed in August 1900, with a capital stock of over $1 million, also went under.[60] Fortunately for the industry, while entry was relatively easy, so apparently, was exit.

The rapid entry into the ice industry during the period of high trust prices undoubtedly meant that the public's "famous victory" only speeded the inevitable. For all its ruthlessness, the trust was unable to raise entry barriers to a degree sufficient to allow a large monopoly profit. Its attempt to realize that profit brought a rash of new competitors, decreasing the price and eroding the trust's market position. As the *Times* predicted in the spring of 1900 "It may turn out that the hoggish monopoly has outwitted itself by its hoggishness."[61] "Its recklessness has endangered the health, if it has not insured the death, of the goose relied on to lay the golden eggs."[62]

Was the action of the trust's management in raising prices and inviting entry and condemnation really so irrational? For the longterm health and viability of the American Ice Company, the move was clearly unfortunate. The troubles of the company "really date to the outburst of public condemnation and disfavor in 1900."[63] The stock, selling at $49 in the spring of 1900, fell to $4¾ in 1903 during the general stock market decline.[64] Reported profits dropped from close to a million dollars in 1900, to $650,000 in 1901, to a *deficit* of $162,000 in 1902.[65] The American Ice Company was clearly in dire straits. *Ice and Refrigeration* reported in the spring of 1903: "If a second cool summer with limited demand for ice should come, no holding company scheme could save the big 'ice trust' from dissolution."[66]

CHARLES W. MORSE

While the company and common owners of the stock were severely hurt by the ice trust's attempted "hold-up" of the community, the president of the corporation certainly was not. Though an identity of interests between the owners and controllers of a corporation is sometimes assumed, in this case, what was good for Charles W.

Morse was not very good for the American Ice Company. While even Mayor Van Wyck lost money[67] on this weirdly overcapitalized venture (most of the $60 million capitalization was pure "water"), Charlie Morse is reported to have withdrawn from the corporation in 1901 with over $12 million![68]

Since Morse played such a crucial role in the formation and actions of the ice trust, it is of interest to digress a bit and briefly examine his colorful and checkered career. Morse was far more of a promoter, speculator, and financial manipulator than he was a conservative or conventional businessperson. After his reign as "Ice King" at the turn of the century, he turned more intensively to shipping and banking. By 1907, through a series of brilliant operations, he managed to achieve something close to a monopoly of coastwise shipping from Bangor to Galveston and became known as "the Admiral of the Atlantic." The panic of 1907, however, found the Heinze-Morse banks at the storm center; an investigation resulted in Morse's indictment and conviction for false entries and the misapplication of funds.[69]

While Morse argued that "there is no one in Wall Street who is not daily doing as I have done,"[70] this "fat, squatty little man" with the "masterful inquiring eyes" was sentenced to a fifteen-year term in the Atlanta penitentiary. Every exertion by Morse's friends and relatives to secure a pardon or commutation of sentence from President Taft proved unavailing. Finally, in 1912 Harry Daugherty, later attorney general in the Harding cabinet, contracted with Morse for a retainer of $5,000 and promise of an additional $25,000 in case of success to secure his release. A commission of doctors examined Morse and reported he was suffering from Bright's disease and could not last the year. Taft reluctantly signed a pardon. However, Daugherty's fee remained unpaid, and the attorney general's office received information that before his examination, Morse had drunk a combination of soapsuds and chemicals calculated to produce the desired temporary effects. President Taft later charged he had been deluded in the whole affair, adding that the case "shakes one's faith in expert examination."[71]

In 1916 Morse again made news with a grandiose scheme for organizing an American transoceanic shipping combination. This assumed reality with the formation of a holding company, the United States Shipping Company. The company prospered during the war, but in the subsequent "war frauds" investigation Morse was again indicted. Before that case could be brought, he was further indicted on the charge of using the mails to defraud potential investors. Before this "mail frauds" case was complete, Morse was adjudged too ill to stand trial. He was placed under guardianship, declared too incompetent to handle his own affairs, and died some seven years later in his home town of Bath, Maine at the age of seventy-six.[72]

THE AMERICAN ICE COMPANY AFTER 1903

Morse and his immediate successor seemingly attempted to milk the corporation dry before the crisis of 1903 and the stockholders' revolt. Before that corporate emergency, the common public stockholder had been virtually powerless to take any action. She was unable to discover the actual ownership of the company (it took a court order to get the official listing during the 1900 Tammany-trust investigation), or the actual control (because of the numerous dummy directorates), or even the earnings of the trust. The *Times*, for example, gave this seemingly tongue-in-cheek account of the 1902 stockholders meeting "It was understood beforehand that the officers of the company would violate the precedent of the past annual meetings and submit a statement of the actual earnings of the company. The corporation regularly pays 6 percent annual dividend on preferred stock, 4 percent on common.... No precedents were violated however."[73]

The stockholders' meeting in 1903 was a very lively affair. The American Ice Company had just announced a deficit for the preceding year, and stock prices had broken to $4¾. A number of prominent stockholders charged, among other things, that the officers of the trust had declared dividends when there were no earnings, had paid unnecessarily liberal commissions for the sale of bonds, had purchased the Knickerbocker Steam Towage Company at an excessive price benefiting a few insiders in the trust's management, and had used the power of the trust to enhance their own holding in an independent ice company. It was from the pressure of these minority stockholders that an investigating committee, albeit a conservative one, was eventually formed to examine the charges and generally report on the condition of the company.[74]

The report of the stockholders investigating committee helped to document the extent of the trust's overcapitalization and corporate mismanagement. While capitalization had been reduced from $60 to $40 million, the committee reported that the company's real property was worth only $15 million and there was "nothing between this and the preferred stock." The $25 million in common stock, in other words, represented pure "good will."[75] (Note the irony.) The financial difficulties of the company were attributed largely to the payment of unearned dividends. The milking of the corporation was further attested to by the fact that 1903 marked the "first time in several years that the company made liberal expenditures" to improve its real estate.[76] Many of the other charges against the trust were seemingly not examined. Morse undoubtedly made things difficult by generally keeping no books and "destroying all records of deals soon after they were closed."[77]

In 1904 Wesley Oler took over as president of the American Ice Company. Oler was a friend of Morse and a member of the original trust, but he was a sound businessperson and stayed with the company for many years, making it a profitable, if not a growing, concern. Oler died in 1927, two years before the corporation reached its all-time peak sales of $20.8 million and all-time peak profits of $3.4 million. The firm was finally absorbed around 1960, with its sales still in the $15 to $18 million range.[78]

In 1905, Oler again reduced the company's capitalization, but book assets still remained largely "good will account, water rights, and patent rights." These became of less and less value as the natural ice properties were discarded and displaced by manufacturing plants. By the early twenties, virtually all of the business of the American Ice Company was in manufactured ice. Yet, it was well into the Depression before all the natural ice properties were written off.[79]

The American Ice Company made numerous attempts to diversify-into the distribution of coal and wood, the repair of wagons, the distillation of water, and so forth-- but the sale of ice continued to provide the vast majority of its revenues into the late twenties and thirties, when electric refrigeration became more common. In 1941 the American Ice Company was still the second largest distributor of manufactured ice in the country, with 50 percent of its $12 million gross sales coming from ice, the rest from fuel oil and laundry services.[80] Of interest in the diversification attempts of the company was the change in its charter made in 1907 to allow it to "acquire, own, equip, operate, and dispose of steamships."[81] This scheme, however, seems to have been quickly dropped when the "Admiral of the Atlantic" was indicted and sent to prison.

Probably the most intriguing episode of the Oler regime occurred in 1906 when a true ice shortage hit New York City, which still relied on the American Ice Company for about half its ice.[82] The general shortage was so acute that for a while, in September, the company was essentially without ice as its fully laden Maine schooners were fogbound in the Atlantic.[83] Prices, of course, were high that year, and the trust made handsome profits, but the company had obviously learned from its 1900 experience. In March, the trust announced its intent "to do everything possible to prevent an increase in public indignation."[84] In June the trust declared that, no matter what, families would not have to pay more than 40¢ per 100 pounds. If prices were to increase, the burden would be on hotels, stores, and other large customers. Further, the 10¢ piece (25 lbs.) would remain on sale.[85]

CONCLUSION

Like many turn-of-the-century trusts, the American Ice Company succeeded in gaining monopoly control over the market. The ice trust, however, had more problems than most in maintaining that position, in some part due to the high visibility and essential nature of the product, but primarily because of the easy entry into the industry. When the trust did abuse its limited economic power, raising prices and decreasing the services associated with the product, these actions proved quite detrimental to its own long-term welfare. (The long-term welfare of the corporation, however, was of no great concern to its early president, whose primary interest was in securing his own short-run profit.) Three years after its formation, the American Ice Company was on the brink of bankruptcy.

While the American Ice Company was only one of the many monopolies formed at the turn of the century, the ice trust was nevertheless a historical phenomenon of some singularity. Among other things, the disclosure of the Tammany-trust connection caused political ripples, and the newspaper crusade demonstrated the effectiveness of public outrage, especially when coupled with strong underlying economic forces. Basically, however, the year of the ice trust provided a unique, if not very pleasant, experience for many residents of New York City-- and a lot of money for Charles W. Morse.

FOR DISCUSSION

1. What was the true economic effect of the public outcry against the ice trust? What would have happened had there been none?

2. Does the nature of the product actually affect whether or not the government will interfere in a market? Is the public more likely to demand the regulation of consumer goods industries? Of conspicuous industries? Cite some examples.

3. Economists generally assume that corporations try to maximize profits. Is this a fruitful assumption? A valid one? Is it more or less likely to be accurate for small or large companies?

4. Can you name the president of IBM, GM, GE, or Exxon? Are corporate executives today less conspicuous than they were in 1900? Less identifiable with a specific company? Explain. What is the economic effect, if any?

5. What are the arguments for and against national (vs. state) incorporation laws? What is the purpose of having corporate charters?

6. Does it ever make sense for a profit-maximizing monopolist to price so high as to attract entry? Explain.

7. Should the government worry about horizontal mergers in industries with low entry barriers? Why or why not?

NOTES TO CHAPTER 19

1. J. W. Markham, "Survey of the Evidence and Findings on Mergers," in National Bureau of Economic Research, *Business Concentration and Price Policy* (Princeton, N.J.: NBER, 1955), pp. 141-82.
2. John Moody, *The Truth about Trusts* (New York: Moody Publishing, 1904), pp.4531-69.
3. Henry Seager and Charles Gulick, Jr., *Trust and Corporation Problems* (New York Arno, 1929), p. 61.

4. Moody, *The Truth about Trusts*, pp. 205-86.
5. *New York Times*, February 2, 1906.
6. "Some Facts on Present Conditions in the Ice Trade," *Ice and Refrigeration* (July 1906): 16.
7. *New York Times*, March 2, 1906.
8. John Moody, *Railroad and Corporate Securities*, annual, 1905-1915.
9. *New York Times*, May 6, 1900.
10. Richard O. Cummings, *The American Ice Harvests* (Berkeley University of California Press, 1949), p. 87.
11. Moody, *The Truth about Trusts*, pp. 227-28.
12. As late as 1913, Milwaukee officials estimated the cost of an efficient municipal ice plant at $150,000. Jeanie Wells Wentworth, *A Report on Municipal and Government Ice Plants in the United States and Other Countries* (New York: M. B. Brown, 1913), pp. 60-62.
13. Oscar Edward Anderson, Jr., *Refrigeration in America* (Princeton: Princeton University Press, 1953), p. 114.
14. *New York Times*, May 6, 1900.
15. "Ice Trade Notes," *Ice and Refrigeration* (February 1902): 54.
16. "Ice Trade Notes," *Ice and Refrigeration* (November 1909): 191.
17. *New York Times*, May 9, 1900.
18. Ibid., May 4, 1900.
19. Ibid., May 6, 1900.
20. Ibid.
21. Ibid., March 6, 1900.
22. Ibid., March 26, May 5, June 6, 1900.
23. Ibid., June 6, 1900.
24. *Ice and Refrigeration* (August 1901): 46.
25. Ibid., May 7, 1900.
26. Ibid., May 6, June 2, 1900.
27. Ibid., April 15,1899.
28. Ibid., May 4, 1900.
29. Ibid., May 5, 1900.
30. Ibid., March 26, May 7, May 8, 1900.
31. "Ice Trust Exactions," *The Outlook* May 19, 1900, p. 144.
32. "Ice and Politics," *The Independent*, May 31, 1900, p. 1331; Owen Wilson, "Admiral of the Atlantic Coast," *Worlds Work* (April 1907).
33. *New York Times*, June 3, June 10, 1900.
34. Ibid., June 12, 1900.
35. "Ice and Politics," *The Independent*, May 31, 1900, p. 1331.
36. Ibid.
37. *New York Times*, June 10, 1900.
38. "Ice and Politics," *The Independent*, May 31, 1900, p. 1332.
39. "Ice Trust in Politics," *The Outlook*, June 16, 1900.
40. *New York Times*, May 8, 1900.
41. "Robert A. Van Wyck," *Dictionary of American Biography* (New York: Charles Scribner's Sons, 1934).

42. *New York Times*, May 6, 1900.

43. Ibid., April 26, 1900.

44. Ibid., May 29, 1900.

45. Ibid., April 20, 1900.

46. "New York's Ice Trust," *The Outlook*, June 9, 1900, p. 328.

47. *New York Times*, June 26, June 29, July 4, July 7, July 13, 1906; "Ice Trade Notes," *Ice and Refrigeration* (April 1908): 209.

48. Wentworth, *A Report on Municipal and Government Ice Plants*, p. 66. The call for municipal plants in 1900 was cooled by the Tammany-trust connections.

49. *New York Times*, April 26, 1900.

50. "Ice Trust Outrage," *Gunton's Magazine*, June 1900, pp. 515-19.

51. *New York Times*, May 16, May 20, 1900.

52. Ibid., June 8, 1900.

53. Ibid., June 29, 1900.

54. Ibid., November 15, November 18, 1900.

55. Ibid., May 9, 1900.

56. Ibid.

57. *New York Times*, May 10, 1900.

58. "Ice Trade Notes," *Ice and Refrigeration* (August 1906): 59.

59. *New York Times*, April 23, 1901.

60. Ibid., October 23, 1903 .

61. Ibid., April 26, 1900.

62. Ibid., May 7, 1900.

63. American Ice Company Stockholders Committee Report, 1903, quoted in Moody's *Manual of Industrial and Miscellaneous Securities*, 1904.

64. *Wall Street Journal*, October 24, 1903, quoted in Moody, *Truth about Trusts*, p. 479.

65. Moody, *Truth about Trusts*, p. 227.

66. "Ice Trade Notes," *Ice and Refrigeration* (May 1903): 197.

67. The mayor sold all his stock in June 1900 at a slight loss (*New York Times*, November 10, 1900).

68. See Wilson, "Admiral of the Atlantic"; also "Water Still Freezes," *Fortune*, May 1933.

69. "Charles W. Morse," *Dictionary of American Biography* (New York: Charles Scribner's Sons, 1934).

70. "Current Literature," February 1910, p. 153, quoted in *Dictionary of American Biography*.

71. *New York Times*, November 16, 1913, quoted in *Dictionary of American Biography*.

72. "Morse," *Dictionary of American Biography*.

73. *New York Times*, March 12, 1902.

74. Ibid., March 11, April 29, 1903; "Ice Trade Notes," *Ice and Refrigeration* (April 1903): 163.

75. "Ice Trade Notes," *Ice and Refrigeration* (January 1904): 59.

76. Ibid.; *New York Times*, November 21, 1903.

77. John E. MacDonald tried to sue Morse for $200,000 in 1904. The above is from Morse's testimony. See *New York Times*, October 25, 1904; ``Ice Trade Notes,'' *Ice and Refrigeration* (November 1904): 188.

78. Moody's, and then Poor's *Manuals of Corporate Securities* 1900-1960.

79. Moody's *Manual of Railroad and Corporate Securities* 1904, 1905, 1912, 1924; "Water Still Freezes," *Fortune*, May 1933.

80. Moody's (Poor's), 1941.

81. Ibid., 1907.

82. *New York Times*, September 24, 1906.

83. Ibid., September 23, 1906.

84. Ibid., March 14, 1906.

85. Ibid., June 10, 1906.

VI POLICY

INTRODUCTION

While most of the essays in this book have some bearing on policy matters, those in this section focus specifically on policy issues. However, these chapters are not intended to prescribe correct policy. Instead they are designed to help illuminate basic postulates, normative aspects, and the general approach of microeconomic theory.

The first two chapters emphasize that people respond to government policy-- they "move last."

Chapter 20 examines the difference between food supplements and cash transfers. Microeconomic theory implies that there may actually be no difference at all. This chapter describes the assumptions required to reach that interesting conclusion.

Chapter 21 discusses the notion of risk compensation. When a safety improvement is made, an individual is able to take more risks. Such actions increase utility, but the overall level of safety is not raised as much as if there had been no offsetting behavior. The possibility of a substantial compensatory response must be taken into account when determining optimal public policy.

The next essay contrasts risk avoiding individuals (Nervous Nellies) with risk seekers (Dangerous Dans). The latter group are among the last both to use safety devices and to buy insurance protection. This fact provides one possible justification for mandatory safety requirements and/or mandatory insurance.

Chapter 23 asks a fundamental, normative question: How should we determine whether physicians are geographically maldistributed? Similar questions could be asked about the spatial appropriateness of police patrols, fire stations, coast guard vessels, ambulances, or even public libraries. This chapter explores the nature of Pareto optimality compared to other, potentially more equitable, ideals. The purpose of the chapter is not to provide answers but to encourage thought about the proper criteria for judging outcomes.

20 FOOD SUPPLEMENTS

In the 1970s the Colombian government instituted a food-supplement program in Bogota designed to raise the nutritional intake of participating families up to minimum standards. As explained in nutritional texts, the program followed the precept that "the supplementary feedings provided should be calculated on the basis of the amounts needed to cover the deficiencies of energy and nutrients."[1] Thus, if a typical lactating woman was currently consuming 1,500 calories per day and the recommended minimum dietary allowance was 2,500, the program would provide a supplement of 1,000 calories per day-- an amount just sufficient to make up the deficit.

The expectations of the program appear to have been misplaced. While caloric intake increased, the increase was significantly less than the amount of the food supplement. This was the case even though every member of the family received supplements. Interestingly, this result should have been expected even if-- perhaps particularly if-- the supplements were the exact kinds of foods normally purchased by the family.

In-kind supplements are often similar to equivalent income supplements. A little introspection helps convince most people of this fact. Assume that you typically go to twenty movies a year at $6.00 per ticket. Now imagine that the government decides to send you, at the beginning of each year, fifteen free tickets good for movies of your choice. You may attend more movies, but it is doubtful that you will increase the number to thirty-five. Instead, you will use some of the fifteen free tickets to attend movies you would have gone to see anyway. You can, and an economist says you rationally should, treat the free tickets as equivalent to receiving $90.

The same principle held true for the low-income families in Bogota. The food supplement allowed them to decrease their food *purchases* and use that money to buy other needed goods and services. Given the food supplement, the family altered its purchasing patterns in order to increase its well-being.

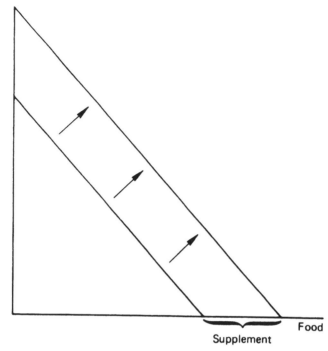

Figure 20-1

The conclusion that in-kind transfers are equivalent to income supplements follows directly from the microeconomic model. In jargon, the gift of movie tickets or food does not affect the relative prices of goods. The marginal opportunity cost of purchasing tickets or food-- the cost in terms of other goods forgone-- is unchanged. There is no "substitution effect," only an income effect. Figure 20-1 shows such an effect on the family's budget constraint.

If the opportunity cost of marginal food purchases were altered, this would produce a substitution effect. Lowering the price of every item of food the consumer decides to purchase, for example, will increase food consumption more than would an income transfer of equivalent value. U.S. public housing subsidies change relative prices and are thereby different than income supplements.

If in-kind supplements are similar to equivalent income transfers, this has important policy implications. It means that the U.S. food stamp program is primarily an income redistribution scheme. The analysis may also imply that the exact form of foreign aid-- whether economic, military, or foreign exchange-- should make little difference to the recipient country. Some economists have even suggested that educational programs such as Head Start are tantamount to direct cash transfers.

Public compensatory education programs essentially increase the "endowments" of some children in poorer families. The increase in the wealth of these families produced by the increase in endowments would induce a redistribution of parental time and expenditures away from the children being compensated and toward their other children and themselves. That is, the induced own "compensatory programs" by parents help defeat the intent of public programs. Although family wealth rises by the full extent of the increase in the endowment of a child participating in a compensatory program, the total (parental included) investment in that child may only rise by a small fraction of the increase in his endowment. The fraction depends on the contribution of his endowment to family wealth, the family's income elasticity of demand for child quality, and so forth.[2]

THE ASSUMPTIONS

Many assumptions are required to equate in-kind transfers with cash supplements. Some are not always realistic. First, the decisionmaker is assumed to have a unique, stable utility function that she singlemindedly attempts to maximize. In the real world, of course, individuals may fall into habits and routines that are costly to change. These may be differentially affected by the form of the supplement.

More importantly, the appropriate unit of analysis is often a group rather than an individual. Some individuals do not have well-defined tastes; for most groups it is impossible to have a set of transitive preference orderings.[3] In the real world, the provision of specific goods to the household may well affect intrafamilial purchase compromises differently than would a gift of cash. Providing military goods to a foreign government may strengthen the military's position in the overall budget struggle vis-a-vis nonmilitary applicants.

Second, product and market information are assumed to be complete. For the Head Start program to be equivalent to a cash gift, parents must have not only full control over family resource allocations but also complete knowledge about their children's educational activities, outside as well as inside the home.

In the real world, supplements may influence people's information and tastes. In the Bogota program, when food supplements were combined with nutritional education, the increase in caloric consumption was significantly larger than the additive effect of each policy pursued separately.[4]

Third, transaction costs are assumed to be negligible. For food supplements to be tantamount to income transfers, the recipient should have the option of costlessly selling the food at market value. In the real world, of course, selling costs, particularly for individual households, can be large. Selling food stamps in the United States is illegal, and while black markets develop, the price of the stamp is materially less than its face value.[5] Figure 20-2 shows the effect on the family's budget constraint if food supplements can be sold at only one-half their market price.

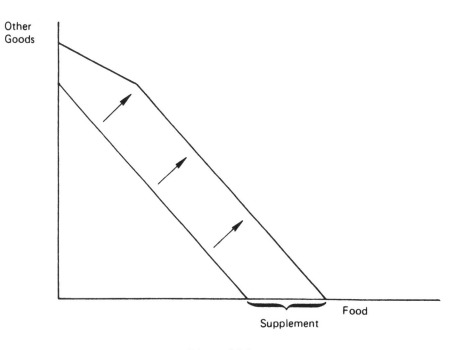

Figure 20-2

The inability to sell food supplements at market prices and the transaction costs in terms of finding a buyer and negotiating a sale, represent the main reasons that economists perceive such in-kind transfers as being potentially different from income.[6] Assume that food is a homogeneous good. If a family receives X pounds of supplemental food per period and willingly consumes X pounds or more, economists assume it is unconstrained by the in-kind transfer; the gift of food is identical to supplementary income.[7] If, however, the family consumes fewer than X pounds (i.e., no food is *purchased*), the gift may be a constraining one and, making the usual economic assumptions, may be less valued by the recipients than the market-equivalent amount of money.

Food, of course, is heterogeneous. If there are resale transactions costs, then, ex post, the economist can assume the recipient is not constrained only if the post-supplement consumption of each and every commodity and variety equals or exceeds the in-kind transfers. In Bogota, the food supplement program decreased fat consumption; this was largely because powdered skim milk was provided, whereas recipients would usually have preferred to drink liquid whole milk.[8]

CONCLUSION

There is a saying in the environmental sciences that "you can't do just one thing." The implication is that all aspects of nature are interconnected; a change in one area produces reactions elsewhere. In-kind transfers also cause responses. A family receiving an in-kind supplement will respond by readjusting its purchases to increase its well-being.

As an empirical analysis of the U.S. food stamp program concluded:

> The main finding is that the naive view that food stamps are restricted, in-kind transfers is largely incorrect, when applied to actual recipient households. Instead the program primarily provides general purchasing power. . . Consequently, the program is much more effective as a provider of income than as a stimulus to the demand for food.[9]

In-kind transfers, however, are rarely *identical* to an equivalent amount of supplemental income. That implication of simple microeconomic theory requires strong assumptions that are not usually satisfied in the real world. In U.S. studies, for example, an additional dollar of bonus food stamps generally has a significantly greater impact on food consumed at home than does a dollar increase in money income.[10] In Bogota, while food consumption increased by far less than the amount of the supplement, the increase would have been even smaller had the supplement been in terms of money rather than food.[11]

FOR DISCUSSION

1. "A gift should be something the recipient would not have bought for herself. Otherwise, you might as well give cash." Explain and comment.

2. For the same cost, can government increase food consumption more by lowering the price of food than it can by giving the food away for free?

3. Do you believe parents would spend significantly less (educational) time with those of their children receiving Head Start help? Why or why not?

4. "To determine the effect of an in-kind supplement, all one needs to know is income elasticities." Comment.

5. If in-kind transfers are primarily income supplements, why are taxpayers typically more favorably disposed to the former than the latter?

PRICES AND CHOICES

NOTES TO CHAPTER 20

1. A. V. Bailey and A. Raba, "Supplementary Feeding Programmes," in G. H. Beaton and J. M. Bengoa, eds., *Nutrition in Preventive Medicine* (Geneva: World Health Organization, 1976), p. 301.
2. Gary S. Becker and Nigel Tomes, "Child Endowments and the Quantity and Quality of Children," *Journal of Political Economy* 84 (August 1976): 5156.
3. Kenneth Arrow, *Social Choice and Individual Values* (New York: Wiley, 1951).
4. Catherine Overholt, S.G. Sellers, J.O. Mora, B. de Paredes and M. G. Herrera, "The Effects of Nutritional Supplementation on the Diets of Low-Income Families at Risk of Malnutrition," *American Journal of Clinical Nutrition* 36 (December 1982): 1153-61.
5. Maurice MacDonald, *Food Stamps and Income Maintenance* (New York: Academic Press, 1977), p. 57.
6. Edwin Mansfield, *Microeconomics: Theory and Applications*, 4th ed. (New York: Norton, 1982), p. 69; Steven Call and William Holahan, *Microeconomics*, 2nd ed. (Belmont, CA: Wadsworth Publishing Company, 1983), pp. 50-52.
7. MacDonald, pp. 52-59.
8. Overholt et al.
9. MacDonald, p. 58.
10. Ben Senauer and Nathan Young, "The Impact of Food Stamps on Food Expenditures: Rejection of the Traditional Model," *American Journal of Agricultural Economics* 68 (February 1986): 38; Christine Ranney and John Kushman, "Cash Equivalence, Welfare Stigma and Food Stamps," *Southern Economic Journal* 53 (April 1987): 1011-1027. However, evidence from Puerto Rico and Panama suggest that food stamps and donated food are virtually equivalent to a cash transfer. Barbara Devaney and Thomas Fraker, "Cashing out Food Stamps: Impacts on Food Expenditures and Diet Quality," *Journal of Policy Analysis and Management* 5 (1986): 725-41; Robert Moffitt, "Estimating the Value of an In-Kind Transfer: The Case of Food Stamps," *Econometrica* 57 (March 1989): 385-409; David Franklin, Marielouise Harrell, and Jerry Leonard, "Income Effects of Donated Commodities in Rural Panama," *American Journal of Agricultural Economics* 69 (February 1987): 115-22.
11. Overholt et al.

21 RISK COMPENSATION

My son is five years old. Though he cannot swim, he is wise enough never to go into water over his head-- unless he is in an inner tube or life vest. Then he is willing to venture into deep water.

The wearing of a flotation device alters my son's behavior. He is safer at any particular depth while in a life vest, but once he puts one on, he places himself in more inherently dangerous situations. This natural and rational response is well understood by safety officials. Indeed, they believe that the change in behavior may be so great that they ban flotation devices at many public recreational areas, including pools, ponds, and lakes, as well as the ocean.

The notion of risk compensation is a familiar one to the economist. It is merely a restatement of the general theme that incentives matter-- that changing the expected costs or benefits of various activities affects behavior. The concept of risk compensation says that making things safer often induces people to take more risks. This does not imply that the overall level of safety will not be raised, only that it will not be increased as much as if compensatory actions had not been taken. There are myriad examples of risk compensation-- of individuals behaving more cautiously in dangerous situations, less cautiously in safe ones. Soldiers walk more gingerly when crossing minefields than when crossing wheat fields. Motorists drive more carefully on wet roads than on dry ones; in icy conditions, they take curves more slowly if driving with regular tires rather than with studded tires.[1] Circus performers take fewer chances when practicing without nets.

The improvement in razors over the last one hundred years has increased not only the amount of shaving but also the speed of shaving. Anyone who has tried to shave with a knife or even with a straight razor knows how exceedingly dangerous that can be. The safety razor has enabled people to shave more often and less carefully.

The birth control pill, by reducing the risk of unwanted pregnancy, is credited with increasing sexual activity among Americans. By providing the pill, parents hope to avert pregnancy in their teenage daughters but fear promoting and condoning promiscuity. In contrast, AIDS, by increasing the risks associated with casual sex, has altered lifestyles among high-risk groups.

Experience and training usually reduce the risk associated with particular activities; yet experienced and trained individuals tend to place themselves in hazardous situations more often than inexperienced individuals do. Beginner ski slopes are populated by novices. Good skiers are more likely to attempt the more dangerous-- and more exciting-- hills.

Increased skill and improvements in safety enable the individual to undertake more of the activities she prefers but formerly avoided because they were too dangerous. Improved braking ability allows speed to be increased. The introduction of road and automobile lighting permitted automobiles to be driven at night.

In contact sports, protection of the body allowed participants to hit with greater force without sustaining injury, enabling them to inflict more punishment on their adversaries. Padded gloves let boxers swing harder without breaking their fists, permitting them to pummel opponents with more brute force. Football helmets "did such a good job of protecting the wearer that tackling and blocking techniques (spearing and butting) were adopted using the head and helmet to receive the brunt of the initial impact."[2]

In baseball, the introduction of the batting helmet in 1952 decreased serious head injuries (1951 was the last year a player in professional baseball was killed by a pitch). It also changed player behavior. Hit-by-pitch totals increased significantly (see Table 21-1). "One can see why that would happen; the batting helmet would diminish both the pitcher's fear of killing someone, and the batter's fear of being killed, which would cause more players to crowd the plate and more pitchers to work inside."[3]

MAGNITUDE OF THE RESPONSE: HYPOTHESES

The size of the compensatory response to safety regulations will depend on the particular circumstances. Some suggestions follow concerning factors that may affect the magnitude of any offsetting behavior.

The compensatory response to safety regulation is likely to be large when the perceived reduction in risk is large.
Conversely, if the actual reduction in risk is small, and perceptions are accurate, the absolute amount of offsetting behavior is likely to be small. For example, if only one aspect of many important ones is made safer (e.g., a living room chair is made less flammable, the side vehicle door is made more crash resistant), it is unlikely to lead to significant changes in behavior. The risk-taking behavior of airline pilots is unlikely to increase substantively if their seat-belt anchors are strengthened or their cushions made more flame retardant. There will be little noticeable impact on overall parental supervision if the already minuscule chance of their children choking on

Table 21-1. Hit Batsmen per 100 Games (*helmets introduced 1952*).

	American League	National League
	(5-year averages)	
1932-36	27	33
1937-41	25	30
1942-46	26	28
1947-51	32	32
1952-56	41	36
1957-61	42	38
1962-66	42	45
1967-71	47	43
	(20-year averages)	
1932-51	29	31
1953-72	43	41
Percentage increase	48%	32%

toys or swallowing them is reduced by alterations in toy design.

Individuals act cautiously to reduce property loss as well as to increase human safety. Where property protection is important, changing the injury risk alone may not result in a large compensatory response. Researchers have had difficulty finding evidence of offsetting driver behavior following the mandating of seat-belt use in Canada.[4] One reason may be that the overall costs of risk taking were only marginally reduced. Property loss was largely unaffected. The wearing of seat belts has little effect on the likelihood of collision and does not decrease vehicle damage once a crash has occurred. Moreover, seatbelts do not eliminate the possibility of serious injury. Thus the overall size of the compensatory response might be expected to be small. The researchers may also have simply missed some compensatory actions actually taken. They examined only a few behaviors (e.g., following distance and average speed). It is therefore not surprising that little compensatory response was found. But there are a large number of other ways that drivers might alter their "risk taking" (e.g., signaling and car maintenance). By analogy, it would be difficult to detect significant changes in consumption caused by small income increases, particularly if one studied only the purchases of milk, shoes, and records.

Whatever the actual reduction in risk, the individual must perceive a change for safety regulations to elicit any offsetting behavior. If the driver is unaware that the windshield is more shatterproof or that the steering column has become collapsible, no compensatory response is to be expected. If, however, the improvements in safety are substantial, the motorist may eventually become aware of the general reduction in risk without ever needing to understand the underlying cause. Some long-run compensatory response is then plausible.

The compensatory response is likely to be large when desired, close substitutes exist.

Mandatory standards may simply require what one is already doing or intending to do. The net effect of the law is then negligible. Or the requirement may be to do something similar. The compensatory response may then be large; the law again has little net safety value. A landlord about to purchase photo-electric smoke detectors will refrain from doing so if the city passes an ordinance compelling the installation of ionization detectors. The landlord may provide no detectors at all if the city requires a sprinkler system.

On the other hand, suppose a property owner has no intention of protecting neighborhood children from the "attractive nuisance" caused by her unfilled swimming pool. In such circumstances, a requirement for fencing can reduce hazards, with little offsetting response. There is little possible substitution effect. The owner has not planned to do much to increase safety, so there is little she can eliminate.

The compensatory response is likely to be large when the benefits from increased risk taking are large.

Increased vehicle safety may result in higher and more variable speeds. This is most likely if speed provides great thrills or time is very valuable. When the opportunity costs of being careful are high-if there are large benefits from risk taking-there is likely to be a significant compensatory response.

The costs of safety are often substantial. Caution as a batter may mean bailing out on inside curve balls and failing to hit pitches on the outside of the plate. Being careful as a skier means going slower and skiing down less exciting slopes.

The compensatory response is likely to be larger in the long run compared to the short run.

The response to changed circumstances is typically larger over longer time periods (just as demand and supply curves are more elastic in the long run). In the short run, certain factors are fixed; individuals temporarily may be locked into past decisions. Even vast improvements in the fire services can be expected to have very little short-run impact on the flammability of the existing housing stock.

Individual conduct can usually be altered more readily than can capital equipment,[5] but even an attempt to change behavior can have accompanying costs. Past actions become habitual, and habits are often difficult to break. In addition, risk perceptions may be slow to respond to changes in the environment. There are empirical indications that the repeal of helmet-use laws and the subsequent reduction in helmet wearing increased caution by cyclists, but this offsetting effect was substantially greater over longer time periods.[6] Of course, the effect was never so large as to eliminate the extra danger caused by the lack of adequate head protection.

The compensatory response is likely to be larger for interventions reducing the probability compared to the severity of accidents.
There is empirical evidence that criminal behavior is more influenced by changes in the probability of apprehension and conviction than by changes in the severity of punishment. Drunk driving is better deterred by increasing the likelihood of arrest than by the threat of Draconian punishments.[7] Similarly, reductions in the probability of an accident may invoke more offsetting behavior than equal reductions in the likelihood of serious injury once an accident has occurred. Improvements in brakes and tires may cause more compensatory response than similarly (ex ante) beneficial improvements in energy-attenuating design or hospital trauma units.

The compensatory response is likely to be larger when the safety improvement affects the individual or her family rather than strangers.
The well-being of oneself and one's loved ones typically represents a larger component of the utility function than the health and happiness of strangers. Safety regulations that primarily decrease the risk to others may not significantly affect the decisionmaker and will therefore elicit little compensatory response. Automobile drivers are unlikely to alter their behavior if hood ornaments are made more flexible to reduce the danger to pedestrians. Few airline pilots or bus drivers will take more chances if passenger protection is increased.

Among strangers, the compensatory response will be larger among groups that elicit a stronger feeling of protection (e.g., children, the disabled). If the hazards they face are decreased, offsetting behavior is likely. Lifeguards do not need to be as alert if children are relegated to shallow pools. Motorists can speed through school zones during mandated classroom holidays.

OTHER INDIRECT EFFECTS

The repercussions of mandatory safety regulations or training programs are varied. As opposed to risk-compensatory behavior, some responses may actually increase the total level of safety.

Mandated safety features may remind an individual of the hazards she faces, prompting her to take needed precautions.[8] The seat-belt buzzer may prod the forgetful and the lazy not only to buckle up but also to drive with care. The installation of smoke alarms may awaken residents to existing fire hazards, inspiring them to replace the old stove or rewire the house.

Training programs, by increasing competence in particular circumstances, may increase the likelihood of individuals voluntarily exposing themselves to certain hazards. This is risk compensation. But an aspect of training is to teach people how to avoid dangerous situations. Pedestrians are taught to cross only at intersections. Deep-sea divers are enjoined against going down alone. Swimming instructors advise not to swim where the current is strong.

Federally mandated safety standards have raised the price of automobiles.[9] This may reduce the demand for new cars, causing people to travel less or take other forms of transportation. These substitutes may be more safe or less safe than the forgone automobiles. Bicycles, mopeds, motorcycles, and older cars are probably less safe. But safety may be substantially increased if, instead of motoring, individuals walk, take the subway or bus, or do not travel at all.

Requiring safety equipment may increase the demand for complementary safety devices. Unhelmeted hockey players may not wear mouthguards for the sake of appearances. Mandated helmets, by sufficiently concealing the head and face, eliminate the short-run vanity reasons for refusing adequate tooth protection. Hip pads may prove too constraining to the unencumbered rugby player. But they provide little competitive disadvantage to otherwise fully equipped football combatants.

CONCLUSION

In the economic model, the goal of the individual is to maximize her utility. Safety is but one aspect of the utility function. The individual's goal is not to maintain a particular level of risk,[10] but to garner the highest total utility. The rational person ensures that the last dollar spent on all goods and activities brings the same additional benefit. The gift of additional safety (e.g., improved roads) or the requirement of additional safety purchases (e.g., airbags) affects the current equilibrium. Since the individual "moves last," she will make adjustments, shifting her purchases and actions to attain a new utility maximization.

The theory of risk compensation says that decreasing hazards typically lead the individual to take more risks. The reduction in hazard reduces the cost of risk taking or the gain from caution. The individual responds to these changed incentives.

While microeconomic theory describes individual behavior, any empirical testing is typically done in the aggregate. A decrease in commodity price may not actually induce all or even most consumers to buy more of the product, but enough will, so the total amount demanded will increase. Similarly, not everyone is expected to exhibit an identifiable compensatory response to mandated safety requirements, but enough should, so there may be a noticeable effect in toto.

The size of the effect depends on many factors. This chapter suggests a few possibilities. The total compensatory response will be larger the greater the perceived reduction in risk and the more the individual has previously spent to reduce that risk. Any offsetting behavior will be larger in the long run, for interventions that reduce the probability rather than the severity of injury, and for safety measures that affect oneself and one's family rather than strangers.

The potential policy dangers of a compensatory response are greatest when the offsetting activity not only exposes oneself to increased hazard but also endangers others. Less cautious driving, for example, increases risks to pedestrians, cyclists, and other motorists, as well as to the driver herself. Football helmets enable wearers not only to take more risks with their own heads (e.g., crashing into goal posts) but also to use their heads more destructively against opponents. By contrast, less cautious shaving imposes few direct costs on others.

Economists delight in exploring and exposing the unintended consequences of policy actions. They emphasize that such responses may be varied. It is certainly possible that some of the indirect effects of safety regulations may be to further reduce the risk. For example, safety requirements may serve to remind individuals of the hazards they face, or they may increase the demand for complementary safety products.

However, the typical response to safety improvements is likely to be offsetting rather than additive. As the probability or cost of accident declines, people are able to behave less carefully. They act to increase their utility while decreasing their safety. The magnitude of the compensatory response depends on the situation and must be taken into account when determining optimal policy.

FOR DISCUSSION

1. What has been the effect of computerized word processing on the cost of initial typing mistakes? On the speed of typists and the number of initial mistakes made?

2. Why are "speed bumps" put in certain roadways? Don't these increase the danger for vehicles traveling at any particular velocity? If the placement of speed bumps makes sense, what does this imply about the expected size of the compensatory response?

3. Relate moral hazard to risk compensation.

4. "Drivers, knowing their cars are safer, get cocky and knock-off more pedestrians and bikers."[11] Is this a reasonable description of the economist's notion of risk compensation?

5. In September 1967, all drivers in Sweden were obliged to change from driving on the left hand side of the road to driving on the right. In September, the traffic fatality rate fell by half. By November, it was back to normal.[12] Discuss.

6. Which individuals are likely to display the greatest compensatory response to safety standards? Small children? Adolescents? Careful planners?

7. Smokers who switch to lower yield cigarettes or who cut down on the number of cigarettes consumed increase their intake of mainstream smoke from each cigarette.[13] Relate to risk compensation.

8. In the winter, motor vehicle accidents per mile driven are higher than in the summer months. But fatalities per mile driven are substantially lower.[14] Relate to risk compensation. Are there other possible explanations?

9. Cite three examples of increased hazards reducing risk-taking behavior; of decreased hazards increasing risk-taking.

10. Describe two methods by which the theory of compensatory response might be tested empirically.

NOTES TO CHAPTER 21

1. K. Rumor et al., "Driver Reaction to a Technical Safety Measure-- Studded Tires," *Human Factors* 18 (1976): 443-54.
2. James G. Garrick, "Injuries are Complex; So Are Solutions," *New York Times*, September 28,1986, p. 513.
3. Bill James, *Baseball Abstract* (New York: Ballantine Books, 1985), p. 133.
4. L. Evans, P. Wasielewski, and C.R. von Buseck, "Compulsory Seat Belt Use and Driver Risk-Taking Behavior," *Human Factors* (1982): 41-48; Adrian Lund and Paul Zador, "Mandatory Belt Use and Driver Risk Taking," *Risk Analysis* 4 (1984): 41-53.
5. David Hemenway, *Monitoring and Compliance: The Political Economy of Inspection* (Greenwich, CT: JAI Press, 1985).
6. John D. Graham and Younghee Lee, "Behavioral Response to Safety Regulation: The Case of Motorcycle Helmet-Wearing Legislation," *Policy Sciences* 19 (1986): 253-73.
7. H. Laurence Ross, *Deterring the Drunk Driver* (Lexington, MA: Lexington Books,1 1981).
8. P. Slovic and Baruch Fischhoff, "Targeting Risk," *Risk Analysis* (1982): 226.
9. Robert Crandall, Howard Greenspecht, Theodore Keeler, and Lester Lave, *Regulating the Automobile* (Washington, DC: Brookings, 1986).
10. G. Wilde, "A Theory of Risk-Homeostasis: Implications for Safety and Health," *Risk Analysis* 2 (1982): 209-55.
11. Jerry Flint, Reviews of Robert W. Crandall, Howard Greenspecht, Theodore Keeler and Lester Lave, "Regulating the Automobile," *Regulation* (September 1986): 51.
12. John Adams, "Smeed's Law, Seat Belts and the Emperor's New Clothes," in Leonard Evans and Richard C. Schwing, *Human Behavior and Traffic Safety* (New York: Plenum Press, 1985).
13. Neal Benowitz, Peyton Jacob, Lynn Mozlowski, and Lisa Yu, "Influence of Smoking Fewer Cigarettes on Exposure to Tar, Nicotine and Carbon Monoxide," *New England Journal of Medicine* 315 (1986): 1310-13.
14. Leonard Evans, "Human Behavior Feedback and Traffic Safety," *Human Factors* 27 (1985): 555-76.

22 NERVOUS NELLIES

Should motorists be required to buckle up? Should motorcyclists be forced to wear helmets? Should landlords be required to install smoke detectors? These issues are controversial. There may be no "correct" answer concerning the appropriateness of such mandatory safety regulations. Many arguments exist on both sides.

Two well-known and related reasons for safety regulations are the existence of externalities and moral hazard. Each person chooses the level of safety that balances her costs and benefits. An externality can exist if her failure to take safety precautions reduces the health or safety of others. Moral hazard occurs if insurance insulates her from the financial cost of accidents. If moral hazard and/or externalities are present, the individual may not sufficiently take the costs of carelessness into account, and she may not take sufficient care. By requiring the individual to exercise care, regulations can help restore behavior to the social optimum.

There are many reasons to resist the imposition of safety requirements. Regulations, for example, typically reduce individual liberty and freedom of choice. This essay is not designed to discuss all the pros and cons of safety legislation. Instead, its intent is to describe two related concepts that have relevance for the debate; these tend to provide additional support for mandatory safety regulations. The theories, termed "selective recruitment" and "propitious selection," are based on differences among individuals in their preference for risk.

SELECTIVE RECRUITMENT

Who wears their seat belts? Assume that individuals have different tastes for risk. At the extremes are "nervous nellies" who are highly risk avoiding and "dangerous dans" who are risk prone. Nervous nellies take all sorts of safety precautions; dangerous dans take few. Under these assumptions, risk-avoiding individuals--

nervous nellies-- will tend to wear their seat belts; they will also tend to drive cautiously. Conversely, the risk seekers-- dangerous dans-- will tend to do neither. Some theoretical considerations work in the opposite direction. For example, individuals who are hazardous drivers should, ceteris paribus, derive more benefit from buckling up, and thus be more prone to do so. In addition, according to the theory of risk compensation,[1] once an individual buckles up, the expected injury severity from a collision decreases, and the motorist may drive more recklessly.

Seat belt use has been studied extensively.[2] The evidence shows that belted motorists are less risky drivers than unbelted motorists. Belt wearers are less likely to tailgate and to drive drunk; they are less likely to commit traffic violations and to be involved in traffic accidents.

Studies also support the idea that safety belt users are risk avoiders, not only as motorists, but in other situations. For example, frequent belt users are less likely to smoke and more likely to exercise and visit the dentist regularly.[3]

In the 1970s and early 1980s, belt usage rates in the United States averaged about 14%. In late 1984 New York passed the first mandatory seat belt law; now the vast majority of Americans reside in states with such laws, and usage rates have risen to almost 50%. The newly-belted motorists tend to be below average risks. The process by which safer-than-average drivers switched to belt-wearing has been labelled "selective recruitment".[4]

Selective recruitment is a descriptive term for an observed empirical phenomenon. A possible theoretical explanation is based on differences in taste for risk. But whatever the reason, the fact is that additional drivers recruited to belt-wearing tend, on average, to be the safer ones from the pool of previously unbelted drivers. The nervous nellies seem to be the first to wear their seat belts. The drivers most at risk for injury are among the last to buckle up. Put another way, increasing belt usage appears likely to reduce serious injury and fatality at ever increasing rates.

Selective recruitment has clear policy relevance. It means that raising belt usage from 0% to 50% will have less impact on injury reduction than if 50% of motorists chosen at random become wearers. It also implies that increasing usage rates from 50% to 100% will more than double the life saving attributable to seat belt use.

Although not everyone may comply, regulation has the power to compel safer practices on the part of many who might not otherwise adopt them. Some of those whose taste for risk is higher and whose behavior is riskier-- those who need it most-- may be induced to follow the safety requirements.

PROPITIOUS SELECTION

A phenomenon related to selective recruitment has been noted in the insurance field and has been labelled "propitious selection."[5] The theory contrasts different people with different tastes for risks. Consider a simple model in which an individual can purchase a safety device and/or an insurance contract; owning the safety device does not alter the insurance premium. The theory suggests that very risk averse individuals (nervous nellies) will tend to purchase both the safety device and the insurance. Risk prone individuals (the dangerous dans) will tend to purchase neither.

Many factors influence the relationship between risk taking and insurance purchase. Two that work against the force of propitious selection are adverse selection and moral hazard.

The price of insurance is often based on an average rate for an entire class. Within each class, some potential insureds will be better-than-average risks while others are worse than average. The people who know they are worse than average will be most likely to desire the insurance contract. This is the adverse selection problem.[6]

Once a person purchases insurance, some of the possible losses will be reimbursed by the insurance company. Since she does not bear the full consequence of a calamity, she has less incentive to take precautions. This is the ex ante moral hazard problem.[7]

The implication of adverse selection is that those who buy the safety device become less likely to buy the insurance. Moral hazard suggests that those who buy the insurance become less likely to purchase the safety device. For any individual, the safety device and the insurance are partial substitutes. By contrast, propitious selection suggests that the individuals who purchase the safety device are likely to be risk avoiders and are thus likely to purchase the insurance.

Whether the forces for propitious selection are stronger than opposing forces is an empirical question. In many instances they seem to be. For example, an analysis of seat belt use in Iowa found that among injured motorists, those who were belted were more likely to be medically insured.[8]

Another investigation found that individuals who never drink-and-drive are more likely than other motorists to be covered by motor vehicle liability insurance.[9] Differences in preference for risk, rather than in income levels, is probably the reason for the relationship: while higher income motorists are more likely to be insured, they are also more likely to drink-and-drive. Holding constant income, education, age and other factors, the individuals who are risk avoiders-- e.g., who have yearly medical checkups, avoid food additives, carefully monitor their levels of alcohol intake, and don't smoke-- are more likely to have purchased the liability coverage.

Of course, other possible explanations exist for these findings. For example, insurers may effectively market their policies toward low-risk individuals, or experience rating may eventually lead to higher premiums for the more risk prone. An explanation consistent with propitious selection is that risk takers (dangerous dans) practice denial, and buying insurance would be an admission that the risk is a real one.

Whatever the reason, the empirical findings have policy relevance. Those most at risk for injury or loss are often the least likely to be insured. Their lack of insurance can impose financial costs on others-- necessitating the purchase of uninsured motorist coverage or leading to higher premiums and taxes to cover hospital bad debt.

MOTORCYCLE HELMET LAWS

Motorcycling is an extremely dangerous method of travel. As the saying goes: buy your son a motorcycle for his last birthday. Motorcycling is very hazardous even with a helmet, but wearing a helmet does substantially reduce the risk of death and serious injury.[10]

The theory of selective recruitment suggests that the most dangerous cyclists will not wear helmets voluntarily. Propitious selection argues that they will also be the least likely to be covered by insurance. There is substantial evidence on this latter point.

Health insurers do not charge higher premiums for motorcyclists, nor do they distinguish between helmeted and unhelmeted ones. Yet motorcyclists are far less likely than similarly aged automobile drivers to be medically insured, and unhelmeted motorcyclists are less likely than helmeted ones to possess insurance coverage.[11]

In January 1992, California began requiring motorcyclists to wear helmets. Usage rates are expected to rise from around 50% to close to 100%.[12] This essay does not lay out the advantages and disadvantages of such legislation. Instead, the point is merely to assert that the theories of selective recruitment and propitious selection provide some support for the new requirements. Selective recruitment implies that the total injury-reducing benefits from helmet use will more than double. Propitious selection argues that, by forcing the dangerous dans to cycle helmeted, we will substantially reduce the external financial burden they currently impose on the nervous nellies.

FOR DISCUSSION

1. Are there other types besides nervous nellies and dangerous dans? What sort of behavior would you expect from rational ruths?

2. Why are some people very cautious about certain things (e.g., airline travel) while somewhat reckless in other areas (e.g, sports or smoking)?

3. Do people change type? Does change occur as people get older, because of the influence of those around them or what they read and hear, or because of some other factor? What implications would such malleability have?

4. Did the spread of condom use to prevent transmission of the AIDS virus follow the pattern of selective recruitment? Why or why not?

5. In which insurance markets do you expect propitious selection to be relatively stronger than adverse selection?

NOTES TO CHAPTER 22

1. Sam Peltzman, "The Effects of Automobile Safety Regulation," *Journal of Political Economy* 83 (1975):677-725.
2. Leonard Evans, P. Wasielewski and C.R. von Buseck, "Compulsory Seat Belt Usage and Drivers Risk-Taking Behavior," *Human Factors* 24 (1982): 41-48; Leonard Evans and P. Wasielewski, "Risky Driving Related to Driver and Vehicle Characteristics," *Accident Analysis and Prevention* 15 (1983):121-36; Leonard Evans, "Belted and Unbelted Driver Accident Involvement Rates Compared," *Journal of Safety Research* 18 (1987): 137-44; Leonard Evans, *Traffic Safety and the Driver* (New York: Van Nostrand Reinhold, 1991); J. M. B. Mayas, N. K. Boyd, M. A. Collins and B. I. Harris, *A Study of Demographic, Situational, and Motivational Factors Affecting Restraint Use in Automobiles* (Report DOT HS-806-407, U.S. National Highway Traffic Safety Administration, 1983); Thomas Perneger and Gordon S. Smith, "The Driver's Role in Fatal Two-Car Crashes: A Paired 'Case-Control' Study," *American Journal of Epidemiology* 134 (1991): 1138-45; David F. Preusser, Allan F. Williams and Adrian K. Lund, "Characteristics of Belted and Unbelted Drivers," *Accident Analysis and Prevention* 23 (1991): 475-82.
3. B. A. Jonah and John J. Lawson, "Safety Belt Use Rates and User Characteristics," in U.S. National Highway Traffic Safety Administration, *Effectiveness of Safety Belt Use Laws: A Multinational Examination* (Washington DC: DOT-HS 807-018, 1986); Michael J. Lichtenstein, A. Bolton and G. Wade, "Derivation and Validation of a Decision Rule for Predicting Seat Belt Utilization," *Journal of Family Practice* 28 (1989): 289-92.
4. Leonard Evans, "Human Behavior Feedback and Traffic Safety," *Human Factors* 27 (1985): 555-76.
5. David Hemenway, "Propitious Selection," *Quarterly Journal of Economics* 105 (1990): 1063-1069.
6. David Bickelhaupt, *General Insurance* (Homewood, IL: Richard D. Irwin, 1974).
7. Mark V. Pauly, "The Economics of Moral Hazard," *American Economic Review* 68 (1968): 531-37.
8. David E. Nelson, Timothy D. Peterson, Terence L. Chorba, J. Devine Owen and Jeffrey J. Sacks, "Cost Savings Associated with Increased Safety Belt Use in Iowa, 1987-88," (1992): in press.
9. David Hemenway, "Propitious Selection in Insurance," *Journal of Risk and Uncertainty* 5 (1992): 247-51.
10. John D. Graham and Younghee Lee, "Behavioral Response to Safety Regulation: The Case of Motorcycle Helmet-Wearing Legislation," *Policy Sciences* 19 (1986): 253-76.
11. Bernard Bach and Edwin Wyman, Jr., "Financial Charges of Hospitalized Motorcyclists at the Massachusetts General Hospital," *Journal of Trauma* 26 (1986):343-47; Timothy Brady, Robert Szabo and Laura Timmerman, et al., "Cost of Orthopedic Injuries

Sustained in Motorcycle Accidents," *Journal of the American Medical Association* 254 (1985): 2452-53; Linda Lloyd, Mary Lauderdale and Thomas Betz, "Motorcycle Deaths and Injuries in Texas: Helmets Made a Difference," *Texas Medicine* 83 (1987): 30-33; Frederick P. Rivara, Barbara G. Dicker, Abraham B. Bergman, Ralph Dacey and Clifford Herman, "The Public Cost of Motorcycle Trauma," *Journal of the American Medical Association* 260 (1988): 221-23; Belavadi S. Shankar, Ammen I. Ramzy, Carl A. Soderstrom, Patricia C. Dischinger and Carl C. Clark, "Helmet Use, Patterns of Injury, Medical Outcome and Costs among Motorcycle Drivers in Maryland," *Accident Analysis and Prevention* 24 (1992): 385-96.

12. Insurance Institute for Highway Safety, *Status Report* (March 14, 1992): 4-5.

23 OPTIMAL LOCATION

The 1981 Graduate Medical Education National Advisory Committee Draft Report[1] implied that if information on physicians' efficacy were available, the correct locational pattern for doctors could readily be calculated. In other words, if we knew the contribution that each doctor in every geographic location made to health, it would be obvious where society would want physicians to locate. This chapter questions that conclusion. It argues that a necessary first step is to reach some consensus on the definition of optimal geographic allocation. What is considered proper policy will fundamentally depend on the exact criterion chosen.

Are doctors in the United States geographically maldistributed? Most health analysts believe that they are. The evidence generally cited to support this contention is the disparity in physician-population ratios across regions. For example, in 1990 the number of doctors per 100,000 population was 320 in New England and only 181 in the East South-Central region (Alabama, Kentucky, Mississippi, and Tennessee). The number of physicians per 100,000 population in New York State was 342; in South Dakota it was 166.[2]

Is this evidence convincing? Certainly not in itself. Almost all health analysts believe that many other factors matter when one is judging geographic distribution, including the specialty distribution of doctors, the distribution of other health workers, the productivity and working hours of doctors according to location, the geographic distribution of illness, and the mobility of patients. Probably the most important and fundamental issue, however, is agreement on a way to evaluate alternative patterns of location. Without such an agreement, it is difficult to talk logically or intelligently about the concept of maldistribution.

An examination of the literature on economics and health care reveals four plausible but fundamentally different definitions of an ideal geographic distribution.[3-6] This chapter describes these four goals, presents a simplified example to highlight the large potential differences among them, and makes an argument for the possible primacy of one of them. The main purpose of the exercise, however, is to illustrate how the perception of maldistribution can depend on the definition of what is optimal.

THE IDEAL DISTRIBUTION

The four standards suggested in the literature are economic efficiency, health maximization, equal doctor-population ratios, and equal health status.

Economic Efficiency

This criterion is the one most widely used by economists for judging outcomes. The effect of any economic activity is typically divided into its "equity" and "efficiency" components. Equity aspects deal with the fairness of the distribution of wealth and happiness. Economists claim no special expertise in determining which outcomes are most equitable; instead, they focus on the efficiency aspects of policy. The idea of a perfectly efficient situation (in the jargon, "Pareto optimality") is one in which everything has been done that helps any person without harming anyone else. Economists argue that all actions that increase the happiness of some people without decreasing the happiness of others should be undertaken. Such transactions are generally accomplished in the free market by voluntary exchange.

Assuming that all persons adjust their purchase decisions to maximize their happiness, a perfectly competitive economy will ultimately lead to economic efficiency. Therefore, if every market (including the market for doctors' services) were perfectly competitive, the free market outcome would be economically efficient.

The criterion of economic efficiency differs from two of the other standards in that the concern is with persons, not regions. The criterion is fundamentally different from all the other standards in that it takes every person's total happiness into account-- happiness as derived not merely from health care but from all possible goods and services. The criterion does not, however, deal with issues of equity.

The next three criteria deal solely with health or the availability of health care. Neither the happiness of doctors nor the satisfaction ("utility," in economic terms) that the population derives from other goods and services is considered.

Health Maximization

Like economic efficiency, this criterion is concerned with persons, not regions. This standard could be met, yet there might still be a very unequal geographic distribution of both health and health care.

The next two goals contain ideas of geographic equality or fairness among regions.

Equal Doctor-Population Ratios

Much of the discussion of physicians' location seems to imply that equality of physician-population ratios is the desired goal. Achieving this objective, however, guarantees equal access to health care only if many other conditions are fulfilled. The criterion, moreover, says nothing directly about the health and happiness of either doctors or patients.

Equal Health Status across Regions

This goal incorporates a concept of equity in terms of health outcomes. A problem with this criterion and the previous one is that by redefining regional boundaries, different patterns of optimal location can emerge. It is only by describing these goals in relation to individuals (e.g., "equalizing health status among individuals") that this problem can be eliminated.

A SIMPLE EXAMPLE

Consider a society in which there is only one medical resource. This resource is doctors. All doctors are identical, and the number of doctors is given, fixed at ten. There are two areas in the society, Blue and Green, populated by equal numbers of people. A doctor practices entirely in one location or the other. Patients receive medical care only in their own area. There are only two states of "health": people are either alive or dead. The only health concern is thus mortality. There is complete information about the impact of doctors on mortality. If permitted, each doctor is assumed to try to maximize his income.

Table 23-1 gives the fees that doctors can command, which depend on the effective demand for doctors and the supply of physicians' services. For simplicity, these fees are specified in terms of physicians' net incomes rather than the price per service. The assumption is that all doctors work a standard number of hours and that their services are always fully used. In the example, the Blue area is willing and able to spend more for doctors than is the Green. Those in the Blue area may care more about their health. In the real world, their higher effective demand probably means that they are richer. In any event, in a free market, they will be able to buy more physicians' services.

Table 23-2 gives the impact of doctors on mortality. The crucial postulate is that their effect is not identical in the two areas. In the example, the Green area is poorer

Table 23-1. Demand for Doctors in the Hypothetical Blue (Richer) and Green (Poorer) Areas.

	Number of Doctors Demanded		
Income of Doctors	Blue Area	Green Area	Both Areas
Thousands of Dollars			
$20	14	8	22
40	12	5	17
60	11	3	14
80	10	2	12
100	9	1	10
120	7	0	7
140	6	0	6
160	5	0	5
180	3	0	3
200	2	0	2

than the Blue. We know that in the United States, poorer regions and states have considerably higher mortality rates than do richer ones.[7,8] People in the lower socioeconomic classes have vastly higher death rates from home and motor vehicle accidents. They are more prone to commit suicide.[9] Although they are poorer, their per capita cigarette consumption is higher, as is their mortality from lung cancer. They are more likely to die from cirrhosis of the liver.[10] Doctors are not very effective at preventing or curing such problems. It is thus reasonable to assume that with equal physician-population ratios, the poor region would still have higher mortality. Even if most doctors practiced in the Green area, those people might still have a high death rate.

Table 23-2 also assumes that the number of lives saved by an additional doctor is not identical in the two areas. We know that medical care is more successful at ameliorating some conditions than others. There is also evidence that health problems differ among income classes.[11] We would thus expect that the contribution or an additional physician to health would vary between regions.

The four goals imply radically different locational patterns for doctors.

Economic Efficiency

Economists have shown that in the long run a perfectly competitive society is economically efficient. Assume for the moment that the market for physicians'

Table 23-2. Effect of Doctors on Mortality in the Blue and Green Areas.

Number of of Doctors	Blue Area			Green Area	
	Number of Deaths/Year	Number of Lives Saved by an Additional Doctor		Number of Deaths/Year	Number of Lives Saved by an Additional Doctor
0	190	-		240	-
1	130	60		190	50
2	107	23		157	33
3	87	20		143	14
4	70	17		133	10
5	54	16		125	8
6	39	15		118	7
7	25	14		112	6
8	14	11		107	5
9	10	4		103	4
10	10	0		100	3

services is perfectly competitive, and allow the market to allocate the scarce supply of doctors. The market, of course, is the way by which the United States rations most goods and services, including meat, housing, toothpaste, electricity, yachts, and doctors' services.

Demand for doctors is determined by many variables, including tastes, income, and other prices. Each person chooses the dollar value that he places on having a doctor available, and each supplier locates so as to maximize his own satisfaction (utility). Doctors' locational decisions are affected by pay and living conditions, among other things. Assume, for simplicity, that each physician desires only to maximize his income. This will tend to equalize the incomes of doctors in both areas, for any income discrepancy will lead doctors to shift locations. In the example, there will be a long-run equilibrium with nine physicians in the Blue area and only one in the Green. All doctors will make $100,000 per year. (A preference for living in a more affluent neighborhood could skew the distribution of doctors even further toward the rich area.)

Although the Green area has a lower health status than does the Blue, effective demand causes more doctors to locate in the Blue area and more lives to be saved there. The Blue population gets most of the health care because it is willing and able to pay for it. In equilibrium, 10 people per year will die in the Blue area, as compared with 190 in the Green.

This result is economically efficient-- if the physicians' service industry is perfectly competitive. Even if it were, this outcome could be questioned on grounds of equity. The society may not want the rich to receive this much more medical care than the poor do. Yet if the situation is economically efficient, it is impossible to help some people without hurting others.

In the real world, of course, the market for doctors is not perfectly competitive. Thus, the current method of allocating physicians-- the free market-- may be neither equitable nor economically efficient.

Health Maximization

This is a slightly different criterion of efficiency. What is to be maximized in this instance is health, not some idea of total utility. Other aspects of welfare are given zero weight. In the example, the goal would be to minimize the total number of deaths in the society as a whole. Given this objective, it is instructive to place doctors, one at a time, in either location. Since the example has been constructed so that the marginal effect of doctors is continually decreasing, this is an easy task. The first doctor should go to the Blue area, saving sixty lives. A second doctor would go to the Green, saving fifty. Examining the marginal effect of doctors tells us the optimal location of each successive doctor. Use of this criterion will tend to equalize the marginal effectiveness in both areas. With ten doctors, seven should go to the Blue area, three to the Green. The marginal benefit of the last doctor in each area is fourteen lives saved.

There are two more doctors in the Green area than the free market would provide. The reason is that although Blue patients are willing and able to pay more for the services of these physicians, these two doctors can save more lives if they are located in the Green region. This solution results in 25 deaths in the Blue area and 143 in the Green. Any other allocation of doctors will increase the total number of deaths in the society.

It should be noted that the physician-population ratios in the two regions are still unequal. Health status is also uneven across regions; there are many more deaths in the Green area than in the Blue. In addition, achieving the goal of health maximization means that certain voluntary trades-for example, money for health-must not be allowed, even though they would represent free market choices and hence, according to economics, could well increase the utility of all parties.

Equal Doctor-Population Ratios

A potentially more equitable arrangement than either of the above solutions might be the equalization of the doctor-population ratios in both areas. Given that the populations in the two areas are identical, this implies an equal number of doctors in each. There will be five doctors in the Blue area and five in the Green. This will result in 54 deaths per year in the Blue area and 125 in the Green.

More people (although different people) would die in this situation than if the goal were to maximize health, because the fourth and fifth doctors in the Green area would save fewer lives than they would if they were located in the Blue region. It should be noted, moreover, that in the real world equal doctor-population ratios do not ensure that equal amounts of health care will be given to persons of the same age with identical health problems. That would be the case only if large numbers of other conditions were fulfilled: for example, equal health status across regions, equal health-care facilities, equal working hours for physicians, equal productivity among physicians, and equal knowledge among patients. The prime virtue of the objective of equalizing physician-population ratios seems to be that the data are easily collected.

Equal Health across Regions

It might be argued that none of the above criteria leads to a fair allocation of doctors. After all, many more people would be dying in the Green area than in the Blue. Equity considerations could lead some to suggest trying to equalize mortality rates in each region. This criterion might be especially appealing if mortality rates were primarily due not to behavioral patterns (e.g., smoking, drinking, speeding, or overeating) but to factors that are less controllable by the patient (e.g., discrimination, pollution, congenital defects, or occupational hazards). To meet this goal would require having eight doctors in the Green area and two in the Blue. One hundred seven people would die every year in each area.

Although this allocation might be said to provide some equity across regions, there are many things that it does not do. It does not lead to equal physician-population ratios. It does not result in the same amount of medical attention for people with similar diseases. And it means a lower average health status for the society than could be achieved with the same resources.

Table 23-3 summarizes the various distributions of doctors for the four criteria.

CHOOSING THE PROPER CRITERION

The selection of the proper criterion depends on one's values. There is no scientifically correct choice. However, one might argue for the maximization of health as the most suitable of these goals. It combines an element of efficiency as well as one of equity. It deals with efficiency in that it maximizes the physician's contribution to human health-- assuming that each person counts equally. This equal

Table 23-3. Distributions of Doctors in the Blue and Green Areas under the Different Criteria.

Criteria for Distribution of Doctors	Number of Doctors		Number of Deaths		
	Blue Area	Green Area	Blue Area	Green Area	Total
Free market	9	1	10	190	200
Minimizing total deaths (maximizing health)	7	3	25	143	168
Equalizing doctor/ patient ratios	5	5	54	125	179
Equalizing death rates	2	8	107	107	214

weighting also provides a strong element of fairness or equity. With respect to their health, all people are weighted the same, whether rich or poor, male or female, black or white. However, the criterion does not take doctors' incomes into account.

With certain assumptions, the goal of health maximization can be made consistent with the criterion of economic efficiency. Scitovsky argues that the equitable distribution of health care may be a collective good.[12] Decentralized decisionmaking will not lead to an economically efficient outcome, even in perfect competition, and it may be appropriate to use collective or governmental action to help secure the desired market-specific egalitarianism.

IMPLEMENTATION

Assume that the Blue-Green society decides that the ideal pattern of location for physicians is the one that minimizes death. How can it ensure that seven doctors will locate in the Blue area and three in the Green? There are many methods that it could use to try to achieve this goal. For example, direct market incentives could be employed. Demand for health care in the Green area could be subsidized. This would attract doctors from the Blue area, but at the same time it would increase the incomes of already well-paid physicians at taxpayers' expense.

In the real world, since new and young physicians are the most mobile, policy is usually directed at affecting their locational decisions. The placement of medical schools and the selection criteria for medical applicants can modify the geographic distribution of physicians; so too can the tying of students' subsidies to future work in underserved areas.

The stick as well as the carrot can be used to alter physicians' patterns of location. Doctors could be more heavily taxed in areas where their marginal contribution to health is low, or licensure could be limited in these regions. The purpose of this chapter, however, is neither to describe all the possible methods of achieving a more desirable geographic distribution of physicians nor to recommend the best strategy. Instead, the aim is more basic to emphasize that before the proper strategy can be determined, we must first agree on what locational pattern we find desirable.

REAL-WORLD PROBLEMS

If maximization of health is selected as the most appropriate objective, there are many practical problems that must be faced. In our mythical Blue-Green society, health is defined simply in terms of life or death, but in the real world a key difficulty is deciding on the measurement of health-on the relative weightings that might be given to setting a broken finger and to ameliorating the symptoms of hay fever. This is not a trivial problem. Although a consensus might be reached on some weightings, unanimity is unlikely. It should also be emphasized that if the goal of health maximization were a strict one, people would not be allowed to trade off fixing the broken finger for any other good or service.

There are other problems. Should the criterion imply that curing a ninety-eight-year-old of pneumonia is equal to curing a twelve-year-old? Or if the duration of benefit is included, what discount rate (if any) is appropriate? The issues are similar to those that have to be resolved in cost-effectiveness analysis.

Our simple example was abstracted from many other practical problems. In the real world, the doctor is but one of the many components in the provision of health care. Other medical resources include drugs, appliances, x-ray machines, hospitals, and nurses. These can be used in various proportions. Doctors themselves are not homogeneous; some are surgeons, some pathologists, and some obstetricians. Some provide higher quality care than others. Some work longer hours. Some work more productively. Thus, society should not be as interested in the number of doctors as in the amount and quality of medical services rendered.

In addition, some medical care may be delivered without any input from doctors. Nonmedical practitioners who sometimes provide health services include emergency medical technicians, midwives, lifeguards, and grandmothers. There are also many ways to reduce the need for medical care, such as smoking less, improving sanitation and diet, and exercising more.

In the real world, doctors and patients may be mobile across regions, although travel does entail costs. Moreover, society's concern is not really with the availability of medical services but with access to them. The real-world problems of empirically determining ideal patterns of location for doctors can thus be enormously difficult. The essential first step is to agree on what is meant by "the optimal location of doctors."

FOR DISCUSSION

1. Would a different approach be appropriate for analyzing the optimal location of food stores? Should health care be treated differently than other goods or services? Than food?

2. In determining the optimal spatial distribution of police patrols, do equity considerations imply that we should try to equalize the chances of residents being mugged? Of muggers getting caught?

3. Is the distribution of income or wealth a good measure of "equity"? When is it not? Does equity imply fairness? Fairness to whom?

4. Do efficiency and equity criteria encompass all reasonable goals for society? What about "friendliness" or "virtue" or "generativeness"? Can these be subsumed under the efficiency rubric?

5. Is a Pareto optimal always Pareto superior to a nonoptimal? When might it not be?

6. Think of another reasonable criterion besides the four listed for assessing physician locational patterns.

NOTES TO CHAPTER 23

1. United States Department of Health and Human Services, *Report of the Graduate Medical Education National Advisory Committee*, vol. 1, Summary Report (Washington, DC: Government Printing Office, 1981), p. 96.
2. Gene Roback, Lillian Randolph and Bradley Seidman, *Physician Characteristics and Distribution in the U.S.* (Chicago, IL: American Medical Association, 1992).
3. R. Fein, "On Achieving Access and Equity in Health Care," in J. B. McKinlay, ed., *Economic Aspects of Health Care* (New York: Prodist, 1973), pp. 23-56.
4. L. C. Thurow, "Equity versus Efficiency in Law Enforcement," *Public Policy* 18, no. 4 (1970): 431-62.
5. M. Katz, "The Supply of Physicians and Physicians' Incomes: Some Projections," *Journal of Health Politics, Policy and Law* 2 (1977): 227-56.
6. D. A. Kindig, "Health Manpower the Right Place," in *Health Manpower Issues* DHEW publication no. (HRA) 76-40 (Washington, DC: Government Printing Office, 1976).
7. M. Lerner and R. N. Stutz, "Mortality by Socioeconomic Status, 1959-61 and 1969-71," *Maryland State Medical Journal* 27, no. 12 (1978): 35-42.
8. Lerner and Stutz, "Have We Narrowed the Gaps Between the Poor and the Non-Poor? II. Narrowing the Gaps, 1959-1961 to 1969-1971: Mortality," *Medical Care* 15 (1977): 620-35.

9. "Socioeconomic Mortalitiy Differentials by Leading Causes of Death," *Statistical Bulletin* 58, no. 1 (1977): 5-8.

10. United States National Center for Health Statistics, Vital and Health Statistics, Series 10, no. 131, *Use Habits Among Adults of Cigarettes, Coffee, Aspirin, and Sleeping Pills: United States, 1976,* DHEW publication no. (PHS) 80-1559 (Washington, DC: Government Printing Office, 1980).

11. "Socioeconomic Mortality Differentials," p. 5.

12. T. Scitovsky, *Papers on Welfare and Growth* (London: George Allen & Unwin, 1964), pp. 250-62.

VII THE ECONOMIC APPROACH

INTRODUCTION

The economic approach is different from that of other professional disciplines. Chapter 24 compares the way economists, lawyers, doctors and public health officials tackle the issue of injury prevention. The essay emphasizes the simple, critical idea of opportunity cost (scarcity) and examines the question of when markets work well and when they don't.

Chapter 25 applies the economic approach to a particular industry, the market for health care. It argues that, for an economist, the two most important aspects that differentiate this market from many others is the low level of consumer information and the high level of insurance coverage.

In a fundamental sense, microeconomic theory is a theory of rational behavior. The theory describes how individuals should act in order to maximize their utility and typically assumes that all individuals will try to act in this manner. In this sense, alcoholics, criminals, and saints are treated alike. The principal distinction among them is that they have differing preferences and desires.

In a light vein, Chapter 26 takes a look at the Bible from an economic perspective. The focus is (a) on the notion of scarcity, which is discussed with respect to the story of the creation and the teachings of Jesus and (b) on rational behavior. All three chapters in this section are designed to show how an economist might approach various topics and to further illustrate the way economists think.

24 INJURY PREVENTION

Injuries are a major public health problem. Although less than 10% of U.S. fatalities are due to injuries, compared to diseases, injuries disproportionately kill the young. Over half the people who die in the United States before the age of 40 die from injuries. Almost one third of injury deaths are intentional (suicide and homicide), about one third involve motor vehicles (including motorcycle and pedestrian fatalities) and almost one third are caused by other accidents (falls, fires, drowning, etc.)

This chapter focuses on unintentional injuries. It (a) contrasts the economic approach with those of other disciplines; (b) gives the economic rationale for government intervention in markets to improve safety; (c) discusses the concern that deregulation in the airline industry might reduce safety; and (d) analyzes the idea that "rich is safer."

PROFESSIONAL APPROACHES

Various professions provide quite different perspectives on understanding and reducing our unintentional injury problem. For example, the medical and legal-liability approaches focus on the individual decision-maker, while the public health and economic approaches take more of a societal orientation.[1]

Medical providers typically interact one-at-a-time with individual patients. The focus of attention tends to be on those factors most accessible to the physician's influence-- behavioral factors under the patient's control. To the extent that doctors are interested in prevention, they try to ensure that their patients follow safe practices-- wear their seat belts, buy smoke detectors, etc. Changing the individual's behavior is seen as the key to prevention.

The public health approach is community rather than individually based. A major goal is to make the environment safer, so that fewer injuries will occur. Public health officials are concerned with keeping people out of harm's way-- ensuring that telephone poles are set away from the roadside, that pajamas are nonflammable, that aspirin bottlecaps are childproof, that cigarettes are fire-safe, that baseball bases break-away to reduce sliding injuries. Public health officials believe the medical profession's emphasis on healthy lifestyles can be carried too far and may inappropriately "blame the victim" for problems when they occur.

Legal liability typically involves a one-at-a-time, case-by-case approach and uses lawsuit results not only to compensate the victim but to penalize those people and institutions who injure others. The idea is that someone is at fault for the incident and that fault can be determined and the guilty party punished. This ex post or after-the-fact approach can help deter unsafe activities that cause injury to others.

The economic approach focuses on the system. The policy goal is to create the right incentives so that decentralized decision making leads to the optimal number of injuries. The optimal number is typically greater than zero. Economic theory emphasizes that there can be too much as well as too little safety.

A fundamental concept in microeconomics is the notion of opportunity cost. Resources-- land, labor, machines, raw materials-- are limited. Using them to produce ever safer products means that fewer resources are available for other worthwhile endeavors such as education, medical care and entertainment.

Advocates for injury prevention favor regulations that require every new dwelling to have a sprinkler system, every swimming pool to have both outer and inner fencing, every car to have airbags and stronger bumpers. These prescriptions will lower our injury toll. They will save lives. They will prevent severe injuries. They will reduce pain and grief and misery. The issue remains-- are they worth it? They well may be, but the economist argues that the costs as well as the benefits must be examined. It is always possible to make products safer. Where is the appropriate place to stop?

The economic approach assumes that people are rational, that they weigh the costs and benefits of alternative courses of action. Economists ask the same from policymakers. Society, like the individual household, has limited resources. The prime cost of using resources in one way is that they cannot be used to do something else.

GOVERNMENT INTERVENTION

In a capitalist system, individual households and firms interact in the marketplace. Much effort has been made to determine when the "invisible hand" of the market works well, and when public policies can improve the situation. The goal of the economist is to help provide correct incentives so that the decentralized decisions of the market will lead to the optimal.

If markets were perfectly competitive, we would have the optimal number of injuries (in long run equilibrium). Typically, of course, there are instances of market failure. Two important problems are the absence of adequate consumer information and the existence of externalities.

Consider the problem of information. A typical consumer purchases small quantities of many items. It is not rational or even possible for her to become expert concerning the quality and safety of many of these products and services. When consumers have poor information, the government might improve the market outcome by requiring the provision of useful information or by providing the information itself. Examples include nutritional labelling requirements, octane ratings, contents labelling, tire grading and automobile stopping distance information.

Another alternative is to set mandatory requirements. Governmental regulations can prohibit the manufacture and sale of items deemed to be unsafe-- products that consumers would not want to purchase were they fully informed. More common than product bans are requirements that the item meet minimum standards.

The Consumer Product Safety Commission is a federal institution whose mission is to reduce injury. This small agency has responsibility for many products, although it has no authority over some of the most important injury-related commodities-- guns, alcohol, and motor vehicles.

Commission activities include the collection and dissemination of injury information, the banning of products, the promotion of voluntary safety standards, the promulgation of (a few) mandatory standards, and the recall of substandard and dangerous products. While some of the Commission's actions have been controversial, there have been various success stories, many involving low cost methods for protecting children. Because of consumer information problems, without Commission involvement, the market would have worked too slowly, or not at all.

Over the years the Commission has banned lawn darts, clacker balls (which can fly off their strings), and kites made of aluminized polyester film (an electrical hazard). It helped promote voluntary standards for playpens to reduce the chance of asphyxiation, and for strollers to lower the likelihood of pinching and crushing the fingers and hands of infants. It administers the Refrigerator Safety Act which requires refrigerators doors to be able to be opened from the inside (children had suffocated when trapped in discarded refrigerators) and the Poison Prevention Packaging Act which calls for child-resistant packaging to prevent youngsters from accidently swallowing dangerous households substances. It helped ensure that small toys are made with radio-opaque plastic so that, if swallowed, physicians can see the items by X-ray. It wrote flammability regulations for children's sleepwear. (In 1971, before the sleepwear standard was issued, the Shriners Burn Institute in Boston reported that 34% of their burn injuries involved sleepwear. By 1977 the percentage was zero.) The mere presence of the agency, created in 1972, has helped to energize industries and individual firms to produce safer products.[2]

Another economic rationale for government intervention is the existence of externalities. Motor vehicles, for example, cause over 45,000 deaths in the United States each year. Many traffic victims are killed by the reckless actions of other motorists. This externality creates one rationale for traffic rules and regulations-- speed limits, traffic lights, etc. Without such rules, for example, motorists might drive faster than optimal. They would be concerned with their own time and safety, and put insufficient weight on the costs that speeding imposes on others-- the increased risk of serious injury.

Governmental policymakers must take the problems caused by externalities into account. Whether or not to raise the speed limit -- e.g. from 55 mph to 65 mph-- requires a careful weighing of the costs (more injuries) versus the benefits (time savings). Similarly, allowing right-turn-on-red saves time and gasoline, but increases pedestrian fatalities.

Individuals' concern for relative position also creates important externalities.[3] This can be seen most vividly in sports, which typically involve beating or losing to others. For example, should ice hockey goalies be required to wear face masks? Not so long ago goalies had a choice of whether or not to wear face protection. Assume that the goalie's mask reduces serious injury by 50%, but also reduces goaltending effectiveness by 5%. If, as coach, your sole goal were winning the next game, would you want your goaltender to wear a mask? If a goalie wanted to play the next game, do you think he would insist on wearing a face mask? What percentage of goalies in a highly competitive league would wear masks? While the "market" solution might be all goalies going maskless, all might be better off with a rule requiring masks.

Similarly, consider two equal hockey teams, trying to decide whether to wear hockey helmets. The helmets substantially reduce injury, but perhaps ever so slightly lessen vision and mobility. Each team wants to win the next game. A prisoner's dilemma game neatly summarizes the problem (Figure 24-1). Not wearing the helmets may be the dominant strategy for each team, leading to the outcome each ranks third. Both teams are better off (fewer injuries, no change in the probability of winning) if everyone is required to wear helmets. Individual

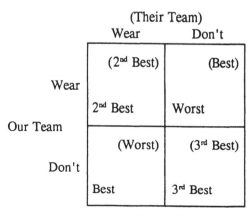

Figure 24-1

hockey players might not wear helmets voluntarily, but all might want the league to mandate them.[4] Similarly, teams may also be happy that tripping, slashing, spearing, charging, cross-checking and high-sticking are illegal. They will also want to outlaw steroid use and the carrying of weapons on the ice.

AIRLINE DEREGULATION

The injury rate may be influenced by economic regulations as well as by safety rules. Airline deregulation, which began in 1978, substantially reduced the real price of airline service. Was there any effect on safety?[5]

The elimination of the Civil Aeronautics Board and with it the government sponsored cartel increased competition in the aviation industry. While the Federal Aviation Administration, which has responsibility for airline safety, was not directly affected by deregulation, concern was voiced that increased price competition might result in reduced maintenance and repair. Competition might also increase the number of airlines in financial difficulties, and firms experiencing a decline in profits often reduce expenditures on safety.

The evidence shows that, after deregulation, airlines kept their old planes longer before replacing them. The increased demand caused by the price reductions lead to more airport congestion and more danger of aircraft collisions. Nonsafety aspects of service quality fell-- there appeared to be significantly more problems for travellers due to lost baggage, overbooking and delays.

On the other hand, in terms of outcome, it is difficult to find empirical support for a reduction in safety. Air collisions, and passengers killed in air crashes fell significantly in the 1980s. Of course, air crashes are rare events; a few dramatic catastrophes could skew the results. In addition, injury rates have been falling on virtually all forms of transport.

Economists emphasize that the market provides incentives for safety. Air crashes are newsworthy. Airlines and aircraft manufacturers may lose customers if their safety comes into question, and insurance companies may raise premiums. Airline stock prices fall after major catastrophes. Although airlines do not advertise safety so as not to increase the fear of flying, crashes also reduce passenger demand for the air service of that particular company. Even absent FAA inspections and fines, airline executives ignore safety at their own financial peril.

Whatever the direct effects of deregulation on airline safety, we can be assured that deregulation increased overall *transportation* safety. By helping to lower market price, deregulation induced many people to use planes rather than automobiles. Plane travel is far safer than driving. The total number of lives saved by this change in transport mode is estimated to be far greater than the total number of lives lost each year from all air crashes. Cheaper skies mean safer highways.[6]

RICH IS SAFER

Being rich provides various benefits. The wealthy can purchase more goods and services than the poor. They can also buy higher quality and safer products and surroundings. It is therefore not surprising to discover that, for most injuries, the rich have lower risk for mortality and morbidity.[7]

For unintentional and intentional injury deaths, the fatality rate in the richest census tracts is less than one half that of the poorest tracts.[8] The poor have substantially higher fatality rates for deaths by fire, drowning, highway collisions, natural disasters, excessive cold, machinery and also homicide. One of the few areas where higher income individuals have higher death rates is in airline crashes. Plane travel is relatively safe, but the risk for the rich is higher than for the poor simply because they fly so much more often.

Decreased income during short run economic downturns may bring increases in injury related problems. Some evidence suggests that recessions and the accompanying higher unemployment, may increase suicide, homicide, child abuse and other intentional injuries. On the other hand, it is known that traffic fatalities decrease during economic recessions, in large part because miles travelled are reduced.

Changes in permanent vs. transitory income will have differing effects on the injury rate.[9] A temporary increase in income may elicit little change in consumption patterns. A more permanent increase may lead, over time, to the purchase of a safer automobile, a home that is more fire safe due to better wiring and newer appliances, etc.

A prime reason our injury problem has diminished throughout the 20th century is that we have become richer. While a few hazards have increased (e.g., soaring, sky-diving) most have decreased. A permanent rise in the standard of living is usually a very effective way to reduce injuries. Conversely, overly restrictive governmental regulations, even safety regulations, if they reduce real incomes, may be not only bad for business, but may extract a human toll in terms of an increase in injuries.

The distribution of income also effects total injuries. Fire fatalities are strongly associated with poverty, and so are many other injuries.[10] As with most pubic health problems, targeting prevention efforts on the poorest members of society can be especially cost-effective.

CONCLUSION

The economic approach emphasizes the concept of opportunity cost. While safety is an important characteristic of many products, it is not the only important product attribute. People willingly make trade-offs between safety and other things they care about.

Economic theory also emphasizes the role of incentives, and the market does creates financial incentives for safety. Workers demand higher wages when they work at less safe jobs (or conversely, they accept lower wages for a safer work environment). Consumers are willing to pay more for safer products (they will not pay as much for less safe ones). Competitive airline companies that have many crashes will be "punished" by the market. The most important safety effect of airline deregulation was caused by the lowering of prices for air service, leading many travellers to switch from highway to air transport.

Real world markets rarely work ideally. Neither does the government. But government intervention may increase both efficiency and equity when there are major sources of "market failure." In the injury area, the two prime suspects are inadequate consumer information and the presence of substantial externalities.

Finally, to increase safety, a healthy and growing economy is often the best medicine. While money may not buy love, it can reduce the risk of illness and injury.

FOR DISCUSSION

1. What other professions or disciplines might offer a useful approach to the injury problem? How would you categorize that approach?

2. What level of risk is appropriate for sports? Does it matter whether the game is played by amateurs or professional, children or adults?

3. It is "unconscionable" to trade any amount of workplace safety for more economic growth. (Former Senator Harrison Williams, D-NJ). "Quite frankly, I believe when you're dealing in questions related to human life, economic costs are irrelevant." (Congressperson David Obey, D-WI). How would an economist respond to such statements?

4. Some say we should direct more funds towards cancer research because it is a "dread disease." Does this argument make sense? Are there "dread injuries"?

5. Do people who suffer an injury or have had a loved one suffer an injury think differently about safety? How can, or should this perspective be incorporated into benefit-cost thinking?

6. What are other economic justifications for possible government intervention in the market besides externalities and poor consumer information?

7. For what intentional injuries may the rich be at greater risk?

8. Are there more or fewer injuries in jobs which pay the most? Explain.

9. Why are cars built to be able to go over 100 miles per hour?

NOTES TO CHAPTER 24

1. This section is based on Stephen H. Linder, "On Cogency, Professional Bias and Public Policy: An Assessment of Four Views of the Injury Problem," *The Millbank Quarterly* 65, no. 2, (1987): 276-301.
2. David Bollier and Joan Claybrook, *Freedom From Harm* (Washington, DC: Public Citizen, 1986).
3. Robert H. Frank. *Choosing the Right Pond: Human Behavior and the Quest for Status* (New York: Oxford University Press, 1985).
4. Thomas C. Schelling, *Micromotives and Macrobehavior* (New York: Norton, 1978).
5. Leon N. Moses and Ian Savage, eds., *Transportation Safety in an Age of Deregulation* (New York: Oxford University Press, 1989).
6. Richard B. McKenzie, *Airline Deregulation and Air-Travel Safety: The American Experience* (Center for the Study of American Business, Number 107, July 1991).
7. Aaron Wildavsky, *Searching for Safety* (New Brunswick, NJ: Transactions Books, 1987).
8. Susan P. Baker, Brian O'Neill, Marvin J. Ginsburg and Guohua Li, *The Injury Fact Book*, 2nd edition, (New York: Oxford University Press, 1992).
9. John D. Graham, Bei-Hung Chang and John S. Evans, "Poor is Riskier," Harvard Injury Control Discussion Paper, 1992.
10. David Hemenway, "Fire Fatalities: A Smoldering Issue," *Journal of Policy Analysis and Management* 4 (1985): 593-97.

25 HEALTH CARE

Medical care expenditures have been rising rapidly in the United States. In 1960, the average American spent $143 per year on medical care. By 1990, that figure had increased to $2,566. Health care as a percentage of Gross National Product rose from 5.3% in 1960 to 12.2% in 1990.

A LUXURY?

Many people view medical care as a necessity of life-- even as a right. The economic definition of a "necessity," however, is a very specific one. Necessities are defined in terms of the income elasticity of demand: the percentage change in quantity divided by the percentage change in income. A commodity is a necessity if the income elasticity of demand is between zero and one. In other words, the item is a necessity-- like food off the farm-- if, as income grows, although the total amount spent on the commodity rises, the proportion of income spent on the commodity falls. A commodity is a luxury if the income elasticity of demand is greater than one. In other words, for luxuries--like caviar or yachts-- as income rises, the percentage of income spent on the commodity rises.

By this definition, medical care appears to be a luxury! As the United States has grown wealthier over the past half century, the percentage of our national income devoted to medical care has been rising, not falling. Similarly, cross-national comparisons find that, compared to less developed countries, the richer nations spend more of their national income on medical care. Only within countries do we typically find that the rich, while spending more on health care than the poor, spend a lower percentage of their income.

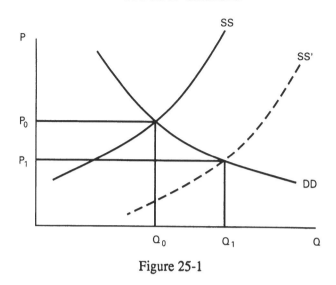

Figure 25-1

INFORMATION

An important way in which the market for medical care diverges from the perfectly competitive model is that information is imperfect. Physicians lack essential information about the efficacy of many procedures. Therefore wide variations in practice patterns can persist among doctors.[1] The federal government has recognized this problem and is currently putting substantial resources into outcomes research aimed at determining optimal treatments for various common ailments.

The more usual information problem in this market is that the patient has difficultly determining the competence of the provider. Patients can generally gain adequate knowledge about service amenities and the interpersonal skills of the provider but not about the technical quality of care.

Patients do not usually know what treatment is appropriate, or often whether they actually *need* to seek professional care. They rely on the doctor for advice. Such dependence on the physician can create problems since physicians are also the suppliers, and are typically paid on a fee-for-service basis. The more services they deliver, the more money they earn. A large amount of empirical evidence suggests that, like all workers, physicians generally respond to financial incentives.

For example, physicians at a chain of ambulatory walk-in centers were initially paid a flat hourly wage. The management of these for-profit clinics believed that their primary care doctors did not have sufficient financial incentive to "build a practice," so they changed the reimbursement package. To give physicians a monetary incentive more in line with the typical fee-for-service practitioner, the firm created a bonus system. Physicians would be paid the higher of (a) a percentage of the gross revenues they individually generated for the firm, or (b) the straight hourly

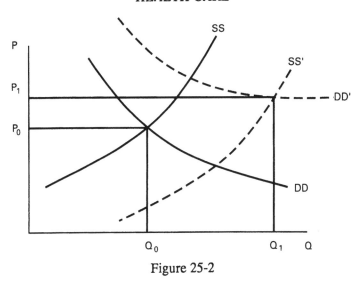

Figure 25-2

wage. One way to increase the firm's revenues was to increase ancillary testing, which was normally done on the premises. A comparison of the practice patterns of the same physicians the winter before and after the bonus system was instituted found that lab tests per patient visit increased 23% and x-rays per patient visit increased 16%.[2]

Physicians can clearly influence patient demand; indeed, their advice is sought because patients are not knowledgeable. The issue becomes, how and under what circumstances will doctors possibly (mis)use their power? The supply of physicians has been increasing in recent years. One fear has been that as the number of patients per physician falls, doctors will compensate by increasing the intensity of treatment per patient served. This variant of Say's Law-- that supply creates its own demand-- has sometimes been termed "supply-induced demand."

How might we recognize such demand inducement? Consider the situation in other markets. In agriculture, we know that bountiful wheat harvests result in an increase in wheat purchased and consumed. But this outcome does not mean that supply creates its own demand. In a competitive market, if the supply curve shifts to the right, quantity consumed rises (Figure 25-1). The reduction in equilibrium price means buyers are willing to purchase more of the commodity. Supply-induced demand in this instance would require that the shift in the supply curve caused a SHIFT in the demand curve (Figure 25-2).

In the medical marketplace, the demand shift might occur if patient preferences are changed by physicians; i.e., patients are told they "need" more services, and so they demand more. If the demand shift is large enough, the equilibrium price might actually rise (Figure 25-2). However, if the demand shift were small, econometricians would have great difficulty distinguishing an induced demand shift from merely a

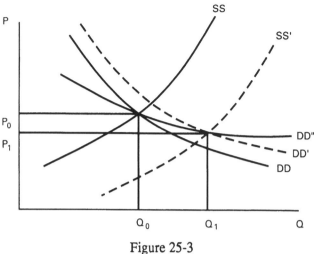

Figure 25-3

more elastic demand curve (Figure 25-3).

Consider another example. University housing is often subsidized, and waiting lists are common. Any increase in the supply of university housing is immediately consumed, without price needing to fall. Again, this finding can be explained without resorting to an explanation of demand inducement; it is completely understandable in conventional neoclassical terms. Price begins below the equilibrium level (Figure 25-4). There is excess demand at the going price, and spaces are allocated using non-price rationing. An increase in supply (a shift in the supply curve) may merely reduce the excess demand; the demand curve need not shift.

In the perfectly competitive model, the product is assumed to be homogeneous. But this assumption is not valid for most goods and services. When the Mets became the second major league baseball team in New York in 1962, more fans attended major league baseball games in New York, even though the Yankees had not previously sold out. The explanation is probably not supply-induced demand, but the fact that the Mets played a different brand of baseball, in a different location, in a different league, and on a different schedule.

This heterogeneity likewise exists in the medical marketplace. Doctors have different abilities and different bedside manners. There is product differentiation among physicians; some patients prefer one physician, some another. When a new general practitioner hangs up her shingle in a small town, the number of patient visits in the town may increase, simply because some residents will take the opportunity of consulting a young physician more attuned to their preferences.

The economic discussion of demand inducement typically portrays physicians as "imperfect agents" who, because of financial considerations, may sometimes act against the best interests of their patients. The more realistic problem in the medical

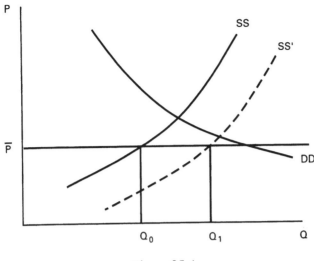

Figure 25-4

market is that patients' preferences are malleable, not fixed. In other words, in the real world much "demand creation" may be caused by doctors imposing their belief system on patients whose preferences are somewhat undefined.

People become doctors because they believe that medical care is an important service, and their training reinforces that belief. Probably few physicians provide services that they believe to be inimical to the health of their patient, or provide services of only minor benefit if the costs imposed on the patient are high. Any demand inducement related to increased physician density probably occurs because doctors have more time to do what they believe useful. Financial considerations simply make it easier for them to justify in their own minds the need for more intensive treatment.

In one test of physician-induced demand, a national sample consisting of hundreds of primary care providers was presented with identical, hypothetical medical cases. These physicians were asked how, in their daily practice, they would normally treat specific instances of congestive heart failure, hypertension and angina. Holding other factors constant, such as subspecialty, board certification and years of practice, physicians who worked in areas with high physician/population ratios chose a more aggressive style of treatment.[3]

INSURANCE

An important reason why demand inducement may be found in medical markets is that consumers are heavily insured. If you are not paying for something, it is easier for a supplier to persuade you that you need it. And there are always many services that might possibly provide some small positive benefit. It is thus not difficult for physicians to increase demand to some degree without seriously reducing patient welfare.

Insurance increases demand. A large randomized control trial, in which households were assigned various levels of insurance coverage, found that individuals facing higher effective prices consumed fewer medical care services.[4] This outcome is to be expected, since rarely are demand curves perfectly inelastic.

By lowering effective price to the buyers and thereby increasing the demand for care, insurance may explain high prices for medical services. But can it explain the rapid *rise* in prices and utilization we see in the United States? It is one thing to believe that monopolies and unions cause high prices; it is another argument to say they create continuous price inflation. Similarly, while greater insurance coverage clearly increases demand-- a one-shot deal-- do we expect that high levels of insurance will lead to continuously rising expenditures?

The dynamic effects of high levels of insurance coverage appear large. Consider a typical market. Sellers urge potential buyers to purchase their product. The prospective buyer is the constraining force. "Buy this encyclopedia," says the salesperson, "so your kids won't fall behind in school." "Maybe," replies the parent, "if it doesn't cost too much." But in a market where all the buyers have close to full insurance, there is no restraint, at least not if suppliers, as in most markets, earn more the more they sell.

Innovation can be divided into two types: process and product. Process innovations are those that reduce the cost-- the real inputs required-- to produce a given level of output. For example, the introduction of the assembly line allowed Henry Ford to manufacture cars more cheaply. Product innovations are those that improve the quality of the product. Examples of product innovations are the numerous advances in engineering and design that make today's cars faster, safer and easier to drive than the Model T. In normal markets, buyers happily reward process innovators, at least those who lower the price as their costs fall. Product innovators are rewarded only if the quality improvement is worth the potential extra charge.

In markets with close to full insurance, buyers do not care much about process innovation; new procedures that reduce the dollar price are irrelevant to their decision of whether and where to seek care. On the other hand, anything that improves quality is desired. Fully insured buyers want to take their business to the highest quality producers, regardless of market price.

Given the high levels of insurance coverage in the markets for hospital care and physician services, it is not surprising that we have witnessed rapid product innovations but few process innovations. This was particularly true during the 1970s when providers received little oversight from insurers and were paid on a cost-plus or fee-for-service basis.

It is common knowledge that people learn from experience. Learning-by-doing can increase productivity quickly, especially for new products. Both medical and surgical treatment of coronary artery disease changed rapidly in the early 1970s. Beta blockers became a common medication, and bypass surgery was introduced. A study found that as doctors gained more experience in these new procedures, medical outcomes improved. However, real costs did not seem to fall.[5] During that period of widespread insurance combined with cost-plus reimbursement, providers were not rewarded for saving real resources. On the other hand, doctors always strive to improve the quality of care, and they are often rewarded by patients, colleagues and administrators for their efforts. Thus, it is not surprising that product improvements were evident, but not process gains. The former were desired by both patients and providers; the latter were not.

The course of events in the market for medical care in the last 30 years is not at all surprising, given the levels of insurance coverage. The driving force is not so much that doctors have a "technological imperative," but that consumers' preferences have been dramatically altered by insurance. Any market, with similar insurance coverage, would probably also experience rapid increases in price, quantity and quality of goods sold.

Imagine the government deciding that playing tennis is vital for people's health. The government begins to fully reimburse tennis instructors-- at whatever price they charge-- for all lessons provided. The quantity of tennis lessons obtained would certainly increase, as would the market price. Perhaps more important, over time, we would observe rapid technological improvements in tennis instruction. Consumers would demand the very latest in computerized tomography and three-dimensional videotapes of their backhands. It is not difficult to continuously find ways to improve a product or service if cost is not a concern.

The economic problem is that the benefits are often not worth the costs to society. There are large externalities; taxpayers and other premium-payers are spending a great deal for many items that may yield only a small benefit to the individual patient-- the extra lab test, the additional patient visit, etc. We are receiving what has been described as the flat-of-the-curve medicine.

Since the key economic factor that distinguishes the medical care market from most others is insurance, many analysts propose changing the structure of insurance in order to bring benefits in line with societal costs. They argue for ways to limit demand. They call for less insurance-- higher co-payments, larger deductibles, requirements for second opinions and authorization before certain procedures can be performed, and the elimination of the tax benefit for purchasing insurance (insurance is paid for in pre-tax dollars while bread, clothing and other necessities are paid for in post-tax dollars).

An alternative method to restrain the system is to give suppliers the incentive to curb usage. We would then have a market in which the consumer wants more, but the seller wants to provide less. One example is the Health Maintenance Organization (HMO). These institutions serve as both insurer and provider. Since they are paid a flat amount of money by each insured to provide all medical services needed, they have a short-run financial incentive to provide less care. HMO physicians certainly hospitalize patients less often than do fee-for-service practitioners.[6]

A similar approach, on a grand scale, has been used by many developed nations. The government insures everyone and gives providers a fixed global budget. In Northern Ireland, for example, hospitals are given a predetermined amount of money to spend as wisely as possible. General practitioners also have a fixed amount for the year, depending on the number and age of the patients who are enrolled with them. The providers must triage-- provide the most important care to those who will gain the most benefit. If high cost-low benefit care is given, they will run out of resources. The patients may ask for more, but those most medically knowledgeable-- the providers-- restrain the system. Of course, this approach is not without problems, but it can successfully hold down medical care spending while ensuring that virtually everyone gets a minimum amount of the most crucial care.

CONCLUSION

The two most important factors that differentiate the market for medical care from the perfectly competitive model are the lack of information, especially by patients, and the presence of insurance. Insurance in the market has led not only to high prices and large quantities consumed, but also to a continually rising quality of services. The problem is not that the latest technology provides no benefit, but that the social benefit may be outweighed by the opportunity costs. At the margin, the resources of society would be better spent on improved education, better roads, etc., rather than on additional medical care.

Other developed countries have adopted top-down budgeting to reduce the pressure for ever-increasing medical care provision. The government-- the prime insurer in many other countries-- limits the total amount that can be spent. The physicians determine what is "good medical practice," and their perceptions, as well as their patients' perceptions, depend in large part on the resources available. Many advanced nations spend fewer resources on medical care than does the United States, without noticeable adverse health impacts.

FOR DISCUSSION

1. Are there items that you deem luxuries or necessities that do not fit the economic definition? Can you think of a better way to distinguish luxuries from necessities?

2. Has a doctor ever encouraged you to accept treatment you didn't think was

necessary? What would you do if this happened?

3. Analyze the markets for cosmetic surgery and infertility treatment. What restrictions, if any, might the government want to impose? What coverage should insurers offer?

4. Would you select other than the most state-of-the-art treatment for yourself if you were ill or injured? What about for your parent, child, spouse or other loved one? What factors are at work in this decision?

5. Can you think of any product innovations that failed or that you did not want to pay extra for? Can you think of any products that have not experienced process innovation?

6. The government provides health insurance to (some of) the poor through Medicaid. What short-run and long-run effects would you expect if the poor received a fixed amount of support for medical expenses in the form of "medical care stamps" similar to food stamps?

7. What impact, if any, does the malpractice system have on demand inducement? On consumer information?

NOTES TO CHAPTER 25

1. John Wennberg and A. Gittelsohn, "Variations in Medical Care among Small Areas," *Scientific American* 246 (1982): 120-134.
2. David Hemenway et al., "Physicians' Response to Financial Incentives: Evidence from a For-Profit Ambulatory Care Center," *New England Journal of Medicine* 322 (1990): 1059-1063.
3. David Hemenway and Deborah Fallon, "Testing for Physician-Induced Demand with Hypothetical Cases," *Medical Care* 23 (1985): 344-349.
4. Joseph P. Newhouse, "A Summary of the RAND Health Insurance Study," *Annals of the New York Academy of Sciences* 387 (1982): 111-14.
5. David Hemenway et al., "Benefits of Experience: Treating Coronary Artery Disease," *Medical Care* 24 (1986): 125-133.
6. Harold S. Luft, "How Do Health-Maintenance Organizations Achieve their 'Savings'?" *New England Journal of Medicine* 298 (1978): 1336-1343.

26 THE BIBLE

When I was young, I was told that there was "baseball in the Bible." It commenced with "in the beginning" (in the big inning) and included Goliath being beaned, Abraham sacrificing, and Noah catching a couple of flies. There was an early prohibition against stealing, as well as people striking out, walking, and, of course, making errors. At the time I thought all this was pretty clever. The present chapter must be considered in the same broad genre. It is a short, light treatment of "economics in the Bible."

This chapter is not about religion or the effects of religion on economics or economic development. It is about a great and influential literary work, the Holy Bible, and tries to illuminate "how an economist might read the Good Book." The focus of the chapter is on the most fundamental concept in economics: the notion of scarcity, especially with respect to the story of the creation and the teachings of Jesus.

It all started with Adam and Eve. In that Garden of Eden where grew "every tree that is pleasant to the sight, and good for food," there was no scarcity. Material goods were plentiful. Supplies exceeded desires, and life was sweet. There was no economic problem and no need for economists. This, indeed, was a paradise.

Then Eve ate the apple. Tempted, she succumbed. She was not following her long-run self-interest. She appears to have been a poor utility maximizer. It might be said that she was simply trying to become like a god; but this was a vain desire that could not be satisfied. At any rate, if you dislike studying economics, put the blame where it belongs. The fault lies with Eve (and that serpent).

Some might argue that Eve simply hastened the inevitable. Following God's command to "be fruitful and multiply," man soon would have overpopulated Eden and eventually the earth. Perhaps the economic problem was just around the corner. We cannot say. But we do know that the eating of the apple so angered God that he cursed the ground, forcing man to live by the sweat of his brow. It may have been then that he made man mortal, "for dust thou art, and unto dust shalt thou return." Mortality firmly established that greatest of opportunity costs-- time-- for man's time on earth was scarce. And, of course, the knowledge of good and evil made Adam and Eve aware of their nakedness, creating a new demand, the need and desire for clothing.

Since the day that Adam and Eve were thrown out of Eden, man has known scarcity. In the teachings of Jesus we find a new attempt to ameliorate "the economic problem." Jesus' method was not to increase the supply of goods (though he did this on occasion) but to urge people to limit their material desires. The story of the rich young man who followed the ten commandments and yearned for eternal life is told repeatedly in the gospels. Jesus said to him: "If thou wilt be perfect, go and sell that thou hast, and give to the poor, and thou shall have treasure in heaven: and come and follow me." He continued: "It is easier for a camel to go through the eye of a needle, than for a rich man to enter the kingdom of God."

An economist perceives this argument in terms of tradeoffs, choices between this life and the next. Riches here will mean pain and unhappiness in the afterlife. It is the meek and the poor in spirit who will receive their "treasures" in heaven. Those who would follow Jesus and his ethical teachings will find their material needs are few. Would all society follow him, total material desires would be much less than potential production, the bliss point well inside the production possibility frontier. People's material demands would be met, and, as Jesus argues, their spiritual needs would be met as well.

For Jesus, the choice between this life and the next is easy. "The kingdom of heaven," he said, "is like unto a merchant man, seeking goodly pearls, who when he found one pearl of great price, went and sold all that he had and bought it." That pearl, the attainment of heaven, is to be valued above all else. It is the supreme goal of the wise person. One should make no tradeoffs. "For what shall it profit a man, if he shall gain the whole world, and lose his own soul? or what shall a man give in exchange for his soul?" For Jesus, the price of a soul is infinite. Remember, for those not gaining admittance to the kingdom of heaven, there shall be "wailing and gnashing of teeth."

Jesus seems to have seen people as too unenlightened to perceive the tradeoff between riches in this life and heaven in the next or too tempted by the immediate pleasures of worldly wealth. His preachings were designed to correct this situation, to reiterate the teachings of the prophets. "Lay not up for yourselves treasures upon earth," he urges, "but lay up for yourselves treasures in heaven." And continuing, "No man can serve two masters.... Ye cannot serve God and Mammon." Or, as Paul writes to Timothy: "The love of money is the root of all evil." Not surprisingly, this fundamental biblical argument is not usually heeded by modern Christians. Perhaps if it were, there would again be little need for economics or economists.

In all his teachings, Jesus' basic conception of people seems quite similar to the economist's. Man tries to follow his own self-interest, weighing the costs and benefits of various alternatives. Therefore, the way to change behavior is to change the payoffs for particular courses of action, or at least to change the perception of the payoffs. This latter seems Jesus' principal role on earth.

For example, Jesus favored giving to the poor and needy. Thus, his arguments to sway people appeal not to their virtue or their social responsibility but directly to their rational self-interest. "When thou makes a dinner, or a supper," he said, "call not thy friends, nor thy brethren, neither thy kinsmen, nor thy rich neighbors; lest they also bid thee again, and a recompense be made thee. But when thou makest a feast, call the poor, the maimed, the lame, the blind: And thou shalt be blessed, for they cannot recompense thee: for thou shalt be recompensed at the resurrection of the just." In other words, give to the poor, for then you will be blessed by God. Such good deeds will be rewarded in the afterlife, just as wicked ones will be punished.

Jesus not only gave spiritual comfort to the poor but also healed diseases and cast out devils. Because the price he charged for these services was very low, queueing resumed, as did competition for favors. The multitudes attracted to him had, at times, to be fed, and this Jesus accomplished by miraculously increasing the supply of bread and fishes; he is also known to have converted water into wine. In our more enlightened era, this practice of freely distributing such scarce material goods could be construed as "dumping" and would certainly be regarded unkindly by the bread, wine, and fishing industries.

In his own day, Jesus did incur great disfavor with the vested interests. He attacked the religious and ruling elite: "Woe unto you, scribes and Pharisees, hypocrites!" And his actions, such as casting out "all them that sold and bought in the temple" and overthrowing the tables of the moneychangers, seemed disruptive of banking and exchange and indeed of the entire economic as well as social fabric of the community. He was killed forthwith.

CONCLUSION

Economists have a particular way of looking at the world. They make certain assumptions and focus on certain aspects of society. The economic approach can be applied to a variety of social phenomena. This paper was a brief, light account of the way some biblical stories struck one economist.

> Of making many books there is no end;
> And much study is a weariness of the flesh.
> (Ecclesiastes)

FOR DISCUSSION

1. What is the effect of burnt (or unburnt) sacrifices on gross national product? On economic welfare? On social well-being?

2. "A virtuous woman who can find/For her price is far above rubies." Can the price of a virtuous woman be put in monetary terms? Should it be? Could putting an economic value on things or relationships in any way "cheapen" them?

3. "A Christian is simply an economic man with special beliefs." Comment.

4. How might an economist view the ten commandments? For example: "Remember the Sabbath, to keep it holy." Does this imply blue laws and forced leisure? "Thou shalt not covet." What are the implications for consumer interdependence? "Thou shalt not steal." What are the implications about the type of economic system? About the cost of law enforcement? "Thou shalt have no other gods before me." Is there any relationship between monotheism-pantheism and monopoly-competition?

5. How important do you think religious beliefs are in affecting economic development? How important are religious institutions? How does the economic system affect religious beliefs and institutions?

APPENDIX

PAYOFF MATRICES

A payoff matrix provides a useful tool for describing and analyzing a wide variety of situations, interactions, and "games." Here we briefly examine a very simple kind of situation; there are two players, and each has two options. There are thus four possible outcomes.

Consider a pure conflict situation. You and your friend are "bucking up," or flipping for nickels. If you match, you win; if you don't, she wins. In Figure A-1 you are row and she is column. Her payoffs are given in parentheses. This pure conflict situation is called a zero-sum game. Whatever you win, she loses, and vice versa. Note that the payoffs in each possible outcome sum to zero. In this simple game, it can never improve your situation to go first or to let your opponent know your selection ahead of time. You should be able to draw the payoffs if two people play "rock, paper, and scissors" for quarters. Games such as poker, chess, and monopoly may be considered more complicated zero-sum games.

	(Her) Heads	Tails
Heads	(-5) +5	(+5) -5
Tails	(+5) -5	(-5) +5

Figure A-1

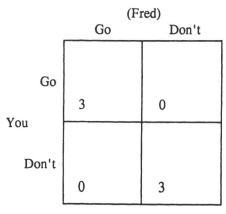

(Fred)

Go   Don't

You

Go

3   0

Don't

0   3

Figure A-2

(Fred)

Go   Don't

You

Go

(3)   (0)

3   0

Don't

(0)   (3)

0   3

Figure A-3

At the other extreme from pure conflict games are pure coordination games. These are cooperative rather than competitive situations. TV's "Match Game," where contestants and celebrities tried to give identical answers, was a successful game show based on pure coordination.

Consider this real-world example. You are supposed to meet your friend Fred at the outdoor tennis courts at 5:00. At 4:40 it begins to mist. You are not sure whether it will clear up or rain and eliminate the possibility of tennis. You cannot locate Fred, nor can he reach you. You thus have two possible choices: to go (walk) to the courts or not to. Fred has similar options. There are thus four possible outcomes. From your perspective, it is important that you both make the same choice. If you both go, that is fine: if the sun shines, you can play tennis, and if it

(Fred)

	Go	Don't
Go	(7) 3	(0) 0
Don't	(4) 0	(3) 3

You

Figure A-4

rains, you can go together for a beer. If neither of you goes, that is also fine, for you have other things you can be doing. But if one of you goes, and the other doesn't, that is not so good. You will be unhappy if you go, and wait, and he never shows up. You will also be unhappy if Fred goes, and waits, and becomes annoyed at you. Your payoffs (in utils) are given in Figure A-2. If Fred has identical preferences, the game is one of pure coordination (Figure A-3).

You would definitely like to be able to inform Fred of your choice. Even if you couldn't communicate directly, it would be very helpful to have a signal to help you coordinate. Perhaps you might have agreed beforehand to telephone WEATHER in such a contingency, and if the chance of rain were less than 70 percent, you both would go. Or you could call a mutual friend, tell her your decision, and have her relay the message. Or better still, you could have prearranged a time and number for one to call the other and agreed on your decision if no call were made.

Let us change the game a bit by postulating that Fred enjoys his walk to the tennis court-- even in the rain. He prefers to meet you, but in any event, he enjoys his "constitutional," and you know this. The payoffs in this new game are given in Figure A-4. We assume that any form of communication is impossible, and no prearrangements have been made. Should you go or not?

An easier question is: should Fred go or not? As in most economic models, we assume that individuals are, or try to be, rational utility maximizers. And any (dis)utility that Fred receives from your happiness or misery is already included in his payoffs. Making these assumptions, we can say that Fred should go. Fred has a "dominant strategy." No matter what you do, he is better off going. Assume he knows you will go; then he too should go, and receive seven rather than zero utils. Assume he knows you aren't going; then he should still go, and receive four rather than three utils. Your choice doesn't affect his decision. He cares about your choice, however, because it does affect his payoffs.

If Fred has a dominant strategy, and you know it and believe him to be rational, then you will expect him to follow his dominant strategy. You will expect him to go. And if he goes, then so should you, and receive three rather than zero utils. In this particular game, if both parties act rationally, no communication is needed to reach the optimal solution for both.

Sometimes decisionmakers following their own self-interest reach an inferior outcome. This is best illustrated by the "prisoner's dilemma" game. Consider this scenario. Two people meet in a bar; they are complete strangers. They decide to commit a burglary and do so successfully. They divide the loot and expect never to see each other again. Unfortunately for them, they are both apprehended and taken before the district attorney. The D.A. knows about game theory and devises an ingenious scheme. Before the criminals can communicate with each other, she separates them, and tells each of them their options and (true) payoffs.

Within the next hour, each will have two choices: to confess or not to. There will thus be four possible outcomes for the criminals, as shown in Figure A-5. If each confesses, each will receive a five-year sentence. If prisoner A confesses and B does not, A will be allowed to turn state's evidence and get off scot-free. B will be prosecuted to the full extent of the law and will receive ten years in jail. The reverse is true if B confesses while A does not. If neither confesses, the D.A. has enough evidence to put them both away for two years. The payoff matrix is given above. What should the prisoners do?

Each has a dominant strategy, and that is to confess. For example, no matter what B does, A is better off confessing. Suppose A hears B tell his lawyer that he (B) is going to confess. Then A should also confess, since by doing so he will receive five rather than ten years. Suppose, on the other hand, that A learns that B is going to keep silent. A should still confess. By confessing, he is not forced to go to jail; if he refuses to confess, he gets two years. Since the game is perfectly symmetrical, B has an identical dominant strategy.

In a prisoner's dilemma game, participants have a dominant strategy. But if each follows that dominant strategy, if each follows his own self-interest, they will arrive at a domin*ated* outcome. In other words, they could *both* be better off if they acted differently. Criminals A and B would both prefer that both refuse to confess. Then each would receive only two years in jail rather than five. Unfortunately for them, without some form of binding contract, each has a strong incentive to confess.

Interestingly, they are more likely to reach the preferred outcome (from their perspective) if certain payoffs are made *worse*. Assume that although they are strangers, both belong to the same organization, such as the Mafia, and that it provides severe penalties (loss of eyes, tongue, fingers) for anyone who confesses. If this threat is credible, the prisoners may be facing a situation such as that described in Figure A-6. Now each has a dominant strategy *not* to confess. If each follows his own self interest, neither will confess, and each will serve only two years.

Payoff matrices can usefully be applied to a wide range of situations involving decisions. For example, in interpersonal relations, should you send Christmas cards

(B)

	Confess	Don't
Confess	(-5) -5	(-10) 0
Don't	(0) -10	(-2) -2

A

Figure A-5

(B)

	Confess	Don't
Confess	(-100) -100	(-10) -100
Don't	(-100) -10	(-2) -2

A

Figure A-6

to particular friends? How should others be addressed in speech? What type of clothes should be worn to a certain function? What time should you arrive at the party? In international relations, payoff matrices might be useful in analyzing whether Country A should recognize Country B. Should it attack Country B? Should battling countries use germ warfare? Should prisoners be exchanged? Should nuclear bombs be employed? And so forth. Payoff matrices are often helpful in highlighting the crucial aspects of the game: how many parties are participating, how many times the game will be played, whether the parties meet in other games, what information is available, whether communication is possible, and what tactics and strategies can prove effective.

The best way for the reader to begin to understand payoff matrices is to draw them and play simple simulated games.

FOR DISCUSSION

1. If both parties cooperate in a prisoner's dilemma game, is the outcome the best for either one? Could either do better by competing?

2. What if the D.A. takes two innocent people and presents them with the game described in Figure A-5? Should either confess?

3. Do you expect more or less cooperative behavior if a prisoner's dilemma game is played repeatedly by the same two people? If communication is possible?

4. Draw a two-person game in which you would prefer to go first and another in which you would prefer to go last. Draw a game in which you would like to decrease one of your own payoffs.

SOURCES

Luce, R. Duncan, and Howard Raiffa. *Games and Decisions.* New York: Wiley, 1957.
Schelling, Thomas C. *The Strategy of Conflict.* New York: Oxford University Press, Galaxy, 1963.

GLOSSARY OF ECONOMIC TERMS

agent.............................. Not a woman

budget............................ What you can't do to a piano

counterfeit....................... What you throw when the sales clerk is slow

C.P.I............................. Advice for a distrustful spouse

debt.............................. What we all are in the long run

discount.......................... Not dat earl

invest............................ Where to keep a pocket watch

liability......................... Skill at prevarication

long run.......................... Marathon

permanent income.................. Earnings of a hair stylist

plant size........................ Height of vegetables

property.......................... What to serve when the Queen comes calling

retire............................ Change a flat

scarcity.......................... Town of haunted houses

sellers........................... Where to keep wine

Social Security................... Confidence from being well-mannered

subsidy........................... Home port of our nuclear fleet

theory of the firm................ "Eat less, exercise more"

withdrawals....................... How southerners talk

NAME INDEX

SUBJECT INDEX

Externalities, 19, 25, 27, 35, 45-47, 89,
97-129, 164, 181-183, 221, 243-245,
255
Extinction, 126

Fashion, 3, 25-37, 88
Federal Aviation Administration, 159,
245
Federal Trade Commission, 152
Fire, 157, 216, 246
Fishing, 125-126, 182
Flowers, 57
Food stamps, 211
Food supplements, 207-212
Free rider, 127

Game theory, 13-14, 125, 244-245, 263-268
Garden of Eden, 259
General Motors, 160
Gifts, 51-61, 78, 79, 128, 194, 210, 218
Golden Rule, 128
Good-faith bargaining, 67, 68
Grades, 137-138, 171-175
Graduate Medical Education National
Advisory Committee, 227

Haggling, 55, 63-69
Head Start, 208-209
Health care, 103-108, 139-142, 149-154,
249-257
Health maintenance organizations, 108,
255
Hedonic method, 135
Height, 42-44, 47
Helmets, 214-215, 216, 219, 221, 224,
244-245
High Noon, 127
Housing market, 66
Hula Hoops, 31

Ice hockey, 244
Ice trust, 189-203
Injury, 215, 221-226, 241-248
Information, 19, 149-150, 153-154, 171,
183-184, 250-253

Innovations, product and process, 107, 153,
254
Institute of Electrical and Electronic Engi-
neers, 159
Insurance, 56, 99-111, 153-154, 222, 253-256
Invisible hand, 45, 128, 242
Irrationality, 186

Japan, 164, 166

Kula, 54-55, 58

Labor market, 66-67
Lawsuit, 242
Learning-by-doing, 254
Licensing, 151-152, 153
Luxury, 194, 249

Magic prices, 14
Marginal analysis, 147-148
Marginal cost, 73, 181, 208
Marijuana, 118, 151
Melanasia, 54-55
Mergers, 189-190
Monopoly, 73, 88, 177-203
Moral hazard, 101-109, 221-223
Motorcycling, 224
Mother's Day, 51

National Bureau of Standards, 164
National Electric Code, 159
National Fire Protection Association, 138,
159
National Highway Traffic Safety Adminis-
tration, 159
National Industrial Conference Board, 162
Natural monopoly, 180
Nervous nellies, 221-226
Nuclear, 167
Nursing home, 139-142

Oil, 124-125
Oligopoly, 66, 166, 167, 172, 180
Opportunity cost, 147, 208, 242, 246,
260

ABOUT THE AUTHOR

David Hemenway received his B.A. and Ph.D. in economics from Harvard. He is a senior lecturer at Harvard School of Public Health, where he continually wins school-wide teaching awards. His previous books include *Industrywide Voluntary Product Standards* and *Monitoring and Compliance: The Political Economy of Inspection*. Dr. Hemenway has written on a wide variety of subjects, including complaints, gun control, arson and statistics. A former Pew Fellow on Injury Control, he is presently deputy director of the Harvard Injury Control Center.